Constitutional Context

THE JOHNS HOPKINS SERIES IN CONSTITUTIONAL THOUGHT
Sanford Levinson and Jeffrey K. Tulis, *Series Editors*

Constitutional Context

*Women and Rights Discourse
in Nineteenth-Century America*

KATHLEEN S. SULLIVAN

The Johns Hopkins University Press
Baltimore

The Johns Hopkins University Press
2715 North Charles Street
Baltimore, Maryland 21218-4363
www.press.jhu.edu

Library of Congress Cataloging-in-Publication Data
Sullivan, Kathleen S.
Constitutional context : women and rights discourse in nineteenth-century
America / Kathleen S. Sullivan.
p. cm. — (Johns Hopkins series in constitutional thought)
Includes bibliographical references and index.
ISBN-13: 978-0-8018-8552-5 (hardcover : alk. paper)
ISBN-10: 0-8018-8552-3 (hardcover : alk. paper)
1. Women—Legal status, laws, etc.—United States—History.
2. Women's rights—United States—History.   3. Married women—Legal
status, laws, etc.—United States—History.   4. Constitutional History—
United States.   5. United States. Consitution. 14th Amendment.
6. Discourse analysis.   I. Title.
KH478.S85   2007
346.7301'34—dc22   2006020808

A catalog record for this book is available from the British Library.

In memory of my father

Contents

Acknowledgments

To gauge the rapid advances of formal equality in the late twentieth century, I only need to think of my sisters. Mary and Carol appeared in any of the Little League booster club programs of the early 1970s in their miniskirts, as supporters of the baseball teams. Helen was soon on the league's first softball team, with a uniform consisting of a t-shirt depicting a softball with a face, hair, and hat. The stitching of the ball made it look as if a tear were running down the face, an endless source of fascination to Maureen and me, who would go on to play in myriad Little League and school teams, with much more refined uniforms. The sudden availability of opportunities was likewise apparent in my educational and professional life. It was somewhat surprising, therefore, to me and others, that I undertook a feminist study that is critical of the theories of the foremothers of the women's rights movement to whom I and other American women owe so much. I am grateful to the following people for their patience, interest, and assistance in carrying out this project.

I have been fortunate to enjoy the mentorship of Gretchen Ritter and Jeffrey Tulis, who made my years of graduate training so rewarding and who continue to offer me their support. Sandy Levinson, Benjamin Gregg, and Pam Brandwein shared their careful criticisms and insights and have made me aware of the pitfalls of this project. If I have not avoided those pitfalls, the fault is my own.

I am grateful for the collegiality, assistance, and intellectual community so generously offered by my colleagues in the Political Science Department at Ohio University, especially Susan Burgess, John Gilliom, Julie White, DeLysa Burnier, and Ron Hunt.

I presented earlier versions of this manuscript at annual meetings of the American Political Science Association, the Western Political Science Association, the Law and Society Association, and the Society for Legal History, and I explored some new ideas at the Georgetown/University of Maryland Constitutional Discussion Group. I thank especially Mark Graber, Ronald Kahn, Keith Whittington, Rose Corrigan, Daniel Ernst, Laura Edwards, Norma Basch, Julie Novkov, and Catherine Frost for their comments and interest. Patricia Strach, Mariah Zeisberg, Linda Tvrydy, Edlie Wong, Priscilla Yamin, and Gwynn Thomas have all read portions of this manuscript; I am lucky to count them among my cohort and friends. I received able research assistance from Hannah Purkey, John Michael McKenna, Lindsey Nelson, Stacy Clifford, and Jessica Giffin, and from the librarians at Ohio University, the University of Cincinnati School of Law, and the Tarlton Law Library at the University of Texas. I thank Henry Tom and the editors at the Johns Hopkins University Press for their expert handling and care of this manuscript.

I am grateful for the patience of Harry and Nora Sullivan, who can now call an end to their sibling rivalry with this project, and to Steve Fetsch, for taking care of all of us. I have had the freedom to complete this book and raise children because of the labor he has provided in the home.

For my unexpected interest in the progressive capacity of the common law in protecting rights, I am indebted to my father, John Sullivan, a traditional man who provided me with some of my strongest lessons in social justice. It would have been nice to talk about this book with him, too.

Constitutional Context

Introduction: Context in the Constitutional Order

Constitutional interpretation is fraught with anxiety. There is always the chance that an interpreter of the United States Constitution will give into his or her own personal and political proclivities, so interpreters take pains to assume an appropriate posture. They may present themselves as religiously faithful or scientifically expert to the undertaking.[1] Such protective measures shield the Constitution's higher-law function from politics, but they present problems of their own. In the effort to behave appropriately, interpreters miss out on opportunities to behave constitutionally. In their labors to act responsibly, interpreters treat vague language as an unfortunate condition rather than an occasion for constitutional construction.[2] The more the faithful and the experts try to get interpretation right, the further the polity finds itself from the opportunity to participate in the task of constitutional interpretation and ongoing construction.[3] The many precautions against wayward interpretation fail to incorporate those limits to interpretive discretion that are found in the political institutions themselves.[4]

Politics in constitutionalism is inevitable and appropriate, even necessary, but its legitimacy suffered, ironically, when the Constitution was interpreted politically in the nineteenth century. In the early decades of that century, recourse to context in constitutional interpretation earned a bad reputation because the political and social contexts were sources of oppression. Both federal and state governments retained ascriptive status on the basis of race, sex, and class.[5] A political reformer who referred to context would encounter impediments to individual freedom in law and social norms.[6] So workingmen's groups, land reformers, abolitionists, and woman's rights advocates produced theories that derived rights of a subject considered without recourse to the subject's place in society. Rights were then employed precisely against those impediments. Activists imbued familiar concepts, such as liberty and popular sovereignty, with an abstraction that had not been used before.[7] The story of the expansion of rights in American history is also the story of rights theories increasingly distanced from the society in which those rights operated. The political subject became a figure of the liberal imagination, the abstract subject endowed with rights, regardless of status. When rights were at stake, it was important to get the interpretation right.

Woman's rights activists offered a particular contribution to this development because their political and legal identities were defined by the rules they sought to overcome. Under the rules of the common law's marital relation, a husband and wife were considered to be one person in the eyes of the law, with the husband representing the partnership and covering his wife's legal identity in a doctrine called *coverture*. Lacking legal personhood for the most part, a married woman could not own property, retain her earnings, have any influence in where the family lived, or make a contract. Although the common law is part of private law, with its protection of property rights and domestic relations, the public law depended on it. William Novak has pointed out that American governance cannot be understood by looking only at the Constitution itself, because the constitutional order was maintained by more than the terms of the document.[8] Massachusetts Justice Lemuel Shaw saw the U.S. Constitution as pertaining only to political rights, whereas matters of civil rights and social relations were left to the states to be taken care of by the common-law social relations.[9]

The call for women's rights occasioned a confrontation between the public law and those public purposes served by private law. Because women's subjugation had served a form of maintenance for the constitutional order, efforts to complete the transformation from status to individual rights had institutional consequences. To claim their liberation, women had to cast doubt on the legitimacy of the status regime at the foundation of the constitutional order.

Tracing this development of rights discourse lends insight into the interplay of law and politics that is at the nexus of legal and social change in the American political tradition. Law influences society, introducing legalistic language and concerns into political discourse.[10] Politics influences law and constitutionalism by imparting meaning to the terms of the Constitution. Keith Whittington has identified the practice of constitutional construction taking place in sites other than the jurisprudence of the courts. The construction takes place through politics carried out on the stage set by constitutional structures. The political realm provides for the transmission of external standards to a document that is routinely viewed as legalistic.[11] While the literature on constitutionalism outside the courts tends to focus on the political branches of government, this study looks at constitutional outsiders, who bring a particular form of political argument to the practice of constitutionalism. Julie Novkov has pointed to the relation between actors within the law and within politics by identifying "nodes of conflict" where various lay, legal, and judicial actors converge and contest the interpretation of the law.[12] Ideas are shaped by the different discourses in which they are taken up; an idea will be expressed differently in a lawyer's brief than in a social movement's rhetoric, and these different expressions will be incorporated into a judicial opinion.

With regard to women's rights, the different discourses emerged across time. In an ongoing exchange of political and legal concepts, woman's rights activists drew their strategies from the opportunities and developments of earlier movements, which began with internal legal change. Property rights had traditionally been part of the common law and were defined so as to serve the public good. Property rights had developed in the early modern period in England. In the early American republic, the fundamental purposes and limits of property were transitioning from considerations of the good of the commonwealth to individualism, a development in service to the needs of a growing commercial economy.[13] The early nineteenth century also saw sustained discussion over efforts to replace the common law with codes. The codification movement was limited in its success, but it reformed some common-law rules and introduced a language of disparagement of the common law. The abstraction and language within these legal discourses appeared quite different when they reemerged in political discourse. Radical abolitionists claimed that natural liberty trumped any constitutional compact over slavery and, in the repression of their speech, likewise developed a civil-libertarian theory of free speech. When woman's rights activists adopted developments in constitutional rights from the abolitionist movement, they drew upon and developed an abstract theory of the political subject.

Woman's rights activists had immediate relations with these movements, which provided them with the tools for construction of constitutional theory. The reform of property law led to the inadvertent conferral of rights with the married women's property acts. The early free love reformer Frances Wright counted Jeremy Bentham, the advocate for codification, among her associates. The codification movement invited a culture of reform, with direct relations between legal reformers, such as Thomas Grimké and his sisters, who would become prominent woman abolitionists. The abolitionist movement proved to be a training ground for women's rights activists and the movement for free speech a springboard to the extension of constitutional rights to women. Aside from making use of these political connections, woman's rights activists strategically drew upon these legacies to carve out a space for their rights. They extended the emerging abstraction in the legal conception of property and the political conception of rights of free speech to construct a theory of woman's civil and political rights.

In adopting concepts from other movements, they introduced new ideas and applications into those discourses. The codification movement had invited a notion that the old British common-law system in operation in the United States was a relic of feudalism and barbarism. The negative connotations of this charge largely fell flat in the 1820s and 1830s in the legal community, but they became more salient later in the century, when the subjugation of women was tied to the common law in political discourse. Woman's rights activists extended the trope of barbarism to the gender hierarchy of the common law, drawing new meaning to the term and extending their opposition to the gendered relations of the common law to the common law itself. Their disparagement of the common law struck at the contradictions inherent in equality within the American political tradition. When the codification movement reemerged in the 1880s, the politicized issue of women's rights would be unavoidable, and defenders of the common law had to contend with the gender hierarchy. The legal and political movements would again diverge, but in their nodes of conflict, they exchanged concepts marked with their own tinkering. The shift from legal to political discourse allowed for the transformation in form, with women's-rights rhetoric borrowing from and altering the legal discourse. As the discourse shifted from law to politics and back to formal law again in more conventional judicial constitutional doctrine, the concept of reform looked different, with consequences for American constitutionalism.

In politics and constitutional law, women's rights would come to be represented as a matter of equality, reflecting the claim of equal protection to challenge the repression of the common-law status regime, but that is not the only form it could have taken.[14] Married women's gradual liberation from their common-law status could have occurred through the doctrine of equality or through the common law's companion, equity, which traditionally offered exceptions to the hardships of the common law. Either equality or equity could have ameliorated married women's subjugation and advanced all women toward a greater share in political rights, but the two doctrines are distinct in their form. When women's rights eventually became a Fourteenth Amendment issue in Supreme Court constitutional doctrine, the Court incorporated the politically developed doctrine of abstract equality rather than the more contextually determined practice of equity.

The achievement of equality over equity has had sustaining consequences not only for women's rights but also for subsequent patterns of rights protection and, even more broadly, for the relation between constitutionalism and politics. The move toward abstraction from status eventually placed the Constitution beyond the reach of corrupting forces, including political constitutionalism. The eventual acceptance of equality, which has been instrumental in invoking a higher law to attack old status-relations and discrimination, certainly ushered in advances for women. This book seeks to recover the historical presence of the common law in constitutionalism and conceptions of liberty in order to identify what was lost in this development.

While this study positions woman's rights activists at its locus, there was no concerted movement geared toward married women's property rights, and there was even dissension among activists — some wanted to maintain the division of labor of the household, others were willing to go as far as divorce reform, and still others were willing to relinquish marriage altogether. These disagreements reflect the larger disagreements of the nineteenth-century women's movement. Some members of the women's movement worked tirelessly for women's suffrage, others were opposed to it. Any of those women may have been part of the temperance movement, or the free love movement, or against those movements. This study looks at the rhetoric and strategies of the public campaign to liberate women from their common-law status as married women. The primary activist that figures here is Elizabeth Cady Stanton, who included married women's rights in the Declaration of Sentiments and continued to pursue them as a goal secondary to suffrage. The woman suffrage movement spilt in 1870, with the American Woman Suffrage Association focusing on suffrage in individual states and the National Woman Suffrage Association pursuing a national strategy, along with other women's rights issues, including divorce reform and married women's property rights. This more comprehensive strategy of the NWSA encompassed a broader recognition of women's rights, and Stanton was a leader. Her attempts to bring egalitarianism to the marital relation drew criticism, from both within and without the woman suffrage movement, that she was undermining the family.[15] Stanton denied this, and, indeed, her own marriage and seven children backed this up, but her theories did challenge the legitimacy of status in American political thought.

When woman's rights activists employed abstract principles against the sources of their oppression, their target was the common law, the system of "judge-made" law derived from feudal England and source of the domestic relations' status regime. American woman's rights activists invoked fundamental American principles to draw attention to the contradictions between rights and status in their effort to abolish the doctrine of coverture. To do this, they presented the common law as persisting at odds with American principles. Their persuasive strategy is most familiarly captured in the Declaration of Sentiments, presented at the first woman's rights convention at Seneca Falls, New York, in 1848. With a simple alteration they rendered the Declaration of Independence's statement of equality to read "all men and women are created equal" and proceeded to list a set of grievances against "mankind" in violation of natural rights of men and women.[16] This classic case of expansion of liberal principles demonstrates that the vagueness of the principles holds out the promise of multiple meanings and extension.[17]

A closer look at the suffragist version, however, indicates that the woman suffragists' application of liberalism was peculiar. The claims of the Declaration of Independence owe as much to common-law liberties as to classical liberal thought. In their invocation of the Declaration of Independence, woman suffragists both proclaimed it a liberal document and reconceptualized liberalism. The Declaration of Sentiments borrowed from the Declaration of Independence, which borrowed from the right to revolution in John Locke's *Second Treatise of Government*.[18] Like Thomas Jefferson, the authors of the Declaration of Sentiments offered a list of grievances that violated natural rights, yet the Declaration of Sentiments significantly departs from its forebears in employing natural rights theory *against* the common law. The theories of Locke and Jefferson had accommodated the common law, the Declaration of Independence resting on principles derived from the common law, and the hierarchy and status of the domestic relations included in John Locke's *Second Treatise*.[19] The original American states retained the domestic relations even after declaring the rights of mankind; after all, the American Revolution was a revolution in political authority but not in the law.[20] By including the rules of coverture among their grievances, woman's rights activists rendered the common law unfamiliar to liberal values and then pitted those liberal values against the common law. In doing so, they did not merely rely on liberalism; they reconstructed it.

When the woman suffragist version of liberalism became definitive of American liberalism, American rights discourse lost an alternative rights theory. Liberalism's loss of the common law might appear to be a welcome one. The classic common-law method, in which judges look to past cases to discern principles with which to decide the case at hand, admits of a conservatism. Suspicion of abstract principles and longing for the common-law methods are familiar conservative sentiments.[21] One need not long for a regression in women's rights, however, to recognize the constitutional resources offered by the common law. Common law's champions have always attested to its adaptability. The common-law method draws its rules from the past but is able to retest and update its rules when they prove to be out of step with a more complex society.[22] This attention to the society in which law operates reflects the contextual nature of the common-law method, which additionally maintains an open-ended approach to big questions. In leaving important questions unresolved, the Court leaves the question open for other institutions to consider, inviting extra-judicial constitutionalism.[23]

These features of vagueness, uncertainty, and the possibilities of multiple interpreters are the same features that render the common-law method unappealing as a guide to deriving rights. Rights have come to be understood in the civil-libertarian tradition, and the contextual basis of the common-law method would likely be less protective of rights. Yet the civil-libertarian tradition elides important questions of equality and power which the common-law method of rights derivation may better accommodate.[24] In his study of nineteenth-century British liberal thought, Uday Mehta demonstrates that the opportunity for understanding the strange and unfamiliar lay in the conservative Burke, rather than in the universal commitments of liberal thought, because Burke, in his localism and prejudice, had the disposition to understand the stranger within his particularity. The universal tenets of liberalism invited the self-perception that they knew and accepted the other, but their level of abstraction hid the imperialistic tendencies of liberalism.[25] Because liberalism's abstract principles are removed from experience, they can overlook the sites of subjection and invite the assumption that they have liberated the oppressed from that subjection. The difference between the common-law method and the abstract principles of liberalism, therefore, is not that the former resists the progress of the latter but, rather, that reform takes place differently. The common-law method of rights derivation remained situated in social context, reflecting the polity it served while it served the needs of that polity.

The common-law method was a historical method of constitutional interpretation.[26] David Strauss points out that current trends in textualism and originalism in constitutional interpretation reflect the impulse to refer to an authoritative source of constitutional meaning. The common-law approach rejects the impulse to refer to an authoritative source for constitutional meaning in text or intent of the framers. Instead, it accepts creative interpretation of the text as a means of gradual innovation, allowing the Constitution to keep pace with the needs of its society.[27] The common-law method more readily embraces politics and uncertainty, and it remains open to multiple interpreters. Common-law constitutionalism operates by inquiring what resources the people need to govern themselves. Justices and other constitutional interpreters could find an answer to that query by referring to social conditions.

Historically, those social conditions included social relations maintained by the common law, with the status regime of the common law serving to establish relations of obligations upon which the larger constitutional order rested. Common-law constitutionalism recognized the importance of social relations for the constitutional order, and it had the capacity to ameliorate the hardships of women while retaining recognition of those obligation for society. But woman's rights activists struck directly at their gendered subordination and called the methods of common-law constitutional interpretation into question, urging recourse to those authoritative sources that were uncorrupted by the historical status regime. When woman suffragists rejected the common law because of the hierarchy of its social relations, they ignored the possibilities for its methods to inform rights theories. More broadly, they called the contextual aspects of the common-law method into question as a legitimate and productive site of constitutionalism. In their move toward a stronger and broader protection of rights, they abstracted rights from the immediate, repressive context. Increasing abstraction was an effective strategy in claiming rights, but it pulled constitutional politics away from the conditions it was addressing in the first place.[28]

Woman suffragists closed off the common-law method by casting the common-law tradition as a barbaric, feudal system of law that was unsuitable for modern Americans. To carry out this project effectively, they incorporated the language of the codification movement's attacks on the common law and cast doubt on the methods and institutions of the common law. The codification movement imported an implicit theory of positivism, which was initially resisted in American legal reform. The employment of this discourse by woman suffragists helped to usher in the latent tenets of positivism. The distrust of practical knowledge, recourse to authority rather than to the people, striving for certainty rather than ongoing interpretation and dispute are all methods of rights derivation that were present in woman suffragists' rights discourse. These features produce methods of rights derivation that are formal and exacting, removed from the messy and uncertain world of politics and human experience. When the woman suffragist version of equality was incorporated into the Fourteenth Amendment's provision for equal protection, it elicited an equality doctrine that is formalistic and, sometimes, absurd in its logic.[29]

By participating in this development and offering a theory of human agency and equality, woman's rights activists were able to contribute to the development of liberal theory and the corresponding denigration of the common-law methods and status. Woman's rights activists were so adept at vilifying the common law that its historical presence in liberalism is barely recognizable now. Rights are now derived by recourse to abstract and ideal principles, with the rights of an imagined rights-bearer defined without recourse to the society in which those rights are to be exercised. The woman suffragists' contribution lay in rendering the common law as "bad" and liberal, natural rights as ameliorative.[30] The juxtaposition between the two closed off the opportunity to recognize the resources of the common law in rights discourse.

Gender has mattered in American political history, so the dismantling of a gendered status regime has had institutional and constitutional consequences. The issue of women's rights forced the public law to encounter the services provided by the private law. But the benefits of a gender analysis cannot be gained by using the usual conceptual categories that accompany standard studies of gender in American political development because woman suffragists were so influential in designing the lens that researchers often use in such studies. The woman suffragists' construction of a good liberalism pitted against a bad common law encourages researchers to reproduce their distinction and to locate rights as a sign of triumph over the status regimes of the past.

This lens is particularly apparent in studies of the limited reform of the married women's property acts. Over the course of the nineteenth century, the rules of coverture were altered by state legislation that conferred rights to married women. Some states began by granting married women the right to own property separate from their husbands, and other states extended additional rights of acquiring, using, and disposing of that property. The initial property acts were followed by earnings acts, which allowed married women to retain their own wages. Despite these reforms, any civil disabilities that were not specifically addressed by statute remained. The capacity recognized in these property rights was not extended to any other rules of coverture left untouched by statute, so a married woman might be able to own her own business and conduct transactions and she might even use her earnings to support her family, but she could have no say in where her family lived.

The limited reform has presented puzzles to today's scholars. If states passed legislation that abrogated this longstanding common-law rule of coverture, then why didn't they interpret the reform statutes to usher in larger emancipation for women? State legislators and judges were not unaware of women's rights and capacities; after all, women had issued their Declaration of Sentiments at Seneca Falls in 1848, in the midst of property reform. Sir Henry Maine announced that modern societies were moving "from status to contract."[31] If this had been the case, then women would have made the transition from the status of *feme covert* to *feme sole* (and perhaps the law would even have abolished the status of *feme* altogether). As married women, however, they retained the civil disabilities of coverture.[32] The married women's property acts gave married women the right to own property, but they exercised that right as married women, as the *feme covert* of the common law.[33]

Studies of the married women's property acts have explained that these laws fell short of emancipating women because they were not intended to liberate women from coverture. The first wave of married women's property acts, beginning in Arkansas in 1835, followed by other southern states, was unrelated to women's rights. These acts secured separate property for women to ensure that it would be free from husbands' creditors in a time of economic panic.[34] The second wave of property acts, beginning in New York in 1848, was the product of wealthy fathers who wanted to ensure that their sons-in-law would be denied access to their daughters' inheritance once the equitable practice of trusts had been altered by code.[35] The limited extent of the reform statutes can also be accounted for by shifts in American culture. The early nineteenth century was a time of regression in women's opportunities. The religious revivals of the early nineteenth century and the development of separate-spheres doctrine, by which women were given a role in the social order that confined them to the domestic sphere, reasserted women's gender and marital status.[36]

Both the origins of the acts and the operation of separate-spheres ideology do much to explain why the reform statutes did not liberate married women from coverture and usher in greater civil and political rights. Scholars cannot resist the conclusion that, nevertheless, the reform statutes should have had the effect of emancipating women. They share a teleological presumption that, even if the reform statutes did not originate with women's liberation in mind, the story of reform should end with women's liberation. Studies might acknowledge the limited reach of the acts in their day but go on to assess the acts for their role in leading to greater rights for women over time.[37] They search for someone to blame for the limited effect of the acts, and judges often emerge as the culprits.[38] That the limited reach of the statutory reforms remains a disappointment and a puzzle reveals the woman suffragist narrative at play. It has the features of a standard Whiggish narrative, with progressive principles and legislation overcoming the obstructions stubbornly retained by the common law.[39] Progress in this narrative is embedded in the principles of liberalism employed against the status of the common law.

Accounts of American political development offer the means to assess limited reform in the attention to liberalism as a heuristic to identify and measure political development or the reform's failure. Liberalism remains practical for gauging American political development.[40] Rogers Smith's multiple-traditions thesis presents a liberalism that has coexisted with nonliberal traditions that are based upon the ascriptive statuses of race and sex.[41] Development is marked by the growth of liberal values, or its failure recognized by the resurgence of illiberal traditions. Under this framework, the limited reach of the married women's property acts make sense as liberal reforms that were limited by the survival of an illiberal status regime. The multiple-traditions thesis neatly parses out the liberal and illiberal institutions operating upon married women's status and experience. By very definition, multiple traditions are defined and categorized as liberalism and its alternatives, whether a more robust republicanism or the more invidious traditions that rest on ascriptive characteristics of race, sex, and ethnicity. Disruptions in progress can be attributed to those enduring illiberal traditions that periodically emerge to restrict civic status. The multiple-traditions thesis explains regression as the liberal doctrine of individual rights and progress stymied by those external historical forces that prevent it from realizing its promises.

The attention to individual rights and freedom from oppression that marks liberal analysis in American politics has drawn attention to the importance of women's citizenship in understanding American political development more broadly.[42] But liberal analysis encounters puzzles similar to those encountered in women's history. The multiple-traditions thesis still does not resolve the puzzle of the limited reform of the married women's property acts. Lawmakers and judges of the time were not unfamiliar with the theories that could have emancipated women. The concerted activism of the woman suffragists in the midst of the passage of married women's property acts only compounds the mystery. It makes the exclusion of women even more poignant and puzzling, because woman suffragists rooted themselves centrally in the American political tradition. As Rogers Smith admits in his study of multiple traditions, "It is not obvious why he [John Locke] and revolutionaries like [Thomas] Paine were so insensitive to the plain case their principles made for female equality."[43] With no ready explanation under the multiple-traditions analysis, the likely explanation for the continued illiberalism in regards to married women is that the defenders of coverture were prejudiced.[44]

When the common law is posited externally to liberalism it emerges as illiberal and its enduring presence only makes sense as base prejudice or dogmatic conservatism. In casting aside the common law as such, researchers miss the opportunity to explore its relation with liberalism. Ken Kersch points out that the Whig narrative of progress obscures ambiguities.[45] Uday Mehta explains that the relevance of the ambiguities of liberalism are lost when seemingly illiberal practices fail to be considered as practices that might serve the institutional maintenance of liberalism.[46] Women's rights are exemplary of this notion. The simultaneous presence of rights and status of women's citizenship was not a contradiction but was, rather, a tension inherent in liberalism. Liberalism does recognize individual rights, but a liberal society has historically relied on status relations to maintain its institutional commitments. The status of the married woman provided for maintenance of the home, care of dependents, and education of children. In the antebellum South, the state counted on patriarchal households to uphold the ideal of egalitarian political relations among white men and to preserve social order. More broadly, the marital relation could serve state purposes of citizenship formation and national expansion.[47] Despite the racial and gender subordination in these instrumentalities, they sustained those social practices and norms needed to produce liberal citizens and the legal sanctions needed to ensure the maintenance of these practices. In classical liberal theory and early American liberalism, the common-law domestic relations played a large role in this institutional maintenance. Certainly these functions were carried out relying on a status and hierarchy that were contrary to individual rights, but they served liberal purposes.[48]

Institutional studies in American political development continue to incorporate the presumptions of a progressive liberalism. Karen Orren and Stephen Skowronek's multiple-orders thesis recognizes institutions originated at different times, so the rules that shaped them drew on different and competing traditions.[49] These institutions come to operate simultaneously, but their different purposes and animating traditions cause them to conflict. This institutional intercurrence becomes the site of tension, conflict, and change.[50] A classic example is presented in Orren's study of American labor law. Originally housed in the judiciary, labor law was informed by the common-law relation of master and servant. It was only when labor law was transferred to the legislature during the New Deal that it was informed by the legislature's animating liberalism.[51] Orren identifies the state of labor law under the judiciary as "belated feudalism," juxtaposing the status relations of the common law to the progressive individual rights of statute, thus incorporating the Whig narrative of liberalism.

When it comes to married women's property rights, however, the multiple-orders thesis does not obtain, and it encounters puzzles of its own. Legislation conferring rights to married women emerged in the first half of the nineteenth century, but there was little demonstration of married women's liberation from common-law status. The status of married women did not make the transition from common law to liberalism when the laws governing it shifted from the judiciary to the legislature. The most common explanation has been that conservative judges resisted the transition, but perhaps the judges were not merely conservative, and perhaps the legislation was not liberal. Rather than attribute these puzzling circumstances to prejudices or conservatism that thwarts liberal progress, it is once again more productive to inquire whether those puzzles suggest that a reconsideration of the received understanding of the juxtaposition of liberalism and the common law is in order.

The survival of the common-law doctrine of coverture does not make sense in standard liberal accounts of the American political tradition because it has already been marked as "bad," an ongoing source of an ascriptive status or a belated feudalism.[52] If this is the case, then one need only recover the progressive common-law tradition in women's rights to challenge the neat dichotomy. Such a recovery, however, is not straightforward. An initial look at the defenders of the common law in the late nineteenth century does indeed bear out the woman suffragist version of a repressive common law sustained by prejudice and resisting liberal progress. As married women gained more rights over the course of the nineteenth century, defenders of the common law justified the remaining rules of coverture by summoning tradition, nature, and God. The language of religion and sin were certainly not illegitimate in nineteenth-century political discourse, but the common-law domestic relations had not needed recourse to religion historically because they were so firmly entrenched in the legal system. By the late nineteenth century, however, the principles underlying the rules of the marital relation were losing their legitimacy, and the religious justifications for married women's status can be better understood as the "last gasp" of the common-law status regime.[53] Defenders of the marital relation sounded like the throwbacks that woman suffragists implied they were at the time. In historical perspective, they appear to be merely clinging to the status quo in the midst of change. The common law certainly continued to promise its own progressive resources. State court judges were offering common-law theories of married women's freedom in the twentieth century.[54] But by that time, married women's status had been taken up by other actors—legislators, U.S. Supreme Court justices, state constitutional convention delegates—who lacked the training of state court judges. The nodes of conflict had invited the exchange of political arguments into law and legal concepts into politics. Faced with making sense of common-law rules, defenders of the marital relation resorted to the dramatic justifications of God, nature, and tradition rather than to the common-law method.

Conflicting representations of the common law reflect its dual nature in the American political tradition. The common law served as both a source of liberty and of subjection in the United States. Its origins in feudalism and the household relations of the feudal lord and his inferiors merit the label "belated feudalism," but the common law enjoys another, competing reputation as a source of liberty.[55] Americans of the revolutionary generation could be heard to refer to it as the "birthright of our liberty" for its part in the "ancient constitution," which included the Magna Carta.[56] Defenders of the common law continually pointed to its ability to preserve its origins and rules while keeping pace with changing conditions.[57]

The common law may have continued to demonstrate the ability to respond to modern challenges, but then it encountered the gendered critique. The husband-wife relation was just one of a set of domestic relations that composed a household. Relations between husband and wife, parent and child, guardian and ward, and master and servant (which encompassed any relation between employer and employed) fixed a status for each party in the relation and respective rights and disabilities.[58] These relations were hierarchical, with the first party in each relation enjoying a higher standing and more rights. A man who was a husband, father, guardian, and employer could serve as head of a household and enjoyed the privilege and was susceptible to the obligations of maintaining and answering for those in his care. The notable subservient in this household was the wife. A single woman enjoyed the property rights of a man under the common law, but once she married, she lost her identity in the eyes of the law. She and her husband became, for legal purposes, one person, with the husband representing their union. Once the reform statutes were passed, some married women claimed that the new right to own separate property implied other rights to acquire, use, and dispose of that property, thus claiming rights that were denied under coverture. This presented a vexing problem at the time. The tension within liberalism, which Locke managed to sustain and the founding generation was happy to adopt, now had to be confronted. Judges responded by balancing rights with the status of married women, not always convincingly and not always sure of themselves. Treatise writers admitted that the principles of coverture were in flux, and they awaited further litigation and judicial decisions to pronounce the effects of the statutes. In the midst of this destabilization of meaning and uncertainty of the common-law rules, woman's rights activists offered their own interpretation by claiming that the married women's property acts were designed to rectify the wrongs done to women in the past. They declared these acts to have dealt the "death-blow" to coverture.[59]

In declaring the married women's property acts to be coverture's death blow, woman suffragists presented the acts as the agents of the abolition of coverture. They placed property rights at odds with status and (their version of) liberalism at odds with the common-law doctrine of coverture. They disparaged the common law itself as a source of rights. They also invoked a particular definition of coverture. The rules of coverture rested on status — a married woman's legal identity covered by her husband's — which conferred certain obligations and privileges of citizenship. In the carrying out of these obligations, the law established a hierarchy, with the wife subservient to the husband. The woman suffragists defined both status and hierarchy as out of keeping with American principles. In doing so, they masked the role that status and its obligations have played in American law and American liberalism.

Woman suffragists invoked equality, first to delegitimize coverture and then to abolish it. In declaring the property acts to be the death blow to coverture, they imbued the reform statutes with egalitarian sentiment that came to characterize the acts in retrospect. It was an effective rhetorical strategy. Under equality, rights are independent of status, at odds with status, and effective in dismantling status. Rights are abstract and universal, and the subject is a bearer of rights prior to any socially determined privilege or disability. This was the form of rights theory that the Supreme Court adopted when launching equality doctrine in the courts.

With this strategy, woman suffragists closed off equity as an alternative model of women's emancipation. In her study of married women's separate property in the colonial period, Marylynn Salmon points out that, in the absence of a legislative effort to alter coverture, colonial judges relied on equitable procedures to reduce the civil disabilities of coverture for individual women. While Salmon points out that equitable procedures were practically available to wealthy women, she suggests that there was already a favorable sentiment toward women's condition and that reform was under way even before the first property act had been passed.[60]

Equity was a resource that could ameliorate the hardships of the common law by providing exceptions. Under equity the status of a married woman remained, even as she exercised her property rights. This construction was reproduced in early judicial interpretations of the married women's property acts, despite the conferral of rights by statute. It is possible that this method of rights recognition could have continued, with states recognizing more property rights while retaining status and the recognition that even a liberalizing society has its social needs. Rather than treating women as abstract individuals, equitable reform could have addressed women's subjugation while acknowledging the reality of women's lives and ameliorating their social conditions.

It is possible to overstate the ameliorative effects of equity.[61] When Mary Ritter Beard criticized the woman suffragist narrative of equality in her 1946 study, *Woman as Force in History*, she complained that the woman suffragists overstated women's oppression because equity was always available to married women to alleviate the hardships of coverture.[62] Subsequent women's historians have pointed out that equity was not widely available, being limited to upper-class women, and that women's subjugation under coverture was, indeed, severe.[63] Without underestimating the material effects of coverture or overstating the corrective force of equity, it remains possible to acknowledge that reform could have continued to operate under the principles of equity and its form of rights derivation. Whether married women found relief through equity or equality was an important distinction, because each relied on a different theory of liberty.[64] Rather than ignoring the obligations assumed in the marital relation, equitable reform could have liberalized them. Instead, equitable corrections to the common law gave way to egalitarian reform, with important consequences for constitutionalism. The situated subject gave way to the abstracted subject, the consideration of what *this* society needs giving way to recourse to an idealized higher law. Today's interpreter who proclaims her faith or expertise in the Constitution effects a posture that distances her act of interpretation from her situated self. This loss of the situated self is a legacy of the need to proclaim the solitary self, who could claim rights despite her social status and repression as constructed by woman suffragists.

The path of reform from law, to politics, and back to law incurred a surprising conflation of positivism and natural rights doctrine, two doctrines that are familiarly opposed to one another in political philosophy. Nineteenth-century positivists targeted natural rights doctrine for its lack of exactitude and its faith in transcendent sources of knowledge. Positivism promised to bring a scientific precision to the derivation of rights. What natural rights and positivism have in common, however, is that they each reject social context. Natural rights promised a delivery from socially derived oppression, positivism from socially derived derivation of rights. In each, social context was irrelevant or anathema to the project of rights. Natural rights took hold in political discourse and positivism was smuggled into legal discourse, with the result that contextually derived rights were rendered suspect and, with this, the common-law method was lost from rights discourse and from constitutional disposition.

Part One recounts the history of the woman suffragist discourse. Chapter 1 traces the use of the language of barbarism in the codification debates. Chapter 2 identifies the invocation of higher law in the abolition movement as abolitionists sought to protect their own rights. It offers a gendered account of the abolitionist movement, pointing out the ways in which woman abolitionists rendered the rights-bearer even more abstract. Chapter 3 finds the woman suffragists blending the derogation of the common law with the recourse to higher law in the liberalism that they invoked to combat coverture. These chapters are attentive to the conditions that made the woman suffragist rhetoric persuasive and to the alternatives that were rejected. The codification debates produced a sophisticated defense of the common law in the face of reform and suggested a common law that could keep pace with modernity. As woman abolitionists modified natural rights theory to overcome women's subjection, the abolitionist Lydia Maria Child urged a rights theory that made use of, rather than escaped, status. Such examples became lost alternatives in the development of liberal doctrine.

The study might end with the triumph of the woman suffragist narrative in Chapter 3 except that the development of rights theory as incurred by the woman suffragists entailed a separation from and delegitimization of the common-law methods in rights discourse. Part Two addresses how this was possible and what loss American rights discourse incurred. Chapter 4 visits the married women's property acts again, this time in the legislative enactment and judicial interpretation in selected states and with a lens that, insofar as this is possible, is not constructed from the presumptions of the woman suffragists. This chapter resists the "good/bad" dichotomy of rights/status in the theories of the woman suffragists. It avoids foisting this dichotomy on an institutional analysis that presumes a progressive liberalism to have been housed in legislatures while conservative feudalism was retained in courts.[65] This chapter demonstrates that judicial interpretation was not due simply to the social conservatism of judges but to an accommodation of the common law in a collaboration of judges and legislators. Members of both institutions sought to reconcile the common law and liberal principles. There was an older rights discourse at work, in which political actors balanced rights with status.

Chapter 5 explains the tenacity of coverture by taking a step away from the husband-wife relation to gauge the change in married women's status within the domestic relations. As economic conditions became more competitive in the years after the Civil War, courts reconstituted the domestic relations by updating the master-servant relation. With the master-servant relation giving way to the employer-employee relation, courts remade the domestic relations as more properly domestic. This is difficult to identify using the woman suffragist version, which equates rights with progress and, paradoxically, deflects attention from the sources of women's oppression at the time of the married women's property acts. The conferral of property rights and the subsequent contract and earnings acts actually entrenched women's status as *feme covert* and provided a means to modernize a status regime.[66] Coverture proved to be remarkably resilient, and the reform statues provided a new means to reassert the old rules, status, and obligations of coverture.

As coverture was discussed at other levels of government its justification took far more bombastic forms. Chapter 6 points to the areas in which the common law's resources were lost from view in political and legal discourse as the common-law rules were defended outside state-level courts. Once common-law rules had been buttressed by recourse to scripture, nature, and tradition, they lent support to the idea that women's subjection was based on stereotypes. These defenses produced a common law that looked like an outdated doctrine for rights discourse, making the woman suffragist narrative appear accurate and persuasive. This loss is apparent in Indiana's constitutional convention of 1850, *Bradwell v. Illinois*, the codification debates of the 1880s, and Elizabeth Cady Stanton's "Solitude of Self." One sees a steady forgetting of the common law in rights discourse and an emergence of coverture as a legacy of mere prejudice.

This study of women's rights is an invitation to resist the liberal paradigm and to recognize the resources of the more organic rights discourse of the common-law method. Engaging in this exercise can encourage an appreciation for what it means to engage in constitutional politics. Embracing politics in constitutionalism means accepting the conditions of American politics, with all its egregious history. It means remaining open to uncertainty of definitive meaning, allowing meaning to emerge through ongoing interpretation and contestation with experience rather than being handed down by an authority. Recognizing the shared history of liberal and illiberal commitments does not require a capitulation to the gender hierarchy of the past. In accepting the limits of liberalism we can recover the radical potential of the seemingly conservative rules and practices of the common law.

PART ONE

The Rise of Rights

CHAPTER ONE

Codification of the Common Law Considered

The common law was British and feudal in its origins, and it vested power in un-elected judges, but it was fairly unproblematic in the early American republic.[1] The English common law was transplanted in the American colonies, and early Americans did not reject these feudal origins or case-law methods after independence. In fact, members of the Revolutionary War generation were likely to refer to the common law as the "birthright of our liberty." They dated the rights of man to the Magna Carta, the charter between King John and his lords in 1215. The jury trial, due process, equal protection, and protection from ex post facto laws and bills of attainder can be found in the common law and the "ancient constitution."[2]

These liberties existed in a society of feudal organization, but the common law was not a vestige of the past.[3] Despite its origins in feudalism, the common law was adapting to its age and circumstances in seventeenth- and eighteenth-century political and legal theories. In the eighteenth century, the common law and liberalism showed signs of converging, with John Locke incorporating the domestic relations in his *Second Treatise on Government* and Sir William Blackstone forming a social-contract basis for the common law.[4] Blackstone's *Commentaries* described a common law that had freedom as its purpose and social contract at its origins, demonstrating that the common law could keep pace with Enlightenment thought. American legal treatises continued to describe a common law that was adaptable to the American experience. The classic common-law treatises of Coke, Mansfield, and Blackstone were joined by an outpouring of legal treatises in the early nineteenth century, including the works of James Wilson, Chancellor Kent, Zephaniah Swift,

Thomas Cooper, Francis Lieber, and others.[5] Such editors as St. George Tucker Americanized Blackstone's *Commentaries.*

The very adaptability of the common law primed it for critical reconsideration, not because it was feudal but because it was cumbersome. After some early attempts to reform the common law, reform projects were undertaken in the 1820s, when the common law in American states was becoming unwieldy.[6] After independence, each state retained its own common-law tradition and relied on the common law to govern criminal law, contracts, torts, and the domestic relations.[7] State court judges practiced the historical common-law method, whereby the judges of the King's Court declared the common law of the land in case after case, with a body of maxims and principles arising from these precedents over time. Each state court system developed its own tradition of common-law reasoning, and the rules began to diverge from state to state. Judicial decisions, gathered in law reports, produced numerous volumes through which lawyers and judges had to sift in order to discern the law. Federalism compounded the problem. Different states were issuing different rules, and lawyers had trouble keeping up with the law, particularly with the increase in interstate commerce. Decisions of appellate courts became enmeshed in the rapidly accumulating law reports, making the common law "maddeningly hard to know" and making it more difficult to do business.[8] The initial impulse toward codification came from practicing lawyers who were frustrated by the sheer volume of law reports issued, compounded by the growth of this trend in each state. They had trouble keeping up with rapid and hard-to-find changes in the laws.[9] This legal situation was not suited for commercial development in a developing, interdependent economy.[10] This moderate group of codifiers within the legal profession sought to shift the location of legal rules from judicial law reports to legislative code. They sought codification for its simplicity.

A more radical movement for codification came from the swell of Jacksonian democratic and antilawyer sentiment in the early decades of the nineteenth century. There was no organized national movement, and the debate did not lay out along party lines; some Jacksonian Democrats were opposed to codification and some Federalists, such as Joseph Story, supported moderate plans for codification.[11] A middle-class contingent of merchants and businessmen worried that their business would be hurt by unclear law, and they reserved specific criticism for lawyers, whose high fees made litigation expensive.[12] In its radical wing, the codification movement took on an antilawyer animus that sought to eliminate legal rhetoric, lawyers' monopoly over the law, and, sometimes, even law itself.[13]

Proponents of codification sought to replace the common-law method of precedent with codified law, which would be passed by legislatures in majority-based stat-

ues, based on principles of law. Rather than requiring a search for the law in the numerous law reports that only trained lawyers could decipher, codified law promised
to be clear and accessible, serving democratic purposes in making the law known to
the people. Such codes would be drawn up by lawyers, however, so the democratic
promise proved elusive.

Despite its pragmatic goals, the legal reform movement of codification invited a
fundamental reconsideration of the common-law method and regulations in the
United States. The philosophical origins of codification promised that the certainty
and scientific methods of positivism would replace the less certain methods of
common-law judicial decision making. The discourse of the codification movement
during the early decades of the nineteenth century proves important not so much as
a study of codification as a reflection of the philosophic position of American legal
thought in regard to the fundamental tenets of positivism.

Despite the emergence of positivism in legal philosophy, American legal thought
in the 1820s and 1830s tended to remain amenable to the less precise and more flexible common law. In rejecting the fundamental positivism of the philosophical origins of codification, even advocates of codification reflected a commitment to the
traditional tenets of the American legal system. Despite the diversity in the development of the common law from state to state, William Novak has identified four in-
terrelated components of American common law: a focus on man as a social being,
a relative and relational theory of individual rights, a pragmatic historical method-
ology reflecting pre-Enlightenment thought, and the maintenance of a well-
regulated society in pursuit of the public good.[14] These underlying commitments
proved durable as the common law came under attack in the codification movement
in the first half of the nineteenth century. Supporters of the common law proved to
be remarkably adept at defending the common law's ability to adapt to modern conditions.[15] Common lawyers, and even moderate codifiers, were not ready to give up
the methods and traditions of the common law. In retaining the common law, they
revealed the resources of the common law for rights discourse and political legitimacy.

THE POSITIVIST CHALLENGE TO THE COMMON LAW

Had Americans taken codification seriously, they would have accepted its implicit positivism and rejected the relational, organic aspects of the common law.
Thomas Hobbes lay the groundwork in *A Dialogue between a Philosopher and a Student of the Common Laws of England*, setting up an imaginary conversation between
a philosopher and a lawyer to revive the older debates between Francis Bacon and

Sir Edward Coke. The philosopher was disturbed by Coke's statement that the law could be determined by reason. Because reason is accessible to any man, the lawyer's vision invited anyone to interpret the law and disagree with the sovereign's interpretation, preparing the ground for disobedience and disarray. The lawyer qualified Coke's statement by explaining that Coke was referring to artificial reason, the reason acquired by "long Study, Observation, and Experience" of law, thus delimiting the multiple interpretations to the practicing jurists.[16] The philosopher remained disturbed even by judicial independence, so he dismissed artificial reason as a mere art that does not constitute law, asserting, "It is not Wisdom, but Authority that makes a Law."[17] Lawmaking was restricted to those possessing the authority to make law, precluding a more customary notion of law as emerging from the community. Law is what the sovereign hands down, not what the members of the community (or judges) build up. When lawmaking was posited in the sovereign, the meaning was clear and certain, because there would be no conflicting interpretations to the sovereign's authoritative dictate.

The sovereign could rely on reliable methods for right use of reason. In *Leviathan*, Hobbes explains that Coke and other common lawyers begin their analysis mired in particulars, basing their premises on unreliable information gleaned from their own experience, precluding the scientific method: "Where men build on false grounds, the more they build, the greater is the ruine."[18] With proper use of reason, the law could be elevated to a science. "Hobbesian reason . . . has precisely the opposite genius, seeking always to clarify and simplify, to deal in certainty, not nuance."[19]

Certainty and simplicity were the goals that Jeremy Bentham set for himself in his own dispute with a common-law jurist. As a teenager, Bentham attended Sir William Blackstone's 1765 Vinerian lectures at Oxford. These lectures would form the basis for *Commentaries on the Laws of England* and serve as an exposition of the common law for readers in both England and the United States throughout the next century. Bentham reacted to those lectures in a series of works, published in his lifetime and posthumously, deriding the common law and the natural law foundation that Blackstone had identified.

Blackstone did not understand himself to be perpetuating a feudal doctrine. He presented the common law as a legal system that was compatible with modernity.[20] He borrowed liberally from the philosophers of his time, sometimes citing passages right from Locke or Montesquieu to connect the common law with modern thought.[21] For Blackstone, common law's modernity was evident in its freedom from both foreign influences and the Church. He viewed the challenge to modernity not in common law's feudalism but in the authority the Catholic Church, whose influence had been retained through civil law in continental Europe.

Blackstone deflected the problem of the feudal-modern tensions within common law by introducing a conflict between civil law and common law.[22] In emphasizing this distinction he could demonstrate the common law's freedom from the church, and the common law's secularism became evidence of its modernism. Seeking to reintroduce training in British law, Blackstone expressed his concern that the English were relying on civil law so much that they were forgetting their own British heritage. Touting the Britishness of the common law allowed Blackstone to distinguish it from the legal systems of other European nations. The civil law, which was the system of law derived from ancient Roman law, was used in such Catholic countries as France and Spain. Blackstone pointed out the common law's distance from the Church at various points in the *Commentaries,* saving his most pressing attacks against the Church for his characterizations of civil law. He dated the revival of Roman law to the discovery of the Justinian pandects, in 1137. The civil law then came into vogue in western Europe and "became a favourite of the popish clergy," who brought the civil law to England.[23] Blackstone presented the presence of both the civil-law and common-law traditions along a religious/secular dichotomy: The "monkish clergy" adopted the civil law, while the nobility and laity retained the common law. Since the civil law had been written it was easily kept alive by the clergy in universities, whereas the study of the common law was in danger of falling into disuse. He explained that the civil law would have taken over the common law had it not been for a "peculiar incident," the centralization of professors of municipal law into the court of common pleas. A collegiate order developed, and rudimentary law schools, separate from the clergy-run universities, appeared. In these institutions, the rules of the common law were passed down, such rules being "so liberal, so sensible and manly."[24] Discerning the rules of the common law was a manly endeavor, one in which those who studied the common law had to do the work for themselves. They had to determine what the law was rather than having the meaning of the law handed down to them from some higher authority.

Judicial decision making likewise protected freedom. For Blackstone, the common law was the product of judicial decision making over time, but those decisions were themselves all in accordance with natural law. Adhering to past decisions provides a means of keeping society in touch with the natural law, just as adhering to custom "carries with it internal evidence of freedom."[25] Under Roman law, anything could be written into law as long as it was procedurally legitimate; even a tyranny could be legitimate under written law.[26] In contrast, Blackstone presented the com-

mon law as operating under the constraints of a constitutional order. He saw the common law as serving a kind of constitutional foundation, limiting the substance of legislative statutes that could be passed. As the common law "probably was introduced
by the voluntary consent of the people," the people's freedom was protected from
transient majorities.[27]

Blackstone's efforts to demonstrate that the common law valued manly legal construction and freedom did not persuade Bentham. Blackstone's assertions, such as
his speculation that freedom "probably" rested at the origins of the common law,
were the kind of statements that exasperated Bentham. Bentham disapproved not
only of Blackstone's inexact methods for locating freedom but even of his recourse
to freedom, an abstract, indeterminate principle that offered no fixed meaning or
guidance for determining and interpreting law. Blackstone's identification of natural
rights, an effort to keep the common law up with modernity, provided the opportunity for Bentham to launch a rationalist attack on the common law for being uncertain and, hence, unstable.

After attending Blackstone's lectures, Bentham spent years deriding the common
law. He pointed out that it was not enough to wrest lawmaking away from the
Church; the law also had to be released from the authority of obscure language and
ideas, which included the abstract language of freedom. Bentham considered recourse to general principles to be a tool bandied about by those in power to obscure
their power and illegitimacy. Ten years after he had heard Blackstone's lectures, Bentham responded with his "Comment on the Commentaries," an unpublished manuscript that was discovered among Bentham's papers in the late nineteenth century.
In "Comment," Bentham chastised Blackstone for his vague definition of law, for his
indifference to the promulgation of law, and for his interpretation of the language of
law.[28] He ridiculed Blackstone's pointing to the antiquity of law as a source of authority.[29] The methods of judicial interpretation were unreliable, because Blackstone left it to judges to tap into the "general reason of mankind" in interpreting the
law. "Good," Bentham responded, "but how am I to come at this general reason . . . ?
I cannot go round the world and count suffrages. I must guess at it by my own."[30]

Bentham proffered another standard: "Had our Author again instead of reason
said utility, he would have said something. He would have referred us for a foundation for our judgment, to something distinct from that judgment itself. He would
have referred us to calculation founded upon matter of fact."[31] In laying down an
incipient theory of utilitarianism, Bentham applied an analytic jurisprudential critique to the common-law method, seeking a scientific calculation to provide certainty in the face of the vagueness and discretion of common-law methods.

Bentham continued to pursue this critique and his own positivist theory, coining the term *codification* to refer to the drawing up of a clear, concise code by an authoritative sovereign. This was not only a philosophic exercise but also a plan for applied reform, and he shopped his codification proposal around to various countries, including England, Spain, Portugal, Italy, France, and the United States.[32] In 1811, Bentham wrote a letter to James Madison, offering to draw up a code for the United States.[33] He made it clear that he was addressing it to the office of the President, not to the person. This is revealing, not only of someone committed to a government of laws rather than a government of men, but also of someone with little familiarity with the structure of American government. It was the state legislatures, not the federal executive, that would write up legislative codes. Madison did not respond until 1816, citing the intervening War of 1812 for the delay. He declined Bentham's offer, noting that the common law was already undergoing reform in the amendments and ongoing changes that had been wrought since it had been established in the colonies.[34] Bentham persisted, pursuing the more productive course of approaching the states. He initially sent his letters to governors, but Governor Snyder of Pennsylvania directed him to the state legislature.[35] Bentham printed general letters to the public, to which he attached the foregoing correspondence with Madison and the governors and a recommendation of Albert Gallatin.

In his appeals, Bentham pointed out that codification would be superior to the common law because it would be comprehensive, certain, and stable. Furthermore, it would be "real law" to replace the "sham law" of the common law.[36] He saw the common law as a referent without substance or legitimacy, and he advised his audience: "The next time you hear a lawyer trumpeting forth his *common law*, call upon him to produce a *common law*: defy him to produce so much as any one really existing object, of which he will have the effrontery to say, that that compound word of his is the name. Let him look for it till doomsday, no such object will he find."[37] An unwritten law was not a legitimate one in legal positivism.[38]

Bentham assured his readers that they should not be wary of him, a foreigner, recommending this reform. In fact, an outsider might be preferable, because a moral scientist could bring the "appropriate knowledge."[39] Reflecting on the positions of the foreigner and the community member, he mused that the foreigner could be useful in supplying the outlines of universal principles, and locals could fill in the details for how these rules would apply in the particular country. The moral scientist's universal rules would not be based on such abstract notions as justice or equality, which were simply indeterminate terms. "It is with trash such as this, that corruptionists feed their dupes. . . . It is with one part of it in their mouths that the holders of power pass for wise."[40] Enlightenment thinkers had freed reason from the subjugation of authority, be it political or religious authority or the "spell of words."[41] Bentham brought the hope of objectivity and science, to be employed with calculations to produce certainty and stability in the legal system. This move toward science was a move away from particularity and tradition. By relying on the methods of the mathematical sciences, which promised clarity, precision, and certainty, the moral sciences, too, could produce clear definitions of words. Once knowledge was freed from authority, including superstition and commitment to tradition, a system of knowledge could be well grounded and expressed in clear principles.

Bentham's positivism held potential consequences for legal interpretation and for citizenship. Under customary law, the meaning of the law rested on practical knowledge. There was no need for an authoritative source to determine or declare the meaning of the law because members of the community knew community rules through their experience of those rules. The positivist, on the other hand, sees rules from an external standpoint, as an observer, and therefore requires that rules be authoritative in order to know that they are the rules. The transition from customary law to positivism therefore entails a shift from community knowledge of truth to legitimation of social policy, from practical judgment to the expert knowledge of positive law, from the customary law of the community to the declaration of officials.[42] The writing of propositions could become the reference point for authoritative, propositional rules and replace practical knowledge.[43] Thus the shift to positive law would result in an alteration in the practice and experience of citizenship. The citizen would no longer have the opportunity to engage in interpretation of law and the state would alter the status of citizen from shaper of the law to subject of the law.

BENTHAM IN AMERICA

If Americans were to embrace legal positivism they would replace practical reason with expert knowledge, replace action with appeal to authority and experts, and replace reference to experience with reference to rules. The transition to positivism in the United States was not made, however, at least, not right away. Despite the adoption of Bentham's language, Americans did not embrace his theory. Bentham was an inspiration for, but not an agent of, the American codification movement.[44] While legal reformers adopted his term *codification*, they did not accept his theories. They employed the concepts of simplicity, clarity, and certainty, but they did not seek clear propositions of truth, nor did they desire the services of an outside expert. They simply wanted law to be clear when they consulted it.

Codification proposals emerged on a state-by-state basis, with codification considered and, in some cases, change effected, but, overall, the product of the movement was slight. There were some state commissions established to investigate the practicability of shifting from the common law to code, and there were some statutory reforms, but even then, codification efforts were limited in their scope in the extent to which they replaced the common law.

With its history of French and Spanish colonization, Louisiana had a civil-law system. Louisiana maintained a tripartite system of law, favoring civil law but also sustaining an American court system and some common-law rules.[45] Edward Livingston, a lawyer from New York and one of the few self-professed Benthamite legal reformers in the United States, was instrumental in writing up a code based on the 1804 Napoleonic Code. Other states with common-law traditions made partial efforts toward codification. South Carolina is notable for its serious interest and debate over codification, but, ultimately, the effort failed to produce a code. Thomas Cooper, another Benthamite, was a South Carolinian who sustained an active public discussion of codification, and Governor John Wilson called for a digest of the law in 1823. Succeeding governors continued to urge the legislature to codify, but the opposition of common lawyers in the legislature never allowed the plan to come to fruition.[46]

Massachusetts considered codification when the governor appointed a commission, headed by Joseph Story, to look into the matter. The commission returned the recommendation that the common law not be abolished but its principles written into clear propositions. This was a moderate proposal, but nevertheless, the legislature took no action at that time.[47] New York achieved some partial codification but is perhaps more notable for its influence on other states. The Revised Statutes of 1828 witnessed a "true, if limited, codification" by categorizing the law by subject rather than writing it down in the order in which it was passed.[48] In 1846, the state constitution called for a code commission, to which David Dudley Field was appointed in 1857. Field committed his late career to the codification of New York state law, and he drafted a set of codes—a penal code, a political code, and a civil code. The drafts lay dormant in the New York legislature for years but circulated throughout the United States and were adopted, partially or fully, primarily in western states and territories.[49] Thus, while the codification discourse percolated in the east, the west was more likely to implement reforms.

By the middle of the nineteenth century, codification was a movement for partial reform rather than a new foundation for American law.[50] The codification movement is notable not so much for its achievement as for the discourse that it generated. Interest in codification invited reconsideration of the common law and analysis of why the United States retained it. The discourse revealed that Americans were committed to the common law, not because they were conservative apologists for the status quo,[51] or because they were elites resisting the tide of democracy.[52] In clinging to their common-law traditions and methods, Americans retained an epistemology, a mode of interpretation, and, ultimately, a conception of citizenship that remained an alternative to the universal, scientific, authoritative methods of positivism.

The American commitment to the common law is reflected in Americans' widespread rejection of Bentham. Despite Bentham's generous offers to codify American law, he was quite unpopular in the United States. Common lawyers found him an easy target for their general disapproval of codification. Reviewing his *Judicial Evidence*, the *Southern Review* pointed to its "obscure, involuted, Benthamee dialect," asserting that "a book, more disgustingly affected, and so nearly unintelligible, it is not possible to produce in the English language, with the exception of some of Mr. Bentham's former works."[53] A subsequent review of Bentham's *Principles of Legislation* pondered whether the publication of another of Bentham's books in the United States was an indication of his increasing popularity, but determined that, when people read it, "it will do nothing to increase that popularity."[54]

Even codifiers were reluctant to be associated with Bentham. The *American Jurist*, a legal newspaper edited by Justice Story's former students and an organ of the moderate codification movement, considered the Benthamite origins of codification to be a liability to American codification efforts.[55] Bentham was referred to as a dreamy philosopher and charged with being out of touch with the American system, remaining a theoretician rather than a practitioner — a criticism that was likely to resonate with both sides of the codification debate, as all the participants tended to be themselves practitioners concerned with how to make the law more workable. Thus, "Benthamite" was an easy epithet for common lawyers to employ against codifiers, and reformers took pains to distance themselves from Bentham.[56]

Bentham's proposal to replace the common law with code was too radical, even for American codifiers, most of whom did not want to relinquish the common law. In endorsing a moderate reform of reducing common-law principles to a written code, Joseph Story was careful to distinguish this project from the more drastic Benthamite overhaul: "We ought not to permit ourselves to indulge in the theoretical extravagances of some well meaning philosophical jurists, who believe, that all human concerns for the future can be provided for in a code speaking a definite language."[57] The *American Jurist* occasionally pointed out that Bentham's views were ill timed, too radical, too intent on revolutionizing the legal system when all that was called for was to fix it: "We are sure that men can never be persuaded to demolish, for the purpose of rebuilding the fabric of law, which constitutes the bulwark of life, liberty, and property,"[58] thus indicating that protection of cherished rights was tied to the common law rather than harmed by it.

When American codifiers adopted terms such as *simplicity* or *certainty*, they did not import the rationalist meaning of those terms. This is evident in the disparate views of France's Napoleonic Code by Bentham and the common lawyers. Americans admired the code, a litany of 2,287 articles, and sought to emulate its simplicity. For Bentham, the Code Napoléon was *too* simplistic. Bentham's notion of simplicity was to reduce ideas to first principles, with codes accompanied by explanatory justifications.[59] For Americans, simplicity held a different connotation and normative status, offering the brevity and simplicity they sought in a workable system of law.

When treating Bentham more directly, the *American Jurist* reflected that he may have been opportunistic in seeking to reform American law not as a service but as a venue from which to implement his theory of utilitarianism. It spent some time casting doubt on utilitarianism itself, noting that the standard of happiness was no clearer a guide than the principles it sought to replace and reflecting that Bentham had hindered reform.[60]

The American codifiers' distance from Bentham is further evident in reformers' treatment of Blackstone. Whereas Bentham saw Blackstone as representing and reproducing everything that was wrong with unscientific treatments of law, the *American Jurist* was content to exercise irreverence, displacing Blackstone's authority by making fun of him. In its first issue, *American Jurist* provided a sardonic biographical account of Blackstone's life and career and suggested that Blackstone was merely an untalented jurist who wrote a mediocre, derivative work that exercised undue influence on American law. The great lawyers in British history are forgotten because they tended to be busy practicing law and not making a name for themselves historically. Blackstone, unable to distinguish himself in legal practice, is only remembered because he instead wrote a treatise. The magazine printed one of Blackstone's amateur poems, "The Lawyer's Farewell to His Muse," wryly noting, "we think it unquestionable that, even looking at the bare consideration of literary fame, Blackstone acted wisely in dedicating himself to the law."[61] The article traced the path of his career as lawyer, judge, and Oxford professor. In evaluating his career, the article pronounced him a shy man, a poor public speaker, and an unremarkable judge. It bestowed the dubious compliments of his being punctual, highly exemplary in his social and domestic relations, and good with his money.[62] Even the *Commentaries*, for which he was known, *Jurist* derided as merely derivative of the work of prior jurists and philosophers such as Sir Matthew Hale and Montesquieu.[63]

This displacement of Blackstone's authority, which was not fatal to the common law itself, merely opened up a space to criticize the common law. It provided the opportunity to change rather than abolish it, a position that comported with that of the moderate codifiers, who wanted to fix the common law's flaws but retain its principles.

MODERATE CODIFICATION IN AMERICA

Supreme Court justice and treatise writer Joseph Story exemplified the moderate codifier's position, a reaction to the accumulation of law reports and Byzantine discovery of legal rules. He wrote the first article in the inaugural issue of *American Jurist*. Story did not think that the common law was inherently unsuitable for the United States. The problem, rather, was that the common law had encountered a modern, commercial society. The courts were overwhelmed, producing volumes of reports in each state, leading Story to remark, "The danger, indeed, seems to be, not that we shall hereafter want able Reports, but that we shall be overwhelmed with their number and variety."[64] The system of federalism, with appellate courts producing common-law opinions in each state, was leading to inconsistency from state to state. This was impractical for a country with an interdependent economy. The response of the moderate codifiers was not to replace the common law, nor to cast doubt on its reliance on judges. The task was to collect judicially derived, common-law principles in more manageable form. The legislature could assist by producing a digest of common-law rules, replacing volumes of law reports with a text reproducing the principles produced under common-law reasoning. Hence the legislature would be put into service to record common-law principles, not to generate rules of its own.

Story's position indicates the limited use of Bentham's ideas. Reliance on written, simplified law would seem to follow the transition from community law to positivism.[65] The codification movement, however, valued simplicity not because codifiers hoped for simple, clear principles derived with scientific methods but because simplicity captured the ease of accessibility to the law that they sought. Codifiers used the familiar language of simplicity but not as legal positivists. With its transfer of lawmaking from court to legislature, the institutional shift to the legislature did not imply any positivist shift to an authoritative source of law, but merely the transcriptions of a recording secretary. To write the law as legislation would not mean that the legislators served as enlightened lawgivers. Common-law methods would still be counted on to produce the principles underlying the legislation.

In 1837, the *American Jurist* printed the report of the Massachusetts Commissioners on the Codification of the Common Law, of which Story and an editor of the *American Jurist* were members. The commission determined that "the common law consists of positive rules and remedies, of general usages and customs, and of elementary principles, and the developments and applications of them, which cannot now be distinctly traced back to any statutory enactments, but which rest for their authority upon the common recognition, consent and use of the State itself."[66] Thus, the legislature need not go outside the common law to determine principles for the code, and it need not engage in the practical project of replacing the entire corpus of the law with a code.

American codifiers fell short of Bentham's positivism in part because they retained a broader sense of scientific method. American codifiers did not fully meet the scientific standards of the positivists, and the common lawyers did not capitulate to the charge that the common law was unscientific. Various understandings of science were circulating in the early nineteenth century.[67] By acknowledging scientific methods in the common law, common lawyers meant that the common law contained principles that could adapt to changing circumstances. The *North American Review* cited Chancellor Kent's finding that the common law "proved to be a system replete with vigorous and healthy principles, eminently conducive to the growth of civil liberty."[68] The common law promulgated its laws through the publication of reports of judicial decisions. Responding to the charge that there were too many reports to keep up with, the article suggested that that was part of the scientific process. Referring to cases as new discoveries, the article explained, "the man of real science does not very often complain of the multiplication of books upon his favorite theme; nor the man of letters, of the numerous works of literature and taste. The comparison furnishes us with a good illustration of the true character of the common law. It is a science, and, like all other sciences, progressive. It perpetually enlarges, and suits itself more and more closely to our wants and circumstances."[69]

Josiah Quincy, president of Harvard Law School, endorsed a notion of practical reason for the derivation of legal principles that connected law to society: "Those, who attain eminence in the profession, necessarily take deep and wide views of the principles of human conduct, and are introduced to an intimate acquaintance with the greater, as well as the lesser, relations and interests of individuals and societies; and this not through cloistered contemplation, but by living, practical observation of the motives of men, of the objects they pursue, and of the uses of those objects."[70]

Common lawyers may have made the case that practical reason was the method of lawyers, but codifiers had an easy time discrediting such practice as a science. The *American Jurist* challenged Quincy's notion in 1838, asking, "But who does not know, at this day, that the science of the law is not to be attained, amidst the cares and ordinary business pursuits of life?"[71] Given the extraordinary number of cases at common law, it required too much labor on the part of lawyers and judges to discern the principles. If the common law could not produce those principles, they could count on scientific advances to derive principles, but positivism was not the only alternative. In looking outside the common law to derive principles, codifiers rejected Bentham's utilitarianism. American reformers found Bentham's formula for discerning principles to be imprecise, an opinion that would certainly have taken Bentham by surprise. Codifiers were stumped as to how to arrive at a standard measure of happiness using the utilitarian principle of the greatest happiness for the greatest number. Furthermore, Bentham was too radical for their comfort. His utilitarian theory, which would be the guide for discerning principles, had little regard for previous socially determined decisions.

Codifiers looked to a variety of outside sources for alternative scientific methods. Timothy Walker's treatise modified the common-law method, using the organizational approach of legal scholars to mediate the voluminous judicial decisions. Codifiers were particularly interested in finding a method that would help them interpret the language of their proposed codes. Asked how they should judge the merits of a work like Walker's they responded, "In a treatise which professes to be strictly elementary, we are not to look for the original speculations of a Bentham. . . . The veteran lawyer will not resort to its pages for new stores of learning, nor the judge seek in them the resolution of a novel and difficult question. We want perspicuity, condensation, clearness and simplicity of style."[72] Walker's text, contained in one volume of only 650 pages, categorized areas of the law and provided the organizing method that would contribute to the clarity of the law. By drawing upon the common principles that were emerging from the varied experience of the common law in the then twenty-six states, he "gave unity and completeness to the system."[73]

Although positivists were skeptical of deducing principles from concepts of natural law, American codifiers had not rejected natural law jurisprudence, as is evident in American Jurist's review of J. D. Meyer's work on codification. Meyer, a German jurist, took the side of codification in an ongoing German debate over codification. In his 1823 work, Meyer criticized the historicist school, the analog of the American common-law defenders. According to Meyer, historicists denied the possibility of a society producing general principles of law. Instead, law grew by accretion: "Law, jus, becomes established by insensible degrees. It is the slow growth of custom and usage. . . . The decision in one case, becomes a precedent for another, until, by repeated instances, it gradually acquires the force of a rule."[74] Meyer cautioned that this method maintained the status quo because "it assumes, as a given or conceded fact, that the existing usages of a nation are always right."[75] There is no outside standard by which to judge the rightness or justice of those customs. The civil law, on the other hand, based its codes on principles of natural law, "the expressions of those sentiments of natural justice, which are engraved on the heart of man by the Author of his being."[76]

The *American Jurist* revisited Meyer's work in 1833, singling out written code as "most conducive to a steady and uniform administration of justice."[77] The method of precedent did not produce general principles or clarity. "By this process the law is brought out only in disjointed fragments; the whole body, as we now have it, is composed of separate and independent cases; of particular applications; and not of general principles."[78] The simple written code, on the other hand, would produce a law that would be clear and known to the common man. Hence the method of the common law resulted in a failure to meet a standard of the codifiers' making—general principles. The codification movement valued general principles, which were clear and simple. They were touted as suitable guideposts because they were derived from principles of natural justice and were capable of being applied to particular cases. Meyer's work turned to an external standard to derive principles, invoking the natural law that so irked Bentham.

The *American Jurist* also reprinted selections of Francis Lieber's *Political Ethics* in two issues, devoting a remarkable number of pages, indicating the importance it ascribed to his project.[79] Lieber was skeptical about precedent, seeing it as an unexamined conferral of authority on "forefathers." He recommended that the law be written down in general principles that could be applicable to particular situations, but he also understood that this left interpretation of the law open to uncertainty. Thus Lieber was committed to the study of hermeneutics to order the interpretation of language. His response to finding the "true" meaning of ambiguous language was not to revert to a positivist calculation but to exercise common sense and good faith.[80] Codifiers could develop guidelines for interpreting language to keep them from going astray, a movement toward objectivity but far short of any scientific calculations for basing legal interpretation on scientifically demonstrable truths.

RADICAL CODIFICATION IN AMERICA

The American codification discourse may have developed as a discussion over the best way to improve the common law rather than as an attack on the common law, but its tone was influenced by the contributions of a few radical reformers, who introduced devastating charges against the common law. A strong contingent of common lawyers resisted the charges and fought back, producing the debates that invited the legal community to wrestle with questions of lawmaking, society, and authority.

Codification discourse in the 1820s proliferated after William Sampson's speech to the New-York Historical Society in December 1823. Sampson sought to defeat the common law by exposing its myths. His speech inspired both codifiers and common lawyers to engage in discussion in magazines and newspapers over the next few years, debating one another and simultaneously promoting or resisting reform in their own states. Instead of conceding defeat, common lawyers responded by flipping the charges Sampson and his advocates leveled, thus revealing the premises and consequences of the positivist sentiments that codifiers were inviting into American law.

Sampson was an Irish immigrant who had been a participant in the Irish rebellion against the British in 1798. Exiled to Portugal, he was imprisoned for uncertain reasons, released, and lived in France from 1799 to 1805, the period in which the Napoleonic Code was instituted.[81] He brought skepticism for Anglo law, first-hand frustrating experience with an overpowering criminal justice system, and familiarity with legal reform in France. He practiced law when he arrived in New York in 1806 and combined his legal experience with his political commitment to reform in his address to the historical society, offering a revisionist history of the common law. He drew attention to the importance of history in the common law in its attention to precedent in judicial decision making and its glowing references to antiquity by treatise writers. Sampson exploited the common law's historical attachment by announcing that the origins of the common law lay not in a golden age but in the practices of barbarous heathens.

Sampson poised his audience for this history by entreaty to their modern sensibilities. He displayed a skepticism toward common-law methods by drawing attention to their "barbarous jargon," "savage antiquity," "veil of mystery," "devotion to idols," "bombastic encomiums," suspect zeal, the duping of Americans, "mummery," "superstitions," and "mysterious essence."[82] He tapped into the rationalist tendency to call authoritative sources of knowledge into question, suggesting that Americans had been duped by those who held expert knowledge of the common law. He recommended that the common law's artificial reason be replaced with the perfection of reason.[83] He explained that questioning tradition was the Enlightenment's last remaining blow to all sources of authority: "Long after they had set the great example of self-government upon principles of perfect equality, had reduced the practice of religion to its purest principles, executed mighty works, and acquired renown in arts and arms, had still one pagan idol to which they daily offered up much smoky incense. They called it by the mystical and cabalistic name of Common Law."[84]

After demystifying the common law, Sampson engaged in a more empirical study of the origins of British law. He returned to the twelfth-century origins of the common law and recollected the practices of the Anglo-Saxons prior to the Norman Conquest. He found British history to be mired in barbarism. The ancient British ancestors were barbarians who failed to cultivate the land, wore animal skins (when they clothed themselves at all), engaged in incestuous, polygamous, and violent family relations, and divined the future by slicing a man in two and reading his entrails. Their wayward ethics rendered them insecure, and the Romans easily conquered them by exploiting their own internal divisions. The Romans improved conditions in England, but they were a "cruel and pitiless race."[85] The Saxons were fierce pirates who worshiped many gods. The Danes were violent and belligerent. Alfred, the British king who is often cited as having brought law to England, was acknowledged by Sampson to have been a successful warrior and leader and literate as well, but his achievements were exaggerated and the Danes nevertheless reconquered England and reversed what he had accomplished. The other British king noted for common-law origins, Edward the Confessor, is cited by Sampson for his meager laws, for taking bribes, and for robbing his mother.[86]

Sampson's ideas had the potential to radicalize legal reform in the United States, but only if they proved persuasive. His lecture launched a flurry of reactions, both favorable and critical. The few Benthamites in the United States eagerly sought to increase their connection with Sampson. Most notably, Thomas Cooper engaged in a public correspondence with him, lauding his methods, by which all mystery in law could be abrogated and, as in the natural sciences, reduced to plain and intelligible principles.[87]

Sampson's identification of barbarism at the origin of the common law was an evocative concept to which legal reformers continually referred. In a review of William Sampson's address, the *North American Review* cast doubt upon the ancient constitution that was a central feature of the common law, remarking, "To talk of the *ancient* common law is to give a false name to the bloody codes of barbarians."[88] The early years of the common law were not marked by freedom or certainty or even viability. They were instead the time when the "feeble, tottering" system had been established. For security, legal systems provide "the reason, wisdom, humanity, and experience of more modern times."[89] The common law, then, should give way to modern methods rather than being retained in modern times. To root modern laws in the tradition of the common law was to "chain the spirit of justice and liberty with the fetters forged in the darkest days of oppression and wrong."[90]

Sampson provided the codifiers with a history that suggested that the common law and codified law belonged to two different ages. *American Jurist* relied on the images of barbarism to point out the unsuitability of such a past for an enlightened age. "Admitting that mankind are growing wiser from generation to generation, how is it possible that rules, and maxims, and usages, which grew out of the circumstances of a dark and barbarous age, should be suited to the present time?"[91]

Recalling Sampson's references to superstition as authority casting a veil of mystery on examination of law, the *American Jurist* acknowledged that common-law practices encouraged "superstitious reverence" of long-held maxims rather than relying on reason.[92] Modern legal thinkers had to assume a critical stance toward the common law and avoid reverence, superstition, and awe. Leveling the charge of barbarism was a sure way to invite such a posture.

COMMON LAW RESISTANCE

Sampson's language of barbarism and superstition was powerful but not definitive. Rather than admit defeat or deny the charge of barbarism, common lawyers challenged the meaning, refusing to allow it the connotation implied by reformers. In 1824, *Atlantic Magazine* reflected on the emptiness of Sampson's barbarism characterization, saying, "There is a great parade of learning to prove, what nobody ever doubted, that the ancient Britons were not many removes from barbarism."[93] Merely associating the early common law with barbarism did not prove anything about the common law.

Other moderate codifiers were able to discern some beneficial qualities in the common law's barbaric origins. In a teleological historical account, in which historical processes moved toward freedom, the *North American Review* found in the barbarian defeat of the Romans in England the loss of refinement and civilization but also "the vigor of nature, contending with the weakness of refinement."[94] Hence even the barbarians had resources that were instructive for a civilized, modern society. In the *American Jurist*, Emery Washburn said, "I trace back [the common law's] history to the rude ages of a half barbarous people, but I find there a stern love of liberty; and, if no more, I there trace the origin of our surest safeguard of personal rights, a trial by jury."[95]

Common lawyers even argued that it was not the common-law tradition but the civil-law tradition that failed to provide adequate protection of rights. While civil-law countries engaged in the Inquisition, for example, the common people of England remained free from state oppression. The barbarians had admirable qualities: "Strange as it may seem, it is nevertheless true, that those hordes of Goths and Vandals that swarmed from the northern hive, and whose name has become a reproach and a by-word for all that is barbarous, are the very people that spread law, language, and liberty over our western world."[96] They were a simple people who contributed to the common law their "love of liberty, its devotion to good morals, and its abhorrence of fraud."[97]

With the connotation of barbarism remaining indeterminate, its potential power as an insult failed to obtain. Sampson and other reformers assumed that *barbarism* would evoke streaming hordes of violent, ignorant warriors. The simplicity of barbarians, however, was not an unappealing image in the 1820s, a time when the common law was under attack not because it limited freedom but because it was too complex. If its defenders could trace the common law back to an original simplicity, they could claim simplicity as part of the common-law heritage. This was a vulgarization of the term *simplicity*, drawing upon a simpler time rather than a simpler method for producing guiding principles in lawmaking. Nevertheless, the indeterminacy of meaning allowed common lawyers to deflate the charges leveled against the common law. Rather than defeating the common law, the codifiers' charges opened up a space for reconsideration of key terms and for common lawyers to level their own counter-charge against codification.

Refusing to concede a negative meaning to barbarism, common lawyers drew attention to liberty. The reformist stance of the codifiers did not necessarily make them modern, as *Atlantic Magazine* pointed out: "The cry of reform, although claimed to be, is not, in fact, a child of modern times: it is as old as ambition, discontent, or usurpation."[98] Furthermore, there have been plenty of reformers in history who reformed the legal system in order to institute despotic governments. The connection between codification and despotism was, on the one hand, an empirical argument that served as a potshot at codifiers. Common lawyers found it useful to point out the many despots who could be classed as progressive: "If Solon was a reformer, so also was Draco: if Brutus was a reformer, so also was Caesar: if Martin Luther was a reformer, so also was Ignatius Loyola: if Henry Laurens was a reformer, so also was Robespierre."[99]

In pointing to the link between despots and reform, common lawyers were doing more than assigning guilt by association; they were implicitly questioning the merits of the positivist tenets that reformers were bringing to bear. Codifiers touted the civil law for its simplicity in comparison to the cumbersome common law. Common lawyers turned that around to inquire *why* it was so simple and whether simplicity really was a feature to be valued. Simplicity was possible because a single voice proclaimed what the law was. People knew the law because someone told them what the law was. This was authoritarian imposition, with one person — or one body — serving as the source of law and, furthermore, as the source of the definitive meaning of the law. "It is not in lands of liberty and equal rights that the business of codifying flourishes. It is commonly the work of despots. A single imperial voice, commanding unqualified instant submission throughout the community, has hitherto ordered, directed, and enforced it in practice. In this manner only can it be promptly, harmoniously, and efficiently done."[100] Hence codified law was despotic because it restricted interpretation of the law. Justinian, for example, was not only the "sole legislator" of the Roman Empire but also the sole interpreter, as was the case for other codifiers: "The will of a single man, of a child, perhaps, as has been justly said, was allowed to prevail over the wisdom of ages, and the inclinations of millions."[101]

Codifiers liked to point out that simplicity was more democratic, because any farmer could read the code, know it, and talk about it. In a letter to Sampson, Charles Watts of Louisiana gushed that codification "would render law, as a science, more level to the understandings of all, to strip it of its unnecessary intricacy, absurd fictions, obsolete and inapplicable maxims, rules, and forms."[102] With these "mysteries" of the law removed, the code would be legible to the common man, a condition that Watts identified in codified Louisiana: "The planters and well informed men have the code in their hand, and discuss it as a branch of politics; while, on the contrary, the community here (in N.Y.) are involved in Egyptian darkness."[103]

Common lawyers were skeptical of this simplicity. Sometimes their criticism was practical; they doubted that all legal concerns could be included in a single code. "The business of fully codifying all the existing laws, we believe, never could be accomplished by one of our free legislatures. We feel almost assured of this, in fact, by actual observation."[104] The *North American Review* determined that the codifiers' objects of certainty, simplicity, and consistency in law were impossible to achieve because "we know that it can never in this way be accomplished, even with the greatest power, genius, and facilities, for carrying it into effect. The various and growing wants and occasions of the law, no human prescience can anticipate."[105] Codifiers could adequately respond to this charge by saying that common lawyers misconceived the codification project, assuming that it would fail because it was not perfect.[106] Codifiers charged that common lawyers were under the misperception that the code had to be written in minute detail, when in fact the code would contain general principles that would be applicable to particular cases.

The common lawyers' doubts about the comprehensiveness of a code reflected a deeper concern. It was not just that the code could not cover all legal issues; a written code with a litany of laws did not capture what it meant to have law. Law was not merely a collection of words on a piece of paper but a reflection of larger experience, in its inception and in its interpretation. Of Sampson's vision of a plain and simple code, *Atlantic Magazine* remarked, "All this is very pretty; it is the *beau ideal* of law;

but we conceive, is much better adapted to the people of Utopia, than to us, with all the imperfections of our human nature."[107]

Common lawyers retained the notion that law grew out of a community and that the law has meaning beyond the words on a piece of paper. To see the law as capable of simplification was to deny this complexity. The only way to simplify the law was to impose meaning upon it. They saw this as despotic as well as impractical; such a practice went against nature, and sooner or later such laws would inevitably need to be changed. The common law was equipped with the means for ongoing adaptability. Hence the common lawyers were able to turn a criticism of the common law into one of its virtues.

Common lawyers were able to respond to concerns about authority in law by reveling in one of the traits that so bothered codifiers — the uncertainty of the common law. Certainty was a feature that codifiers touted as being possible and desirable in a code. Codifiers pointed out that the common-law method, with rules emerging out of the slow and murky process of precedent, did not lend itself to certainty. Codifiers were well aware of the ambiguity of words, which they treated as a problem that needed to be avoided or solved. In a review of the work of the German historicist school, the *American Jurist* noted, unfavorably, that the historicists treated law like a living language. "It is, in its nature, essentially variable, extending and contracting itself according to the condition of the nation, accommodating its flexible character to the manners, habits, and employments of the people. . . . It is, in its nature, essentially incapable of fixity. There is no time when it is stationary and stable, but it is kept in perpetual movement by the varying condition of the nation."[108] Common lawyers were sanguine in their acceptance of this feature of the common law. They did not see the uncertainty of the common law as capriciousness, because the discovery and interpretation of the law would be guided by knowledge of both the law and the community. Hence this was not an "anything goes" endeavor, and common lawyers could state confidently, "In unwritten customary law, on the contrary, vagueness, ambiguity, and uncertainty, are inherent in its essence; they are not accidental specks or blemishes, but are incorporated into its very nature."[109]

Common lawyers refused to cede a connection between certainty and rights. They pointed to uncertainty of the common law as a virtue. Any single rule could be interpreted flexibly, and should a law not be written, the common law "furnishes a rule where written law is at a loss."[110] Codifiers associated the common law with the status quo, specious because it "exhibits itself in national and patriotic feelings; for it assumes, as a given or conceded fact, that the existing usages of a nation are always right."[111] Common lawyers, however, identified a progressive tendency in the flexibility of the common law by identifying its ability to adapt to a changing society over time. The common law was "a more flexible and apt species of jurisprudence, containing an internal principle of reformation within itself, and accommodating itself with equal facility to the advances of science and the changes of society."[112] Under this perspective, the history of the common law, as the colonial system of law derived from England, attested to its strength. The common law was able to survive the American Revolution and take on a life of its own in each state. While detractors would point to the multiplicity of common-law rules that this had produced, making it hard for the common man to know the law and for lawyers to practice law, common lawyers saw this as proof that the common law could adapt to local conditions and to changing circumstances over time. "Its improvement arose from its gradual adaptation of those principles to the condition of the colonies."[113]

Joseph Story was able to combine his concern for scientific and commercial advancement with his respect for the common law. In "Course of Legal Study," an article that he wrote for the *North American Review* in 1817, he lauded progress in moral, political, and juridical science and pointed out the importance of a uniform administration of justice. These concerns did not lead him to seek an alternative to the common law, however, because he found the source of improvement to lie in the common law. "Whatever of rational liberty and security to private rights and property is now enjoyed in England, and in the United States, may, in a great degree, be traced to the principles of the common law, as it has been moulded and fashioned, from age to age, by wise and learned judges. Not that the common law, in its origin, or early stages, was peculiarly fitted for these purposes; for the feudal system, with which it originated, or at least, became early incorporated, was a system, in many respects, the very reverse; but that it had the advantage of expanding with improvements of the age."[114]

The uncertainty of the common law was a liability only if one applied the standards of positivism. When one assessed law as a lived experience, applicable to human affairs, its uncertainty was a virtue: "To a certain extent, law must forever be subject to uncertainty and doubt; not from the obscurity and fluctuation of decisions, as the vulgar erroneously suppose, but from the endless complexity and variety of human actions. However certain may be the rules of the statute or common law, they must necessarily be general in their language, and incapable of a minute and perfect application to the *boundless* circumstances of life, which may modify, limit, or affect them. It is impossible to provide by any code, however extensive, for the infinite variety of distinctions, as to civil justice."[115]

The feudal origins of the common law and its commitment to tradition invited codifiers to construct a feudal-modern dichotomy between the common law and codified law. Relying on such arguments as Sampson's, codifiers could cast codification as the project suitable for moderns and render the common law inappropriate and obsolete. Common lawyers refused to allow this dichotomy to stand. Relying on notions of science and progress, they, like Blackstone, presented the common law as capable of adjusting to modernity. Furthermore, they questioned codification's fitness for a modern government based on popular sovereignty, suggesting that its reliance on authority was itself unsuitable for the modern, American project.

The legitimate source of knowledge was up for grabs in this debate. Codifiers adopted the long-standing positivist concern that law be made known. Common lawyers retained a notion that knowledge was available through routes other than clearly written code. Practical knowledge could transmit understanding of law. This, however, is a messy, uncertain means of acquiring and disseminating legal knowledge.

Common lawyers were able not only to resist the attack on the common law but also to turn the codification argument on its head. They pointed out that the old common law was not so conservative after all, that its very pre-Enlightenment features offered a legal system that, although rooted in feudal origins, nevertheless exhibited a progressive capacity. It could keep pace with modern imperatives. It also offered a method of deriving legal rules that took society into account and offered ongoing interpretation of the law. Rather than being a backward, obsolete system, it offered resources needed as the country developed economically and made new demands on the law.

In the 1820s and 1830s, the common law was still strong enough for lawyers to muster a defense that resisted innovations in legal reform. The common law was still able to make a strong case for itself as suitably modern and capable of innovations. This common-law voice provided a site from which to question reforms that, on their face, seemed progressive and inevitable. The insights of the codification debates were only possible because of the rigor of the common lawyers. Without them, even legal reformers would have been deficient in their reflections on the implications of reform.

Despite the defense by common lawyers, the common law suffered in these debates, because a language of derision toward it had been introduced. The common-law defense was only as good as its champions. Common lawyers fended off the connotations of barbarism in the 1820s and 1830s, but the derisive language remained, available to those who would challenge the common law in the future. If the common law lost its defenders, or the quality of those defenders' arguments, then the charges of barbarism and feudalism, with all their negative connotations, would stick. These early criticisms would reemerge outside of the legal community. The social reformer Fanny Wright, a friend of Bentham's, extended his theory to liberation from repressive social norms. The woman abolitionists Angelina and Sarah Grimké were the sisters and daughters of moderate codifiers in South Carolina. Unable to be members of the legal community at the time, these woman's rights activists translated the ideas of the codification movement into discourse suitable for the political venue, where the derogation of the common law would make a new appearance.

CHAPTER TWO

Abstracting Rights

Because the codification movement did not succeed in replacing the organic development of the common law with the precision of an authoritative and logical code, legal thought did not reject the contextual development of law that was possible under the common law. The law was much more amenable to releasing itself from context when constitutional rights discourse developed under the activism of the abolitionists.

It is well known that the abolitionist movement gave rise to the woman's rights movement by serving as a training ground in political activism.[1] The abolitionist movement also provided woman's rights activists with a theoretical basis for their own rights discourse, as abolitionists developed theories to protect their own rights. The repressive situation in which abolitionists tried to exercise political rights encouraged them to develop arguments for their own constitutional protection by abstracting from the immediate social context. Because women encountered repression in both laws and social norms, they contributed to the burgeoning modern free speech theory.

Inspired by the religious fervor of the Second Great Awakening, the abolitionist societies that began forming in the 1830s denounced slavery as a sin and declared those social and political institutions that sustained slavery to be illegitimate.[2] They appealed to the concept of liberty to claim the individual dignity and freedom of enslaved persons. As they proceeded in their highly organized activities of forming societies, publishing newspapers, holding public meetings, sending petitions to Congress, and mailing antislavery publications to the South, their own rights to engage in such activity were challenged, leading to the need to defend the rights of abolitionists as well as declaring the freedom of slaves. Expressions of abolitionism met with suppression out of fear of inciting slave rebellion in the South or for their purported threat to the stability of the Union.[3] Repression took the form of governmental acts—for example, the Postmaster General's refusal to deliver mail and the gag rule on abolitionist petitions—or more social sanctions of mob violence. The abolitionists responded with justifications for their rights to publish, speak, and assemble.

In articulating their own right of expression, abolitionists formulated an early version of modern free speech doctrine.[4] While historians have identified the development of modern free speech doctrine, they have been less concerned with the availability of alternative theories of free speech that were not taken up. The shift toward the civil libertarian form was neither preordained nor inevitable but was, instead, a chosen strategy that abolitionists used to overcome the many social impediments to their First Amendment rights. The best way for freedom of speech to overcome barriers was for its proponents to rise above immediate experience and present it as a general principle, not determined by political circumstances and not limited by them, either. Abolitionists contributed to the notion that social impediments were, furthermore, unreliable as a source of knowledge and of rights. The petition controversy in particular provides insight into the ways in which the abolitionists constructed free speech doctrine. In responding to the refusal of Congress to consider their petitions with claims of denial of freedom of speech, the abolitionist discourse reveals not only a dynamic of repression versus rights but also the choice of one form of rights doctrine over another. The anti-institutionalism tendencies of abolitionism carried over into abolitionist theories of rights.[5]

Abolitionist methods replaced older common-law methods. The original understanding of freedom of the press was derived from British common law, which limited protection to the absence of prior restraint. Government could not require that publishers of political material acquire a license before they printed. Apart from that, government could repress freedom of the press by punishing the author, printer, and publisher for criminal libel once they did publish.[6] Thus, the Sedition Act, which Congress passed in 1798, making it a criminal offense for anyone to criticize the government, was consistent with common-law protections.

The Sedition Act was vigorously opposed, but even its opponents relied on common-law liberty in their arguments for expanded protection of expression rather than claiming freedom of the press as a general principle. They did not defend freedom of the press as the claim of individuals against repressive government but, rather, as analyses of what it meant to be a government that was ruled by the people and, in turn, what it meant to be a people who rule. Their arguments were still contextualized, identifying those rights as tools needed for political practice. Hence the extent of the rights was structurally determined and embedded in the context of what rights were needed for American government to function.[7] While James Madison's Virginia Resolution urged a more protective notion of freedom of the press, it did not treat this freedom as a general principle.[8] Freedom of the press was one of the tools that American government needed to function.[9] Madison explained that rights in the British tradition were rights against the monarch, whereas Parliament was sovereign. In the United States, the people, possessing sovereignty, both ceded authority to the legislative and executive branches of the federal government and secured rights against the legislature. It was time for a theory that was appropriately American, not in some abstract, patriotic sense, but out of inquiry into what American governance required.

THE RIGHT OF PETITION IN CONGRESS

The right of petition was likewise rooted in context. The right of petition can be traced back to the Magna Carta. It was largely ignored by British monarchs, but it received renewed attention with Sir Edward Coke's 1628 Petition of Right, which set the precedent for petitions to be received by Parliament. Petitioning was included in the British Bill of Rights in 1689, and petitioning was included among those privileges that Queen Elizabeth extended in the colonies.[10] The British government's limited response to colonists' petitions is included in the grievances of the Declaration of Independence. As states developed their own constitutions, some included the right of petition. Although the right of petition was not included in the U.S. Constitution of 1787, it was discussed at the Virginia and North Carolina ratifying conventions and it was included in the First Amendment. In subsequent years, occasional antislavery petitions were sent to Congress. There were other controversial petitions, regarding the national bank, the campaign to stop Sunday mails, Georgia and the Cherokee Nation, and the currency question, and Congress reported on many of these. Petitions asking Congress to regulate slavery in the District of Columbia were different.[11] Slaveholding interests feared that discussion of that power would lead to consideration of slavery and its regulation as a national political issue. They couched their concerns for the stability of the Union, arguing that even discussing slavery would upset the peace and the harmony generated by prior compromises.[12]

Antislavery petitions nevertheless poured in. The American Anti-Slavery Society petition campaign was a broad-based effort with centralized guidance from leading abolitionist leaders, who sometimes provided the text of the petition.[13] The centralized resources allowed for myriad petitions to be circulated widely, most notably in areas with strong abolitionist bases, including New York, Pennsylvania, Massachusetts, and Ohio, and then submitted to members of the House of Representatives and the U.S. Senate. The 24th Congress was inundated with antislavery petitions, but it did not abolish slavery in the District of Columbia as a result; in fact, members spent little time discussing Congress's power over slavery in the District of Columbia. Rather, Congress discussed whether it should receive these petitions.

The conventional procedure for the reception of abolitionist petitions was to receive them, print them, pass them to committee, and let them die there. Members of slaveholding states and their sympathizers sought to prevent discussion of the petitions by refusing to consider them. A move that an antislavery petition not even be received initiated debate over whether the right of petition was being denied petitioners.[14] In the House, Representative Pinckney of South Carolina introduced the gag rule in May 1836: "All petitions, materials, resolutions, propositions, or papers, relating in any way, or to any extent whatsoever, to the subject of slavery, or the abolition of slavery, shall, without being either printed or referred, be laid upon the table, and that no further action whatever shall be had thereon."[15]

Rules resembling the Pinckney Gag were renewed in the House each year until 1840, with the establishment of a House rule that remained in place until its repeal in 1844. The reluctance even to receive abolitionist petitions shifted the constitutional conflict from Congress' power to legislate slavery in the District of Columbia to citizens' right of petition. Despite the repeated issuance of gag resolutions, no one in Congress denied that there was a right of petition; disagreement centered on the extent of that right. Opponents of the abolitionist petitions read the right narrowly—they construed the right of citizens to petition to encompass the right of citizens to address *their own* grievances to government, not those of another.[16] By this reasoning, residents of Massachusetts should have no concern for the situation in the District of Columbia. Furthermore, the right of petition was the right of citizens to assemble and to write and sign petitions, and that was all.[17] Supporters of the abolitionist petitions determined that the right of citizens to petition implied a corresponding duty of Congress to receive that petition.[18]

The supporters of the right of the abolitionists to petition were not necessarily abolitionists or even abolition sympathizers. They nevertheless developed arguments that defended abolitionists' rights by making the right of petition central to citizenship. Supporters imbued the right of petition with sacred connotations by presenting it as a fundamental right located at the core of American citizenship and government structure. Supporters of the right of petition identified the right as existing prior to the Constitution as a "primary, inherent, absolute, and essential right."[19] To cast the right of petition as existing prior to the Constitution, however, was not to rely on it as an abstract principle. Supporters of an expansive right of petition identified it as foundational because it was a right that had been practiced in Anglo-American history. They recounted the role that the right of petition had played in American history and in its British heritage, locating the right in the Magna Carta and in the revolution of 1688, "when the right of the people to self-government was established," and noting its inclusion in the Declaration of Rights of 1774, in state constitutions, and in the Bill of Rights.[20] The right of petition was identified as one of the practices of a people who ruled themselves, as a requirement for that ruling, and as a defining feature of a self-ruling people. The use of popular sovereignty in these arguments was constitutive. Supporters claimed that the right of petition "runs in our veins," was "an inheritance our ancestors brought," and constituted "our heritage."[21] As they defined their background they defined themselves as a people. The act of defining and determining the extent of the right of petition was itself a constitutive process, offering a contextualized derivation of rights, with society serving not as the source of repression but as the means of determining rights.

This organic conception of the right to petition would change as supporters of the abolitionist petitions increasingly associated the right of petition with freedom of speech, thereby relying on principles to trump repressive rules. Representative Slade identified a nebulous spirit, inevitable and incapable of being resisted: "The spirit of free inquiry is the master spirit of the age; it bows to the authority of truth and reason and revelation; but it bows to nothing else. It must have free course, and it will have it; giving life and soul and energy to the march of liberal principles, and destined to shake every institution on earth, which does not recognize the 'inalienable rights' of man, and bow to the supremacy of just and equal laws. And, sir, it shall move onward and onward and onward, until every kindred and tongue and people under Heaven shall acknowledge and glory in the great truth that 'ALL MEN ARE CREATED EQUAL.'"[22]

Slade's optimism in the spirit of inquiry typifies the belief in the spirit of an age. Slade perceived a pervasive spirit, unable to be captured, working its way through social institutions, pushing all obstacles out of its way, altering them until it brought them on the forward march of progress. This imagery represents the reliance on rights as general principles, viewing them as abstracted from their social setting in their construction, with no account for how they were generated. The spirit was not only abstracted in terms of the construction of rights; it also had little regard for the institutions with which it came in contact. It moved "onward, onward, onward," dismantling structures inconsistent with it along the way, regardless of the consequences. Sustaining the delicate compromise of slavery was of little concern when one was moved by such a spirit: "Great principles are always immutable, and cannot be made to bend to circumstances."[23]

Such circumstances included the disruption caused by broaching the topic of antislavery. The discussion of abolition could be labeled as incendiary, and persuasively so. To employ speech on this topic was to unsettle the compact on slavery and subsequently to invite instability into the constitutional order. Arguments for freedom of speech that were contextualized would inevitably encounter the constitutional compact regarding slavery. If one were to construct an organic rendition of freedom of speech, the narrative about who "We the People" are would invariably have to acknowledge people's compact to tolerate slavery, a constraint upon the extent of the freedom. When decontextualized, however, free speech could be understood as a right that preceded and trumped the constitutional compact over slavery. When opponents of the petitions charged the abolitionists with abstraction, they were right. The abolitionists' defenses of freedom of speech were abstracted from social context in the formulation of the definition and extent of that freedom.

Supporters of the petitions were soon charged with being too abstract in their defense of the right of petition, and abstraction itself became a topic of discussion. There were different ways in which supporters of petitions were said to abstract from social conditions. One charge was that abolitionists discussed slavery in the abstract without knowing anything about the lived experience of slaves. Representatives from slaveholding states charged that those in non-slaveholding states "have thrown around it [slavery] all the glooms and horrors that heated imaginations could depict,"[24] when, in fact, slaveholders said, northerners who actually visited slaveholding states would be "completely astonished and gratified at the real condition of things. Instead of meeting with his supposed squalid, trembling, ill-treated set of beings, he finds a cheerful, well-conditioned, laboring people."[25] Slaveholders, of course, constructed their own narrative of the experience of the slave to represent slavery as a safe, domestic relation.[26] Beyond the misrepresentation of the abuse of slavery, however, lay a familiar dynamic for the time—resistance to the use of an abstract concept to explain or reform lived experience.

Opponents to petitions feared another quality of abstraction—they were wary of the zeal that accompanied reliance on general principles. There were members of Congress who were opposed to the content of the antislavery petitions but nevertheless urged fellow members of Congress to receive them, because they anticipated that suppression would further contribute to the principled commitment of abolitionists. Seeing abolitionists as fanatics, Senator Tallmadge did not want to contribute to the excitement—"the food on which abolition feeds"—by refusing to hear petitions.[27] If abolitionists' petitions were not acknowledged, "we cannot fail to satisfy this class that they are engaged, if not in an unholy, in a most unjust crusade against the rights of others."[28] Other members of Congress equated the commitment of the abolitionists to religious zeal, warning that suppression of abolitionist petitions would be received as religious persecution: "By persecution, religious sects, maintaining doctrines the most absurd and the most extravagant—doctrines directly at war with the pure faith and principles announced to the world by the Divine Author of our religion, have been magnified into importance."[29]

The connection between principles and religious zeal was not unfounded. The abolitionism of the Garrisonians, at least, was informed by passionate religious beliefs, with a disdain for slavery that was so absolute that no manmade agreements that tolerated it were to be respected, because they violated God's law. Garrisonians pursued the goal of immediate abolition of slavery regardless of the consequences for existing political arrangements. As Garrison told an abolitionist audience, "It is said that if you agitate this question, you will divide the Union. Believe it not; but should disunion follow, the fault will not be yours. You must perform your duty, faithfully, fearlessly and promptly, and leave the consequences to God."[30] The principles were brought into analysis from a higher realm and wielded against social and political institutions. The development of free speech doctrine would provide political principles to replace the initial religious conviction.

Perhaps the strongest and most insightful of the charges against the abstract character of abolitionist argument was that abolitionists relied on abstract principles but that abstract principles could not be discussed outside their social context. Some members of Congress insisted that the discussion of slavery not be conducted in theory but in relation to legislation. Senator Bouldin viewed the abolitionist argument as a "philosophic dream" that had no real effect on institutional arrangements in the South.[31] Senator Niles was nervous about the discussion that the abolitionist petitions—and the suppression of those petitions—provoked, because it invited theoretical discussion divorced from policy matters: "Resolutions have been introduced presenting, for the consideration of the Senate, sundry abstract questions in relation to this subject, and the constitutional powers of Congress. . . . What is the object of such debate? Is it to settle constitutional or other general principles, and thus put this question at rest? If this is the purpose, I think it will fail. Sir, I have no belief in the utility of the discussion of abstract propositions, totally disconnected with legislation or any practical results."[32]

As the earlier formulation of freedom of the press and the right of petition had demonstrated, it was common to derive principles in relation to constitutional structures rather than in opposition to those structures. The abstracted form was new and allowed for further theorizing, which was disturbing to many. Representative Pickins decried the reliance on equality in the Declaration of Independence and its use as a leveling doctrine, which undermined social structures as it became defined as more than equal political privileges. Disdaining the appropriation of the doctrine of equality, he lamented, "instead of its becoming a doctrine full of light and peace to a world sleeping in darkness and bondage, it becomes a doctrine of universal discord, confusion, and ruin. True, it is an abstract truth; but, like all other mere abstractions, it can have no actual existence."[33] Pickins was using a skeptical argument to limit the extent of equality, but there is a basic understanding of the relationship between principle and practice beneath his pretense: "True and practical liberty, in my opinion, exists among a people who live under a system of ascertained and well-regulated *law* that has grown up from time immemorial out of the experience and absolute necessities of the society that is framed under it."[34]

Pickins echoed the notion that principle is not opposed to society but emerges from it. Principle develops through the practice of a society. Such arguments emerged to counter the activity of the abolitionists, but they reveal just how novel the abolitionists' form of argument was. In resorting to fundamental principles, such as the principle of liberty to counter the institution of slavery or, more specifically, the right of petition and freedom of speech to oppose the suppression of petitions, abolitionists were employing principles in a new way.

The House dropped the gag rule in 1844 in response to partisan changes in House membership and to the persistent efforts of John Quincy Adams, who resisted, defied, and subverted congressional procedures in order to force the discussion over the right of petition.[35] Members of Congress had succeeded in drawing attention to the right of petition and in introducing a more protective defense. They began the move toward abstraction, but they had not developed it beyond a distrust of institutions and an awareness of the progressive spirit of the age. Constitutionalism was also being practiced outside Congress, in those abolitionist newspapers that kept close watch on the congressional debates.

FREE SPEECH IN THE *PHILANTHROPIST*

As detractors had cautioned in congressional debates, the gag rule had the effect of strengthening the abolitionist cause. Northerners who had previously been unsympathetic to the abolitionists began to sympathize with them as the issue was reframed as a fundamental liberty being at stake.[36] The issue became part of a public discourse, and the abolitionist newspapers were ready to frame it. The *Philanthropist* is a case in point. Started by James Birney, of the Ohio Anti-Slavery Society, in January 1836, the *Philanthropist* set out to be "a repository of facts and arguments on the

subject of Slavery as connected with Emancipation."[37] Birney, the political abolitionist, was more measured than Garrison in his opposition to slavery, but he likewise turned to abstraction in defending rights. Rather than deriving his free speech
theory from a notion of sin, he drew it from a conception of truth, which he assumed
would emerge from frank and free discussion. As Birney saw it, hostility to the abolitionists arose from misrepresentation of the movement. If the truth could be
brought to light, and then disseminated, everyone would come to see the validity of
the abolitionist position. His faith in discovery of the truth was so strong that he did
not consider that slaveholding interests might have recognized the "truth" of the
movement and nevertheless opposed to it because of their own calculations and ex-
periences.

The *Philanthropist* reproduced speeches and essays from abolitionist meetings
and newspapers across the country in order to disseminate ideas and information
about the movement. It also devoted space to the slaveholding perspective in a section entitled "Slaveholder's Department." Birney solicited essays from slaveholders
who would like to engage in dialogue in the newspaper. Expecting that slaveholders
would not take him up on this offer, he explained that the newspaper would reprint
"the best *second hand* articles we can possess ourselves of."[38] Birney did not receive
original articles from slaveholders and their sympathizers, but he was able to publish their views and respond to them, thus generating a quasi-dialogue that probably
came as close to a marketplace of ideas as anything that could be sustained at the
time, with the culture of free speech discussed and emulated in the editorial design.

In his first editorial Birney announced that his hope for abolition lay in discussion. Once the evils of slavery and its horrors were revealed, once the effect of slavery on the slaveholder was acknowledged and studied, then public opinion on slavery would grow unfavorable. He was committed to the belief that discussion would
produce truth, and that stifling discussion impeded the discovery of truth and perpetuated falsehood. The *Philanthropist* also set aside space that it called the Dough-
face Department, to reproduce the sentiments of members of Congress from free
states who supported the rights of slaveholders. It reprinted a spoof of a Virginia Resolution that had originally been published in the *Emancipator*, in which dough-
faces swore to such "truths" as two and two do not make four, there is no such thing
as inalienable rights, and the Constitution gives Congress no right to interfere with
slavery in the District of Columbia or elsewhere in the Union.[39]

The *Philanthropist*'s interest in truth indicates that political abolitionists were
able to extend the abstract turn. Whereas abolitionists initially turned to abstract derivation of rights as a means to overcome obstacles that impeded their ability to act,
the political abolitionists distrusted socially derived rights discourse because it im-

peded one's ability to acquire information and to reason. Society impeded knowledge as well as action. Like more radical abolitionists, Birney distrusted context, but
his commitment to truth placed him in the tradition of positivism rather than that
of natural rights.

The *Philanthropist* kept readers informed of developments in the status of postal
delivery of abolitionist literature and closely monitored congressional proceedings
on the right of petition. It posted the roll call votes of the Senate's consideration of
petitions, as well as notable speeches on behalf of the right to petition. In its reports
it presented these events as direct threats to freedom of speech and freedom of the
press.

The *Philanthropist* developed an explicit defense of freedom of speech through
a quasi-dialogue it generated by responding to antiabolitionists. In a series of responses to John C. Wright, author of the antiabolitionist Cincinnati Resolution, Birney constructed a positive argument for freedom of speech. He identified freedom
of speech and freedom of the press as natural, inalienable rights derived from God
and superior to any acts of manmade legislation.[40] He was also able to dispel the notion that free speech merely entailed toleration of points of view, identifying toleration as "not to be found in the vocabulary of republican freemen. Toleration means
something that is *allowed* or *permitted* to us by another."[41] Toleration, he explained,
allows speech to be a right that is dispensed by government, subject to the approval
of authority. The abolitionist alternative, by locating freedom of speech as prepolit-
ical, was able to identify it as a right secured to individuals, preceding and sur-
mounting any action of state power.

The violence of antiabolitionist mobs made it clear that the protection of freedom of speech was not an abstract need. In July 1836, a group of fifteen to twenty
antiabolitionists broke into the printing offices of the *Philanthropist*, dismantling
the printing press, tearing up the paper, and smearing it with a keg of ink. The incident was followed by posters in Cincinnati, with the admonition Abolitionists Beware, noting that the raid of July 12 was only a warning. "If an attempt is made to re-
establish the Press, it will be viewed as an act of defiance to an already outraged
community, and on their heads be the results which follow."[42] The mob violence
against the *Philanthropist* escalated throughout the summer of 1836.

The response was the abstract theory, introduced by zealous evangelical Chris-
tians and modified by political abolitionists, that one should rely on truth rather than
sin to support the rightness of free speech doctrine. The free speech arguments in
Congress and in the abolitionist press were preliminary, with vague references to
spirits of freedom and recourse to Truth. It would take the contributions of woman

abolitionists to develop a theory of an individual rights bearer who acquired the right to free speech prior to entry in this repressive society and political order.

WOMAN ABOLITIONISTS AND FREE SPEECH

The new sympathy for abolitionist free speech was not fortuitous for women. The abolitionist movement had always welcomed women. It enlisted them to collect petition signatures, lecture, write, attend meetings, boycott goods, and make goods for fund-raisers. Many pertinent abolitionist strategies and controversies were, likewise, gendered. Images of both manhood and womanhood were employed to elicit sympathy for those who were enslaved.[43] Women were active participants in the movement, and the "woman question" was one of the internally divisive issues attributed to the splintering of the abolitionist movement in 1840.[44]

Half of the petitions sent to Congress during the petition campaign were signed by women during a time when women were not supposed to engage in politics.[45] In carrying out this public activity, women were straining the boundaries of suitable behavior.[46] As the discussion of the right to petition became a matter of freedom of speech, abolitionist women were threatened with marginalization in the movement because, under separate-spheres ideology, they were not to speak in public. Ideologically, women were relegated to the private sphere in the mid-nineteenth century. As universal white male suffrage defined the electorate as male, politics became identified as masculine, and the public sphere was understood to be competitive, violent, and raucous.[47] Men's masculinity earned them the right to participate, and their masculinity was enhanced by their participation. Women's virtue would be compromised under such conditions, so it was considered inappropriate for women to engage in political activity, which included public speaking. To adopt a rhetorical style of authority and expertise was to behave in an unwomanly fashion.[48] As a young black woman, Maria Stewart challenged both gender and racial mores in her public speaking.[49] The abolitionist movement breached these barriers to women's public speaking by having women serve as agents of the American Anti-Slavery Society and serve as public lecturers.[50]

Women had to contend with the right of free speech in a way that men did not. For men, relying on the abstracted form of free speech doctrine meant that they pitted the abstract right against the constitutional agreement to keep silent on slavery. For women, reliance on the abstracted right pitted them against an entire social order that produced and depended on their gendered behavior and roles. For women to claim freedom of speech threatened a displacement of social institutions and a remaking of their political identity. Women could not merely refer to a nebulous spirit of the age for their abstract theories. They had to overcome both laws and norms of repression, and they could extend the logical arguments of male abolitionists to do so. If "the construction of the Constitution is a matter of opinion, and every citizen has a right to express that opinion in a petition or otherwise,"[51] then woman abolitionists could render constitutional arguments of their own.

Fanny Wright

A forerunner to women in the organized abolitionist movement, the reformer and performer Frances "Fanny" Wright was a student of Jeremy Bentham who relied on his ideas to address social oppression. Wright committed herself to the various liberal and reformist causes of her day, including marriage law, divorce, free love, experimental communities, racial justice, public speaking, and dress. She was committed to overturning repressive social norms and visibly transgressed them. Her charisma and notorious performances rendered her something of a celebrity in her time.

In 1822, Wright published A Few Days in Athens, a work of historical fiction set in ancient Athens. The book was dedicated to Bentham, who was represented in the novel by the philosopher Epicurus, whose principle of pleasure was as misunderstood as Bentham's utilitarianism. In the novel, Theon, a young student of the philosopher Zeon, meets Epicurus as an unnamed "sage" and embarrasses himself by parroting his teacher's derision of Epicurus. Theon has been taught that Epicurus's is a doctrine of impiety, orgies, and rejection of virtue. When he visits the hall of Epicurus, he comes to appreciate that pleasure is the attainment of virtue, not its corruption. As expounded by others, however, Epicurean philosophy seemed to be hedonism. Thus Theon learns that prejudices and misconceptions impede the acquisition of knowledge. Theon must confront these prejudices as he visits his old school and is castigated and shunned by his former friends for his association with Epicurus. His positioning in both schools allows him—and the reader—to assess the tarnished reputation of a philosophy and its best version.[52]

When she came to the United States in 1824, Wright became active in the utopian community New Harmony, she started a free-thought newspaper, the Free Enquirer, and she worked for racial equality, but her most notorious activities were her public-speaking engagements. Having given public lectures out west, she conducted a number of public-speaking series in New York City. Her shocking disdain for social and political conventions and her charisma and theatricality rendered her lectures "high ritual" and cast her as something of a rock star in her celebrity.[53] She aroused panic, and reactions to her talks included outcries, critical reviews, and even a fire set in the midst of one lecture. Wright's boldness and the performative quality of her expressions resulted in criticism directed not only at her arguments but at her character, as well. William Leete Stone, a New York newspaper editor, complained, "It is time we should have done with Miss Wright, her pestilent doctrines, and her deluded followers, who are as much to be pitied, as their priestess is to be despised. . . . She comes amongst us in the character of a bold blasphemer, and a voluptuous preacher of licentiousness."[54] Wright's reputation haunted woman abolitionists as their political activism threatened to breach the demarcation of the separate spheres. Despite their attempts to designate themselves as "ladies" rather than as "citizens" in their activities and maintain a humble posture,[55] the scepter of Fanny Wright hovered. The epithet "Fanny Wrightism" was leveled at women as a reminder when they did seem to cross boundaries.[56]

Angelina and Sarah Grimké

Angelina and Sarah Grimké were committed abolitionists who faced social transgressions of their own. Daughters of a South Carolina slaveholding judge, the sisters became agents of the American Anti-Slavery Society after Angelina wrote a letter to the *Liberator* which was published and well received. The Grimké family was also significant for its political activity. South Carolina was known for its radical politics in the early nineteenth century, particularly with regard to secession and nullification.[57] It was likewise innovative about codification, and came very close to codifying its laws. Some of the primary figures interested in codification were the Grimké sisters' father, Judge John Grimké, and later, their brother, Thomas, both moderate codifiers who led a nearly successful codification campaign, which failed only when South Carolina politics had to attend to economic crises.[58] The Grimké sisters exercised innovative reform efforts both in their abolitionist activity and in their claims for women's rights.

Angelina Grimké fused the political causes of abolition and woman's rights with her first major publication, *Appeal to the Christian Women of the South*, in 1835.[59] She sought to construct a sisterhood of southern women.[60] As free speech occupied abolitionist thought in 1835 and 1836, Grimké determined that this freedom extended to women as well. She talked it over with other abolitionists, not all of whom were supportive. She recounted Gerrit Smith's warning that if she spoke in public, "it would be called a Fanny Wright meeting & so on & advised us not to make addresses except in parlors."[61] Despite such discouragement from other abolitionists, she persisted, proposing a woman's rights resolution at the First Anti-Slavery Convention of American Women in May 1837: "RESOLVED, That as certain rights and duties are common to all moral beings, the time has come for woman to move in that sphere which Providence has assigned her, and no longer remain satisfied in the circumscribed limits with which corrupt custom and a perverted application of Scripture have encircled her; therefore that it is the duty of woman, and the province of woman, to plead the case of the oppressed in our land, and to do all that she can by her voice, and her pen, and her purse, and the influence of her example, to overthrow the horrible system of American slavery."[62]

Although the resolution passed, the vote was not unanimous, as not all woman abolitionists were willing to extend the language of rights to women. Nevertheless, Angelina Grimké persisted in making the case for woman's rights. Later that month, on the eve of her New England speaking tour, she wrote to a friend, "we had just another such [pleasant meeting] at Friend Chapman's, Ann's father. Here I had a long talk with the brethren on the rights of women & found a very general sentiment prevailing that it was time our fetters were broken."[63] Finding a small but welcome audience receptive to woman's rights, she and Sarah launched a public speaking tour through New England in the summer of 1837.

It was not uncommon for woman abolitionists to speak to women audiences, often in the home of a hostess, but the Grimkés spoke in front of "promiscuous" audiences, that is, audiences of both men and women, black and white.[64] This provocative behavior aroused the curiosity of some, who attended and were persuaded by the talks, particularly by Angelina's charisma. It aroused the ire of others, who deplored the blatant violation of social mores. Criticism of the tour and specifically of the Grimké sisters, emerged from fellow male and female abolitionists, from anti-abolitionists, and from members of the clergy, who published the "Pastoral Letter of the General Association of Massachusetts to Churches under Their Care" in July 1837.[65] They alerted churches to the "dangers" raised by the trend of women speaking in public. They argued that in public speaking, women assumed a position at odds with their nature and divested themselves of the protection they enjoyed in their status as dependent women.

The pastoral letter was made public and was intended to humiliate the Grimkés into submission. In response, Sarah Grimké wrote a series of letters and essays that were published as *Letters on the Equality of the Sexes* in 1838. Rather than dwelling on the insults in the pastoral letter, she used the letter as an invitation to consider the ridiculous system of gender hierarchy: "I rejoice that they have called the attention of my sex to this subject, because I believe if woman investigates it, she will soon discover that danger is impending."[66] She sought to expose the power and construction of rules used to justify women's subordination, anticipating, "I am persuaded that when the minds of men and women become emancipated from the thraldom of superstition and 'traditions of men,' the sentiments contained in the Pastoral Letter will be recurred to with as much astonishment the opinions of Cotton Mather . . . on the subject of witchcraft."[67] Just as earlier abolitionists had read the Bible to find a condemnation of slavery, Sarah Grimké could not find in the Bible any support for woman's subordination. Instead, she determined gender hierarchy to be a misguided social tradition. The rules that made women dependent upon men and denied them civil and political rights were themselves unnatural and against the teachings of scripture. She even found in the Bible a command to speak one's conscience: "Cry aloud, spare not, lift up thy voice like a trumpet."[68]

Meanwhile, Angelina Grimké was developing a theory of moral agency. When rights were derived contextually, women's rights were determined by their social status, and thus women could be denied rights because of their sex. To counter this obstacle, she viewed rights as human rights, abstracting the subject from social status and viewing the human subject as a moral being in a state in which "all distinction in sex sinks to insignificance and nothingness."[69] In order to theorize human rights, she abstracted from society and its sex-based classifications. She made this move deliberately, determining that with this method, one could "measure her rights and duties by the sure, unerring standard of moral being, not by the false rights and measures of a mere circumstance of her human existence."[70] To derive rights from social context was to have one's judgment altered by social prejudices that were marred by a system of gender hierarchy.

The ideas and actions of Angelina Grimké and Sarah Grimké contributed to the development of abstracted rights discourse. Because the sisters could not enjoy the development of doctrine from petition to free speech, they made a space for women in abstracted rights discourse by developing the concept of the moral subject who was a bearer of rights prior to society and the status it conferred. Their contribution was not always appreciated by other abolitionists. Angelina Grimké reveals this in a letter composed to both Theodore Weld—her future husband—and John Greenleaf Whittier in August 1837. She defended her "alarming" advocacy of woman's rights, claiming her "letters have not been the means of *arousing* the public attention to the subject of Woman's rights; it was the Pastoral Letter which did the mischief."[71] Grimké thus constructed a narrative in which woman's' rights developed in response to contentious circumstances, obscuring her commitment to and speculation about woman's rights long before critics voiced their objections.

It is striking to recognize how successful the Grimkés' arguments ultimately were. The theories of human dignity and agency that they developed are those on which today's civil-libertarian doctrine depends. The individual is a bearer of rights that existed prior to his or her socially determined status. The individual can invoke those rights to overcome and remove any barriers generated by that status, and indeed, to overturn the status designation itself. To the contemporary liberal, there is much that makes sense in the theory of the Grimkés. Those detractors might be branded as mere sexists who failed to recognize the worth of women's dignity as individuals.

Lydia Maria Child

The contributions of the Grimkés to free speech discourse could be seen as a natural extension of the larger abolitionist trend, except that it was so resisted, even among woman abolitionists. Although abolitionism was a radical ideology in the 1830s, not all abolitionists transferred this radicalism to woman's rights. Woman abolitionists who may have been committed to (if not entirely comfortable with) attending abolition meetings, writing, gathering petition signatures, and boycotting household goods made by slave labor,[72] were less willing to challenge societal norms for the cause of woman's rights, including women's freedom of speech.[73] Some were hesitant because they were conservative; they saw slavery as a sin but were not committed to broad social change.[74] One curious position was that taken by the abolitionist Lydia Maria Child. A friend of the Grimkés, she did not oppose their efforts to claim rights for women, but she did not entirely approve of these efforts, either. Despite her admiration for the sisters, she was reticent to take part in their activities, an absence for which the Grimkés took Child to task. In a letter written to the *Liberator*, Child recalled that "they urged me to say and do more about woman's rights, nay, at times they gently rebuked me for my want of zeal. I replied, 'It is best not to *talk* about our rights, but simply go forward and *do* whatsoever we deem a duty. In toiling for the freedom of others, we shall find our own.'"[75]

The disagreement between the Grimkés and Child is an indication that the transition to abstract free speech discourse was not simple, nor was it inevitable. Not all activists who were supportive of rights for women shared the trend toward abstraction; they must have had some alternative means of discussing and deriving rights. The internal woman abolitionist discourse provided a site for such contestation over alternative theories of rights. Rather than arguing about whether women should have rights or not, they differed over the most suitable way to derive and secure those rights. The problem in recovering this discourse is locating it. This is constitutionalism outside the courts, but also outside any formal branch of government, given women's barriers to voting and representation in government. The abolition movement gave women a rare public platform, and their ideas can be found in their newspapers articles, books, and political tracts, in addition to their personal (although not entirely private) letters. Child's reticence to publicly reprove the Grimkés, however, indicates that this was a disagreement that was not being carried out for all to see. These were activists in the midst of an abolitionist movement that, in the mid-1830s, remained a politically unpopular organization and was already courting the "woman question." Thus, it would have been a political liability to make this internal disagreement public.

Looking at gender, then, in constitutionalism outside the courts, requires the examination of less accessible and less obvious locations of political discourse. In the case of the disagreement between Child and the Grimkés, the discourse can be found just barely hidden in a romance novel. In the summer of 1836, Child published *Philothea: A Grecian Romance*, a historical romance set in fifth-century B.C. Athens. Child did not write her romance novel for lack of access to more mainstream forms of writing.[76] She was an activist and a professional author who was prolific in writing books, newspaper and magazine columns and articles, and poetry. Her decision to include a political message in a romance novel is an indication not of her marginalization but of her choice to place it there. Child employed the form of the romance novel to carve out a space in which she could pit competing sides of rights theory against each other. Attention to this romance novel can indicate not only what theories were being developed in the 1830s but also what forms reveal about the political imperatives that shaped constitutionalism outside the courts.

Philothea anticipated the Grimkés' free speech theory, appearing a year before their speaking tour. The abolitionist free speech discourse that had emerged from the petition controversy was already well under way, so *Philothea* can be seen as Child already staking her position in the controversy that was to intensify in later years. Child was ready to take a position before the Grimkés' controversy; she had already contended with an earlier advocate of woman's rights and a woman's right to speak in public, Fanny Wright, in the previous decade.

Lydia Maria Child reviewed a Wright lecture in 1829. Unlike other detractors, Child did not overreact to Wright as undermining the social edifice with her outrageous acts. Instead, she refused to take Wright seriously. She acknowledged Wright's charisma, noting the "smart sally," sarcasm, and sly machinations of her argumentative style, but she failed to recognize such rhetorical skill as genuine argument. Child saw Wright as dangerous, not in her power to follow through on the sweeping social change she spoke of, but in the influence she could have over her adherents, who would try to act on her ideas. Child worried that the vague term *knowledge*, which Wright so often invoked, would be susceptible to abuse in redefinition and application. She also worried whether Wright's naïve followers would be able to handle the implications of her ideas. Child's 1829 review of Wright was therefore quite flippant, refusing to concede Wright as a force to be contended with.[77] Her reservations about Wright's followers, however, did not disappear, and she presented them more fully in *Philothea*, in which she was able to stage a confrontation between herself and Wright through their counterparts in the story and also to follow the fate of a character who took Wright's ideas to heart, leading to tragic consequences.

Philothea appears as a deviation from Child's politically charged works of the time and a literary refuge from the political controversy in which she was mired.[78] While romance novels can appear to be escapist and trivial, readers of romance exercise agency in their consumption of these formulaic stories.[79] In her preface to the 1845 edition of *Philothea*, Child anticipated that her fellow abolitionists might be disappointed in her retreat into fiction, especially romantic fiction. "This volume is purely romance; and most readers will consider it romance of the wildest kind." She went on to indicate, however, that there was another meaning for the discerning reader: "A few kindred spirits, prone to people space 'with life and mystical predominance,' will perceive a light *within* the Grecian temple. For such I have written it."[80] Hence Child offered a clue that her supposed retreat from politics was only apparent, and she invited the reader to derive the higher meaning in this "trivial" form.

Philothea is the story of a young woman, Philothea, her servant, Eudora, and their respective love interests. When the novel begins, Eudora has returned from studying music with Aspasia, a former courtesan now married to Pericles and responsible for the restrictive citizenship laws that threaten Philothea's marriage. As Philothea expresses her disapproval of the libertine mores that Aspasia has brought to Athenian society, Eudora defends her: "'I think women should judge kindly of Aspasia's faults, and remember that they are greatly exaggerated by her enemies,' rejoined Eudora; 'for she proves that they are fit for something better than mere domestic slaves. Her house is the only one in all Greece where women are allowed to be present at entertainments. What is the use of a beautiful face, if one must be shut up in her own apartment for ever? And what avails skill in music, if there is no chance to display it? I confess that I like the customs Aspasia is trying to introduce.'"[81]

Philothea first encounters Aspasia clad in rich purple robes, reclining on a crimson couch, playing a Doric harp. Philothea notes that she is radiant, voluptuous, and intelligent, but most notably, that her face is not veiled. Aspasia explains her transgression of mores by declaring, "I must see this tyrannical custom done away in the free commonwealth of Athens."[82] Aspasia comments that she would have expected someone as intelligent as Philothea to reject the prejudiced custom as well. Wearing a veil is a custom that, in Aspasia's view, oppresses women. The veil obscures a woman's beauty, which Aspasia finds problematic because beauty is given to women to "be like sunlight to bless and gladden the world."[83] Hence women expose their faces in order to share their beauty with others, to be gazed upon.

Child's presentation of Aspasia's views on veiling is unfavorable—Aspasia begins to inveigh against veiling using terms of women's liberation, but by the end of the conversation, she has digressed into rejecting the veil because it limits women's ability to gain admirers. Aspasia was a caricature of Fanny Wright, and Child, in assuming the voice of Philothea, leveled her own disapproval. Child deflated Aspasia/Wright's argument for women's liberation into Aspasia's superficial opinion about beauty and ego. Philothea, on the other hand, appears to be sustaining a repressive practice, but she has philosophical grounds for retaining her veil in public, explaining that "beauty is given to remind us that the soul should be kept as fair and perfect in its proportions, as the temple in which it dwells."[84] Philothea cherishes her beauty because it reminds her of the Ideal. If women were to reject veiling because of women's-liberation arguments, then they would deprive themselves of the opportunity to discern the design of the gods. Philothea justifies herself when Philothea lifts her veil when the women are finally alone, and Aspasia is taken aback by Philothea's beauty—a poignant moment, considering that Philothea was an idealized portrait of Child herself.[85]

Taken in by Aspasia's influence, Eudora becomes attracted to a married man at the party, provoking her fiancee's disapproval, to which Eudora, ennobled by her contact with Aspasia, retorts, "I will dance with whom I please."[86] She thus asserts her individualism and agency, which she further exercises when she agrees to meet the man in her garden later that night. Philothea confronts Eudora, expressing her fear that "the voice of that siren [Aspasia] is luring you to destruction."[87] Eudora responds, "I have a spirit within me that demands a wider field of action, and I enjoy the freedom that reigns in Aspasia's house."[88] This freedom does not liberate Eudora, however. When he finds out, her fiancée is willing to forgive her, as long as she can admit that she had not agreed to the assignation in the garden. It is not her attraction to a married man or the meeting but her consent to meet him that Philaemon deems unforgivable. When Eudora admits her ill-considered exercise of consent, Philaemon breaks off the engagement and leaves Athens. Eudora was one of those acolytes that Child had worried about in her 1829 review of Fanny Wright.

Philothea rejected the radical, sweeping proclamations of Aspasia because she appreciated the opportunities for enlightenment found in norms, laws, customs, and the physical world. The customs that emerge from a community might reflect a pattern or practice that approximates the ideal natural order, a platonic idea, taken up by the American Transcendentalists, which is easily identified in *Philothea* because Plato himself is present at Aspasia's party.[89] Philothea's alternative to the libertine lifestyle of Aspasia was to exercise freedom in accord with social norms rather than to free herself of them. Philothea took care of the household for herself and her grandfather, but she did not feel repressed by her domestic duties, and she even found freedom in doing them. Because she undertook her duties so willingly, her virtue was apparent, and this earned her the respect of her grandfather and his friends, so she was a welcome guest at gatherings of philosophers and poets. Apart from the subsidiary benefits, even the act of engaging in domestic chores did not therefore prove oppressive: "The intense love of the beautiful, thus acquired, far from making the common occupations of life distasteful, threw over them a sort of poetic interest. . . . The higher regions of her mind were never obscured by the clouds of daily care."[90] Cooking and cleaning were not diversions from her freedom but, rather, opportunities to engage in an activity in which she could absorb herself and achieve transcendence.

Just as *Philothea* taught that freedom could be exercised within norms, so too did Child demonstrate that there was a radical potential in the historical romance. Just as she had elevated women's work to a critical part of the national economy in her domestic treatise, she was also imparting a broader message in the romance of *Philothea*.[91] Many of the plot elements in *Philothea* really did transpire in Greek history.[92] Child needed only to add some fictional characters, alter the life spans of these historical characters, inject transcendentalism into platonic philosophy, and the plot and cast of characters of *Philothea* was complete. Child was accused of both presentism and inaccuracy in reviews of the novel.[93] These apparent errors, however, served to stretch the possibility of the form. In relying on history and then modifying it, Child was performing the theory she propounded in *Philothea*. The historical genre provided the structure in which she could tell a story, but she was not utterly bound by the form. By taking artistic license, she demonstrated the opportunities for manipulation available within the constraints of the genre and the restrictions of one's social and legal status.[94]

The muted voice in *Philothea* illuminates Child's reluctance to endorse the Grimkés' free speech theory. Child objected to the decontextualized subject they constructed. The Grimkés would have thought that their theorizing was synonymous with engagement in the world. In her *Appeal to the Christian Women of the South*, Angelina Grimké offered as advice for "What you can do" to "speak on the subject" of slavery. For Grimké, speaking *was* doing. Child's interest in transcendentalism allowed her to recognize that this was not activity that sufficiently engaged the individual. To "do," according to the Transcedentalists, was to engage in the work of one's position in life, not in its exceptions. To engage was to become consumed in one's work as a farmer, or a priest, or a scholar, or a woman. It was an invitation to explore one's status and to find freedom within its constraints and manipulations rather than seeking to liberate oneself from it.

Because Child was not opposed to rights for women, her disagreement cannot be attributed to the conservative sentiments of abolitionists such as Catherine Beecher, who opposed the goals of women's rights. Child's disapproval helps us to appreciate that the Grimkés' theories were so disruptive because of their abstracted form, which was dismissive of social institutions as a source of rights or a site of their exercise. In public, Child neither publicly denounced nor enthusiastically supported the Grimké sisters' free speech theories. She did vote for Angelina Grimkés' resolution at the First Anti-Slavery Convention of American Women in 1837, and she did appreciate them: in a letter, Child recounted the reaction to a speech that Angelina Grimké had made to the Massachusetts state legislature, noting that the audience made fun of Angelina, calling her "Devil-ina," but she herself recommended to a friend, "I know you would have enjoyed it so much. I think it was a spectacle of the greatest moral sublimity I ever witnessed."[95] Despite her admiration for the Grimkés, she was reticent to take part in their activities, which elicited her comment about her reluctance to *talk* about rights. Child was only reluctant to talk about women's right in the same manner as the Grimkés did. She found it important to retain status because it allowed rights to be exercised in relation to the everyday life of citizens. This meant that she resisted the tendency toward abstraction of the subject away from her sex and gender. "I am not one of those who obtains there is no sex in souls," she explained, "Nor do I like results deducible from that doctrine."[96] In exercising freedom within social status, rights could take the experience of status into account.

Child's explanation for her reticent position was continually guarded, both in her public statements and in her own work. Her feminist agenda was less apparent than her antiracist agenda.[97] Child was much more enthusiastic in her abolitionist writing, with a bold preface to *Appeal in Favor of That Class of Americans Called Africans;* Child beseeched her readers to see the truth of the wrongs of slavery and racial prejudice. In *History of the Condition of Women*, however, she was more reserved, presenting a history of women and not a plea for woman's rights. Her preface to this work is filled with "denials and disclaimers."[98] It would have been impolitic to make this internal dispute public in a movement that was beset with public intolerance and internal conflict over women, so *Philothea* provided the venue for Child to air her opposition to the form of the burgeoning woman's rights discourse the abolitionist rights theories was inviting. The Grimkés' complaint to their friend Lydia about why she did not join them in their advocacy of women's freedom of speech is enacted in Aspasia's questioning of Philothea's wearing of the veil, and Philothea is not afraid to speak out. The Grimkés' discussion of women's freedom of speech was lending itself to abstraction, a form of which Philothea—and Child—was critical.

The abolitionist's development of free speech doctrine was a response to repressive conditions. The abstraction of free speech theory increased as the repression upon each repressive group increased. The objections to this development were generally voiced by antiabolitionists, so there was little discussion of the merits of the form that free speech theory was taking. Child offered an objection and an alternative in her application of transcendentalism, but her ideas did not make their way into the public discourse. When woman suffragists would borrow from the abolitionist rights theory, there would be few alternatives—and few notes of caution about the association of rights with abstraction.

CHAPTER THREE

The Married Women's Property Acts

Death Blow to Coverture?

As the woman's rights movement took shape in the mid-nineteenth century, it drew upon the legacies of the legal codification movement and the political abolitionist movement to assail the common law, one of the primary sources of women's civil and political status. Woman suffragists drew attention to the relations of status and hierarchy in the domestic relations and made it more difficult to refer to the common law as a palladium of liberty. To emphasize the hierarchy of the common law and its unsuitability for the American polity, they turned to the principles of the Declaration of Independence. In invoking the natural rights tradition to dismantle this status regime, they seemed to be relying on liberalism when they were, in fact, constructing a new version of liberalism, wresting it from the common-law relations that had always been a part of liberal theory and American liberalism.

The common-law rules of the marital relation were a source of women's subjugation.[1] Women owed their husbands the labor of household duties and childcare without pay.[2] The rules of coverture established the husband as head of the household, allowing him to choose the family domicile even if he had promised his wife-to-be that they would live elsewhere.[3] Domestic violence was permissible and even advisable if a husband needed to restrain his wife's behavior.[4] The husband could regulate visitors to the home.[5] The husband's status was reproduced in culture in accordance with nature and scripture, and both wife and husband were encouraged to live up their gender roles, as benevolent masters and obedient wives.[6] The loss of property rights within marriage led to the subsidiary denial of many political rights for all women.[7] Nor were the ameliorative possibilities of equity always available to the average woman.[8] Given the hardships imposed upon married women, it is no wonder that woman suffragists seized upon the opportunity presented by the married women's property acts to dismantle the rules of the common law which served as the basis for a second-class citizenship, even if such dismantling was the not purpose of the acts.

THE LEGAL REFORM OF PROPERTY

The origins of the married women's property acts, in both their content and their liberal interpretation, can be traced to the larger movement of legal reform, in which the turn to abstraction was well under way. Historians have pointed to changes in the reconceptualization of familiar political and legal concepts in the early years of the nineteenth century. Consent, for example, developed from a sociological notion of a society consenting to its own laws, to a theoretical reference, to a mythical contract.[9] These developments reflected the ability of politics and law to adapt to changing social and economic conditions. In the early nineteenth century, property law was in the midst of reform as the law adapted to a changing economy. Before the American Revolution, property consisted of both privileges and rights, centered on land. Property rights reflected a static and agrarian conception of an owner's enjoyment with the purpose of maintaining community in the form of economic and social stability.[10] The ethical standards of property rights were poised for change after the American Revolution.[11] Property law could then be used instrumentally to respond to and foster economic growth by accommodating the needs of entrepreneurs and business, releasing property rights from a static, land-based conception to suit the needs of an industrial and a market economy.[12] This development wrought a change in the fundamental notions of property—the ethical community standard, in which property was subordinated to the good of the community, shifted as economic stability became a good in itself.[13] Individual rights became legitimate as serving the good of the state. The ethical notion of fair exchange, which was at the basis of contract law, gave way to the individualist formulation of the wills of the contracting parties.[14]

Property did not cease to serve public functions, but a notable change occurred once the conception of the agent—property owner, contractor, or debtor—was posited on the fiction of an actor removed from his social setting. Older notions of property holders were built upon the social situation of the property exchange, which included social status, because maintaining status was a critical part of the stability that constituted the good society.[15] Reform in property law presaged the shift from status to contract.[16] The actor could present himself as a contracting actor rather than as a father who was contracting, or a master, or a servant, and so on. This was the beginning of the overcoming of status and the rise of abstraction, in that the in-dividual was conceived of without regard to social circumstances or social status.

REFORM STATUTES

The first statutes that granted married women the rights to own property did not reflect the new abstracted individual subject. The first wave of married women's property acts occurred in the South, beginning with Arkansas in 1835 and Mississippi in 1839.[17] These statutes were not a response to agitation for woman's rights; they made adjustments for ongoing debtor-creditor problems. The economic collapse that followed the Panic of 1837 led to an increase in legislation concerning bank-ruptcy, banking, and debtors' rights.[18] In the midst of this economic reform, married women's property acts provided that a married woman's property would be exempt from a creditor's recovery of property should her husband be in debt. These initial acts, limited to southern states, were similar to exemption laws in that they prevented creditors from taking all of a family's property when recovering.[19] Far from embrac-ing liberal freedom for women, they sustained paternalism for married women, act-ing as a legislative form of southern chivalry, thereby maintaining, rather than un-dermining, traditionalism.[20]

The second wave of property statutes, beginning in the 1840s in northern states, was the product of previous legal reforms. The abolition of primogeniture gave fa-thers discretion over the distribution of their property, allowing them to leave prop-erty to their daughters. Any property left to a daughter, however, would pass to her husband when she married, and fathers feared that their family property would be squandered by sons-in-law.[21] Before the advent of reform statutes, fathers could cir-cumvent this arrangement and manipulate the laws of coverture by setting up trusts for their daughters. With the property held by the trustee, usually a close friend of the father, the daughter had access to the property, but her husband, and any cred-itors seeking to recover from the husband's estate, did not. The codification move-ment raised concerns that individuals could defraud creditors if they had access to property that was held in the name of another. A statute regulating trusts was passed in New York, with the unintended consequence of depriving fathers of their prior means of protecting family property from their sons-in-law. The trust statute was, therefore, followed by pressure for married women's property acts from fathers who wanted to secure their daughters' inheritance.[22] New York passed its married women's property statute in 1848 and other states followed.

No state declared that the granting of property rights to married women recog-nized women's civic capacity or served as a prelude to greater rights of citizenship, but the woman suffragists interpreted the acts as such. They spun a narrative in which the married women's property acts signaled just the first stirrings of a larger revolution in women's rights. In retrospect, the New York laws appeared to launch a revolution: "When the State of New York gave married women certain rights of property, the individual existence of the wife was recognized, and the old idea that 'husband and wife are one, and that one the husband,' received its death-blow. From that hour the statutes of the several States have been steadily diverging from the old English codes. Most of the Western States copied the advance legislation of New York, and some are now even more liberal."[23]

Woman suffragists declared that the early reform statutes signaled the death knell of a status regime, reflecting later in the century, "This was the death-blow to the old Blackstone code for married women in this country, and ever since legislation has been slowly, but steadily, advancing toward their complete equality."[24] It was a compelling narrative, and a timely one as well. The emergence of the woman's movement coincided with a period in which the doctrine of coverture was in flux. As the initial property acts were implemented, no one—neither lawyers nor judges nor legal commentators—knew precisely what the status of married women was. The married women's property acts provided married women with certain, limited rights to property and contract, but otherwise, married women's rights remained subject to the rules of coverture. Various groups tried to make meaning of them, either by reconciling them to the common-law rules or by accepting them as a break from the past. The transitional status of married women's rights incurred by the statutes invited a reconsideration and explanation of those rights. The gap in authoritative meaning provided a space for woman suffragists to enter and tell a narrative in addition to those told by legislators, judges, and treatise writers.

TREATISES

Making sense of the married woman's property acts was not as easy for other legal actors. Legal treatises served as practical guides to the law for lawyers who were too busy to consult the many volumes of law reports.[25] As the common law developed, comprehensive treatises gave way to specialized subjects, with a series of treatises on the domestic relations emerging over the course of the nineteenth century. As their publication overlapped with legislative change in the marital relations, domestic-relations treatise writers sought to keep up with and make sense of legislative changes to common-law rules, which differed from state to state, and to account for common-law rules that remained intact. With some common-law rules abrogated but others left untouched by statute, treatise writers sought to identify the re-

maining features of the marital relation. The reform of some rules but not others required them to recur to the principles that underlay the marital relation, but the principles were changing, too. The oldest principle was the unity thesis, which sustained
the legal fiction that a man and woman became one person in the eyes of the law
when married.

Before the waves of the married women's property acts, treatise writers needed little justification for the rules of the marital relation. Tapping Reeve's early domestic-
relations treatise, *Law of Baron and Feme*, first published in 1816, contains no explanation for the husband-wife relation. Lacking an introductory section presenting
the reasons for or theories underlying the rules of the marital relation, his treatise
merely states the condition, commencing with, "The husband, by marriage, acquires
an absolute title to all the personal property of the wife, which she had in possession
at the time of the marriage; such as money, goods or chattels personal of any kind."[26]
Reeve elicited the terms of coverture, tracing rules of ownership, contract, and debt
from the basic rules of the husband's possession of the wife's property. Later editions
did not confront any inherent tension between the rules of husband and wife and
the reform statutes; the third edition references updated reform statutes in footnotes,
but it retains the rule of the husband's right to the property that his wife brought to
the marriage.

James Kent, Chancellor of New York from 1814 to 1823, published the four-
volume set, *Commentaries on American Law*, between 1826 and 1830, supplanting
the popularity of Blackstone in the United States.[27] It was a popular work for its time
and was reissued throughout the nineteenth century, with Oliver Wendell Holmes
serving as editor of the twelfth edition. Kent viewed the common law as remaining
responsive to modern needs, including the needs of a developing commercial economy.[28] His defense of the common law included the domestic relations. Reflecting
the ideas of Blackstone, he explained, "The legal effects of marriage are generally
deducible from the principle of the common law, by which the husband and wife
are regarded as one person, and her legal existence and authority in a degree lost or
suspended, during the continuance of the matrimonial union."[29] The couple's respective civil disabilities and obligations derived from this principle, including the
general rule that the husband "becomes entitled, upon the marriage, to all the goods
and chattels of the wife, and to the rents and profits of her lands, and he becomes liable to pay her debts and perform her contracts."[30]

By the time of the eleventh edition of Kent's *Commentaries*, many states had
passed provisions for married women to own their separate property. For the *Commentaries*, these statutes conferred only rights to property and did not alter the married woman's status as *feme covert*. Hence it was not contradictory for the eleventh

edition to treat the issue, "How far the wife is enabled to act during coverture, as a *feme sole.*"[31] Even in the midst of reform statutes, Kent's treatise continued to find guidance for the reform statutes' interpretation and incorporation in the common law, since the common-law system had long contained provisions for equity. Under equity, a married woman had, historically, been capable of owning separate property and acting as a *feme sole*. Thus the reform statutes did not present a need to abandon the common law if they were perceived as legislative forms of equity.

James Schouler's treatise on the domestic relations, first published in 1870, was typical of the specialized domestic-relations treatises that would emerge in the late nineteenth and early twentieth centuries. Devoted to the relation between husband and wife, it grappled with the state of the common-law rules in the midst of legislative change. Schouler recognized that the loss of a wife's identity was a practice that was unfair to women's individual rights, and he easily rejected the legal fiction of marital unity. This did not result in his rejection of coverture, however. Revisiting the concept, he pointed out that the very notion of coverture assumed that the husband and wife were two distinct people, as the wife had to be a separate person in order to have her identity covered by her husband's. The wife's separate identity and need to be protected from her husband emerged as the reason for coverture. Schouler pointed out that this principle had been in Blackstone all along, as Blackstone noted that the wife's civil disabilities were intended for her protection and benefit, and the rules of coverture could be sustained under this principle just as well as under the thesis of marital unity.

By developing the marital protection thesis, Schouler found new reasons for many of the old rules of coverture. Under the principle of protection, a husband and wife could not contract with each other, not because a person could not transact with himself or herself—the principle comporting with the marital unity thesis—but because the wife was assumed to be acting under her husband's coercion. By prohibiting these transactions, the law was protecting the wife from a husband who was not acting in her best interest. Schouler cast the right of chastisement, which allowed a husband to beat his wife with a switch no larger than his thumb, as inappropriate, belonging to "a ruder state of society," in which power was exercised by brute force.[32] He thereby distanced the common law from its more "barbaric" elements, but he did not dispense with the rules of coverture. Even with domestic violence deemed inappropriate, the husband could still be recognized as the head of the household by wielding the less violent power, "at least by moral coercion, to regulate her movements so as to prevent her from going to places, associating with people, or engaging in pursuits, disapproved by himself on rational grounds."[33] Schouler saw such power as necessary for the husband to remain head of the household. Such a hierarchy might seem out of step with modern egalitarian sentiments, but it could be justified by the perceived need for authority to keep the household from splintering. The husband was head of household not because the home was a site of despotism but because the home was to be harmonious. Schouler retained the traditional privileges of deciding who could be admitted to the home and of choosing the home as well. His reconsideration of the underlying principles is representative of the modernization of status regimes.[34] In expressing his disapproval of the unity thesis, Schouler seemed to bring modern sensibilities to bear on his assessment of coverture, but he mustered new justifications for the rules of coverture and legitimated them as suitably modern.

DECLARATIONS OF INDEPENDENCE

Woman suffragists chose a much different strategy for making sense of the reform statutes. Rather than reconcile the reform statutes with the common law, woman suffragists reconciled them with fundamental American principles, as espoused in the Declaration of Independence. Woman suffragists argued that the rules of the marital relation were inappropriate for a country committed to the rights of the individual. The civil and political rights touted by foundational documents could be extended to the private sphere, thus rendering the hierarchy of the home unacceptable, whether justified by the unity thesis or justified by protection of the wife. The space for redefinition of the marital relation provided woman's rights activists with the opportunity to reject it altogether.

Woman suffragists carried out their attack on the common law by relying on the legacies of the codification and abolition movements. Even when relegated to feminine roles, such as sewing abolitionist emblems onto bags and selling handkerchiefs at antislavery conventions, woman abolitionists found that their success in fundraising could secure them power in their state antislavery societies.[35] Woman abolitionists were, therefore, understandably put off when they were denied seats on the floor of the World Anti-Slavery Society convention in London in 1840. As they later famously recounted the story in *History of Woman Suffrage*, Elizabeth Cady Stanton and Lucretia Mott instead walked around the city, talked about women's exclusion, and formulated plans for a woman's movement, which they realized in Seneca Falls New York, in 1848.[36]

The Seneca Falls convention was announced in newspaper advertisements as a "Woman Rights Convention" featuring Mott as its keynote speaker. The authors of *History of Woman Suffrage* explain that the convention organizers sought a model by which to frame their resolution about woman's rights. "The reports of Peace, Temperance, and Anti-Slavery conventions were examined, but all alike seemed too tame and pacific for the inauguration of a rebellion such as the world had never before seen."[37] When they consulted the Declaration of Independence, they recalled, their enthusiasm rose, and they decided to adopt it, with some modifications to the gendered and historic language and a new list of grievances, articulating eighteen grievances to match the number of grievances the American colonists enumerated against King George.

The Declaration of Sentiments begins with the same language as the Declaration of Independence, with a preamble commencing with "When, in the course of human events . . ." Its second paragraph is nearly identical, with the insertion of "women" into the language, thus altering the famous line to read: "We hold these truths to be self-evident: that all men and women are created equal."[38] The Declaration of Sentiments continues with the language of the Lockean right of revolution, recognizing the rejection of the legitimacy of a government when it has rescinded its contract with the people. To demonstrate the arbitrary power of "mankind," the Declaration of Sentiments then lists a set of grievances. The first grievance is that women have been denied the political right to vote. This is followed by the grievances growing from the doctrine of coverture: "He has made her, if married, in the eye of the law, civilly dead. He has taken from her all right in property, even to the wages she earns. He has made her, morally, an irresponsible being, as she can commit many crimes with impunity, provided they be done in the presence of her husband. In the covenant of marriage, she is compelled to promise obedience to her husband, he becoming, to all intents and purposes, her master—the law giving him power to deprive her of her liberty, and to administer chastisement."[39]

Recurrence to the Declaration of Independence was a common strategy for marginalized groups of the period, rendering a universal meaning to the invocation of God-given natural rights.[40] While this was the pattern that was assumed by social reformers, including the women's rights activists and the American Anti-Slavery Society before them, J. R. Pole suggests that the equality reference would have been understood during the founding period to mean that the American people were equal to the British people.[41] The equality they would have been concerned with was the protection of common-law rights. The British monarchy's offense lay in its arbitrary power in violating those liberties that were part of the ancient constitution, including common-law property rights, which had been violated by taxation without representation.[42] The founding generation considered the common-law tradition to be a source of their freedom. Those common-law origins tended to become obscured when political activists removed them from the historical context and cast them as universal rights against the relations of the common law.

Locke's work incorporated the common law as well. Locke's rights-bearing individual was himself embedded in a series of relations that formed the context for this subject's rights. Certainly these relations serve as a form of patriarchy upon which the social contract rests, as feminist theorists have pointed out.[43] But there was an important institutional role that these relations played in the maintenance of a liberal society that deserves further consideration. The relations were present not only to provide for men's freedom in the public sphere but also to serve purposes of caretaking and ownership on which a liberal society depends.[44] The domestic relations provided a source of multiple identities for the individual. Locke invoked them to rebut Sir Robert Filmer's theory of the subjection of the people by the king, making it clear that the king had political power over his subjects but that those subjects were not wholly subjected. In the private sphere, the political subject could take on other identities, such as father or master or servant. These multiple identities served as a source of freedom, allowing one to be subject in one area without allowing that status to define him wholly.

The political subject was not only free in the private sphere, he was the head of his own household government, the patriarch serving as the husband in the husband-wife relation, the master over his servant, the guardian over his ward, and the parent over his child. Locke discerned distinct reasons for each relation. The origins of the master-servant relation lie in the unequal capacities, or mere laziness, on the part of the servant, the individual who consented to be a servant as an alternative to starving.[45] The inequality of the parent-child relation is justified by the temporary "sort of Rule and Jurisdiction" that parents have over their child, who, while born free, is in a temporary state of tutelage. Parental power is both hierarchical and touching: "The Bonds of Subjection are like the Swadling Cloths they are wrapt up in, and supported by, in the weakness of their Infancy. Age and Reason as they grow up, loosen them till at length they drop quite off, and leave a Man at his own free Disposal."[46] Despite the tenderness of the undertaking, someone must be in charge: "But the Husband and Wife, though they have but one common Concern, yet having different understandings, will unavoidably sometimes have different wills too; it therefore being necessary, that the last Determination, i.e. the Rule, should be placed somewhere, it naturally falls to the Man's share, as the abler and the stronger."[47]

This often-quoted passage is misleading. It suggests that Locke based hierarchy on physical differences between men and women, but that would overstate the presence of natural behavior in his theory. Locke identifies procreation as the end of the marital relation and delineates the roles of husband and wife by this end.[48] The wife's subjection is thus determined both by the terms of the marital contract itself and by her anticipated role as mother. Locke counted on parents to take care of their children and to educate them out of their own feelings of natural affection, a theme that is reflected even in the tone of *Thoughts concerning Education.*[49] As Locke says in the *Second Treatise,* "God hath made it their business to imploy this care on their Off-spring, and hath placed in them suitable Inclinations of Tenderness and Concern to temper this power."[50] Parenthood can even be definitive of joy: "Joy is a delight of the mind, from the consideration of the present or assured approaching possession of a good. A father, in whom the very well-being of his children causes delight, is always, as long as his children are in such a state, in possession of that good; he needs but to reflect on it to have that pleasure."[51]

Locke does not trust these sentiments for institutional maintenance, however. In Locke's account of parenting, parents must continually overcome their natural affection in order to do what is best for the child. It may be instinctive to keep a child safe, warm, and fed, for example, but Locke suggests that parent not keep the child too warmly clothed, that his shoes be thin, that he be bathed in cold water. Such advice would be anathema to parents' sensibilities, and he certainly knew that: "How fond mothers are likely to receive this doctrine is not hard to foresee. What can it be less than to murder their tender babies to use them thus? What! Put their feet in cold water in frost and snow, when all one can do is little enough to keep them warm?"[52] Locke recommended that parents expose children to difficult conditions to habituate them and build their constitutions and fortitude, requiring, too, that parents habituate themselves to these conventions. The very natural fondness that would draw parents to take care of their children would impede the development of reason: "As the strength of the body lies chiefly in being able to endure hardships, so also does that of the mind. And the great principle and foundation of all virtue and worth is placed in this, that a man is able to *deny himself* his own desires, cross his own inclinations, and purely follow what reason directs as best though the appetite lean the other way. . . . Parents, being wisely ordained by nature to love their children, are very apt, if reason watch not that natural affection very warily, are apt, I say, to let it run into fondness."[53]

Parents—mothers as well as fathers—must learn to resist their loving tendencies and to assume the responsibility of being lord and the absolute governor of their children.[54] Parents become so habituated to their role that, by the time the child is of school age under a tutor, the doting parents are absent. At that time the father must be instructed to be familiar with his child.[55] The parents have been socialized to habituate themselves out of their natural affection. The home in Locke's work, then, is only nominally natural. The relations and feelings of family members toward one another have been socialized and naturalized so as to appear to be the proper behavior of intimates. Similarly, the authority of the husband comes not from any natural or brute strength but from convention and convenience. It is property that eventually requires hierarchy between the husband and wife, who have each been able to participate in authority over the children. The material care of children requires laying up goods for their well-being, not only as children but in inheritance.[56] The laws of inheritance prevent one's own property from returning to the common stock after one's death.[57] The care for and education of young children is temporary, needed only until the child attained reason.[58] The imperatives for retaining property alter the parents' identity from the short-term caretakers of their children's development to a permanent identity. With this new identity comes women's subjection. The passing down of property generates an interest that must be kept in common, inviting a renewed need for family unity. Should the wife disagree with her husband, the property would be threatened. Hence the need for a single decision maker, and Locke's placing of this power, almost arbitrarily, in the "abler and stronger" husband.

In placing the power of the husband as head of the household in his physical strength, Locke drew on the image of natural attributes to achieve a social convention. To take Locke's "abler and stronger" passage at face value is to assume that he rested hierarchy on brute force. This reading misses the masking of the structures and obligations within the family. Locke's domestic relations effected status and obligations for both public and private purposes. Parents raised children to be educated and capable of reason, needed in their capacity as citizens. The status of family members retained families and family property.

When Americans relied on Locke's natural rights theory, they borrowed his notion that all men are created equal, but not all men were equal or remained equal. The Americans of the early republic, whether consciously or not, retained the notion of an individual who was both an individual rights-bearer and a member of a status relation within the household. This was true for all the domestic relations, and Americans retained a hierarchical master-servant relation to govern employment until the twentieth century.[59] When the woman suffragists turned the rights of the individual against the domestic relations, they were not merely eliminating the brute force of the husband; they were delegitimizing the status that retained the purposes and obligations of the family. The story of Locke's liberal thought as the lone rights bearer was always a partial story. The woman suffragists defined liberalism by this aspect alone.

Whereas Locke and the American revolutionaries had been able to reconcile liberal principles with common-law status, American women's rights activists, who suffered the brunt of the subjection under the common-law domestic relations, would not ignore the tension between their own capacity and the strictures incurred by the common law. They brought this tension to the forefront and resolved it by eliminating the common law from conceptions of liberalism. The woman suffragists cast the common law and other sources of women's subjection as traditional notions based on no more than stereotype, which stood in the way of progress.

RECALLING BARBARISM

Sir Henry Maine captured the trajectory of progress in his declaration that modern societies were moving "from *status* to *contract*."[60] In his comparative legal history, which spanned centuries, Maine identified the family as the basic unit of society in ancient Rome. In this arrangement of "domestic despotism," all members of the family were subordinated to the single head of the family. This was changing, however, as "the drift of our social relations is from status to contract, from accepting life at second-hand to an original acquaintance with its sources."[61] Maine saw women's subordination in the nineteenth century as an incursion into the development of law rather than an ancient remnant. The Roman system ameliorated women's condition over time, but women in modern Anglo and American societies experienced subordination because of the more recent introduction of external traditions, namely, canon law.[62] Canon law was an intrusion that was responsible for thwarting progress; it maintained status at a time when status was giving way to contract, when the family was giving way to the individual as the basic unit of society.

This transition from status to contract did not obtain easily in the United States in the mid-nineteenth century, even with the radical theories of freedom developed by fellow social reformers. Woman's rights activists continually encountered reformers who did not extend theories of freedom to women. Woman suffragists, former abolitionists themselves, chastised James G. Birney for his commitment to freedom on the plantation but not at his own fireside.[63] If this was an age of progress, then a doctrine rooted in feudalism and entrenched by religion was inappropriate. The key to striking at coverture was to cast it as an illegitimate relic of the past, and the language of barbarism was an appropriate resource. The connotations of barbarism, which remained indeterminate during the codification debates of the 1820s, took on a new resonance when women's rights activists employed it. It was more difficult to defend the hierarchy of the marital relation as modern. The conditions were ripe to invoke the charge of barbarism without the indeterminacy or debate that had marked the earlier codification discourse.

The connection between barbarism and the domestic relations was a significant part of Judge Herttell's early, failed attempt to introduce a married women's property bill in the New York State Assembly in 1837. Recognizing that the common law survived the colonies' rebellion against England, Herttell presented the maintenance of coverture as an oversight. The new states had retained the common law out of habit, custom, and an absence of reflection.[64] If the public were only directed to reflect on the common law, it would find it incompatible with stated American commitments. In order to demonstrate this inconsistency, he invoked the language of the common law as barbaric, pointing out that it "originated in the *dark ages:* — in times of comparative intellectual ignorance, debasement and human vassalage, under an absolute and despotic feudal government and the auspices of mercenary men who were interested in its injustice."[65] He cast this doctrine as repugnant to the Constitution by relying on a synthesis of founding principles. Drawing upon a theory of popular sovereignty, he deemed women to be included in "The People" who are entrusted with natural rights, which he referenced with the Declaration of Independence. The United States recognized women's natural rights by its practice of allowing unmarried women to own property. To deny women their property upon marriage was a violation of their natural rights without due process of law.

The justifications for the denial of property rights to married women, found in references to a husband and wife being one person and one flesh, Herttell dismissed as "absurd *dicta.*"[66] These were ridiculous notions that carried no legal weight. He did recognize, however, the underlying purposes served by these absurd notions — they effected relations and obligations to ensure that both husband and wife would maintain the home and family.[67] Herttell appreciated the underlying perceived need for the marital relation, but he questioned the means by which it was achieved and the attendant subjugation of women.

The language of barbarism was readily available to the woman suffragists in their political rhetoric after the Civil War, when it took on cultural and political currency.[68] In 1856, the newly formed Republican Party platform resolved that Congress, in its power to legislate for the territories, prohibit "those twin relics of barbarism — Polygamy, and Slavery."[69]

Senator Charles Sumner from Massachusetts repeatedly equated slavery with barbarism. One of the early members of the Republican Party, he delivered a four-hour speech, "The Barbarism of Slavery," to the Senate in 1860.[70] In the speech, reproduced for popular reading, Sumner explained that the choice between slavery and freedom was a choice between barbarism and civilization. In 1864, in the midst of the Civil War, Sumner proposed a resolution that equated southern rebellion with slavery, urging that both be crushed. Again, the imagery of barbarism was illustrative in proposing that "it is our supremest duty . . . to take care that the barbarism of slavery, in which alone the rebellion has its origin and life, is so utterly trampled out that it can never spring up again anywhere in the rebel and belligerent region."[71]

Representative Ward, concerned that laws against polygamy were not being enforced in Utah, proposed a resolution providing that the "remaining barbarism of our age and country should be swept (like its twin system slavery) from the Territories of the republic."[72] In his annual message to Congress, President Grant referred to the "remnant of barbarism" remaining in Utah.[73] During and after the war, both slavery and polygamy were referred to as barbaric in congressional records, and they retained their status as relics, vestigial features of society that were poised to be swept away. In the very construction of these features as barbaric, Americans could define the country as modern.

The language of barbarism remained available for the confederacy as well. The Confederate Congress could declare the Civil War to be barbaric because it was an unjust usurpation of power.[74] Federal troops' treatment of Confederate prisoners of war was likewise cited as barbaric.[75] Confederate uses of barbarism were consistent with the notion that use of force was brutish and at odds with modernity. Members of the Confederate Congress could rely on the notion that modern political power was based on legitimate authority and reason rather than on physical force and point to the use of wartime force as an illegitimate exercise of political power.

After the Civil War, the appeal to modernity remained a persistent theme of barbarism rhetoric, and it was easily adapted to the growing racialization of the time. Moderns could be defined by their distance from the primitive, read through a contemporary understanding of white versus nonwhite. Under this reasoning newly freed slaves could be aided in their path to self-governance not by acknowledging their right to human dignity as autonomous individuals but by preventing their "constant tendency to relapse into barbarism."[76] The immigrant Chinese population could be controlled by comparing "coolie labor" to the barbarism of slavery, thereby restricting the entry of those who did not adopt the dress and manners of (Anglo) American culture.[77]

With the rhetoric of barbarism pervading political discourse, woman suffragists were able to employ it in their responses to the Reconstruction Amendments. With the addition of "male" in the Fourteenth Amendment and suffrage protected on the basis of race but not sex, the Reconstruction Amendments reasserted a dual citizenship between men and women.[78] In response, woman suffragists invoked barbarism in its racialized form, contrasting modern America to non-Western, barbaric cultural practices that repressed women. By offering a litany of the repression of women

—foot binding in China, widows throwing themselves on their husbands' funeral pyres in India, divorce customs in Jewish law, veiling in Turkey and Persia—they could associate American women's oppression with non-Western, primitive cultures, thus, in effect, asking American lawmakers if they wanted the United States to be classed with these cultures.[79] Woman suffragists were also able to apply the racialized reliance on barbarism to internal racial categories in the United States. They could denounce slavery as barbaric,[80] but they referred to black men as barbaric when their suffrage was protected under the Fifteenth Amendment.[81] The suffragists' facility in the racialized and modernized rhetoric of barbarism allowed them to shift the focus to relics of barbarism governing women's civil and political status.

Woman's rights activists could identify barbarism in America and, at the same time, exonerate Americans by blaming the inappropriate presence of this barbarism on inappropriate sources of political power. The woman suffragists classified women's status as the product of men's power over women, a power acquired by brute force and, hence, illegitimate. "A survey of the condition of the race through those barbarous periods, when physical force governed the world, when the motto, 'might makes right,' was the law, enables one to account for the origin of woman's subjection to man without referring the fact to the general inferiority of the sex, or Nature's law."[82] War itself could be identified as a relic of barbarism. Woman suffragists identified war as proper only for an earlier stage of human development.[83] War was barbaric because it was violent and because it relied on brute use of power, an idea that suffragists could easily apply to power relations and hierarchy in American law.

The unsuitability of brute force could be attached to the common law. Woman suffragists could point to the Anglo-Saxon customs of the common law as barbaric and its relations as its feudal remnant. "The system of Feudalism rising from the theory of warfare as the normal condition of man, still further oppressed woman by bringing into power a class of men accustomed to deeds of violence, and finding their chief pleasure in the sufferings of others. . . . The whole body of villeins and serfs were under absolute dominion of the Feudal Lords. . . . it was upon their wives and daughters that the greatest outrages were inflicted."[84] By attributing the hierarchy of the common law to primitive abuses of power rather than to institutional imperatives, they established a presence of hierarchy that was based on a clear illegitimacy and could be dismissed as outmoded: "Here are seen the old fossil prints of *feudalism*. The law relating to woman tends to make every family a barony, a monarchy, or a despotism, of which the husband is the baron, king, or despot, and the wife the dependent, the serf, or slave."[85] This was hierarchical and it was, of course, bar-

baric: "That this falsehood itself, the deposit of barbarism tends perpetually to bru-
talize the marriage relation by subjecting wives as irresponsible tools to the capri-
cious authority of husbands."[86]

The response could not lie in resistance. Some male advocates of women's rights
were willing to denounce their own male privilege in their marriage vows, but this
could only stand as a symbolic gesture. Robert Dale Owen vowed, "I . . . declare that
I consider myself, and earnestly desire to be considered by others, as utterly divested,
now and during the rest of my life, of any such rights, the barbarous relics of a feudal, despotic system, soon destined, in the onward course of improvement, to be
wholly swept away."[87] In marrying, Owen took on the privileges and obligations of
a husband whether he wanted them or not. By their calculation change would only
come by dismantling these legal rules.

With the identification of physical power and hierarchy as barbaric, woman suffragists were positioned to call the common-law doctrine of coverture into question.
"Your laws relating to marriage—founded as they are on the old common law of England, a compound of barbarous usages, but partially modified by progressive civilization—are in open violation of our enlightened ideas of justice."[88] By associating
coverture with the practices of the "purely savage tribes" and Asian cultures,[89] they
could confront America with its own self-identification and ask whether it really
wanted to be associated with barbarians and decide to be rid of coverture once and
for all through legal reform.

SWEEPING AWAY BARBARISM

The woman suffragists cast coverture as a mere relic, tragically and erroneously
carried through time by long-standing customs and prejudice. "Behind this wrong
lies the superstition and ignorance of the dark ages. Every error and wrong has its
root growing in the soil of ignorance and undevelopment."[90] They dredged up some
of the darkest practices in American politics and law, but their narrative was not one
of tragedy. They urged Americans to live up to their own ideals and to give in to the
inevitable tendencies of the age. Recognizing the mid-nineteenth century as an age
of progress, a delegate to the 1852 national woman's rights convention urged capitulation to progress as inevitable: "This is a time of progress; and man may sooner ar-
rest the progress of the lightning, or the clouds, or stay the waves of the sea, than the
onward march of Truth with her hand on her sword and her banner unfurled."[91]
They were ready to ride the wave of progress to its logical conclusions. Speaking of
woman's rights at an antislavery society meeting, Sarah Smith said: "Let our course
then still be onward! Justice, humanity, patriotism."[92]

Because the survival of coverture could be attributed to distant dark ages, there was no one to blame. American men in power need not feel embarrassed for supporting the practice; they need only recognize it and live up to their stated ideals. "We by no means make man responsible for all the blunders and barbarisms of his ignorance; we only ask the nineteenth century to shed the dead skin of the past, and bring its customs, creeds, and codes into harmony with the higher civilization we are now entering."[93] This nonconfrontational stance provided an added benefit—it allowed women to jump aboard as fellow travelers in the march toward progress. The rejection of feudalism would mean a rejection of the status relations of the common law. Hence women could be imagined as individuals first and foremost, deserving of the natural rights recognized for all human beings.

Women's rights movements abroad bolstered their case and provided grounds for hope: "When, in old monarchical England, where the best minds are in a measure palsied by the demon of caste, women are rising up in their dignity, throwing off the schackles of custom."[94] The feudal customs were firmly rooted in America, but there was hope that American women would throw off their shackles, too: "These hideous, deforming superstitions still exist in the minds of even many comparatively intelligent women, and never can be eradicated until the laws of the human system are taught in preference to crude doctrines and dogmas."[95] While coverture rested on powerful prejudices, they were, after all, only prejudices, and no match for a society that practiced its principles.

The onward surge would eventually come to pass. Although the married women's property acts were not intended to emancipate women, they had the potential to contribute to a narrative of women's emancipation from the strictures of coverture. The codification of trusts led to the passage of married women's property acts. Discrepancies in women's ability to use that property sometimes led to further reform statutes. Even if inadvertently, one thing was leading to another; when taken together, events did appear to constitute an irresistible wave of progress. Woman suffragists imbued this identification of progress with a particular content and rights with a particular form by reflecting on the status that women should have in this progressive age. "It needs but little observation to see that the tide of progress in all countries is setting toward the enfranchisement of woman, and that this advance step in civilization is destined to be taken in our day."[96] They were able to insert women's rights as another chapter in the onward movement of progress, dating back to the dark ages and continuing into the bright future. As Wendell Phillips said at a woman's rights convention, "Every step of progress the world has made has been from scaffold to scaffold, from stake to stake. . . . Government began in tyranny and force; began in the feudalism of the soldier and the bigotry of the priest; and the ideas of justice and humanity have been fighting their way like a thunderstorm against the organized selfishness of human nature. And this is the last great protest against the wrong of ages."[97]

The woman suffragists were thereby able to make the case for women's rights by rendering their claim consistent with American traditions and tendencies as they presented those traditions and tendencies. The Declaration of Sentiments emerged as a homage and a best reading of the Declaration of Independence although, in fact, it was a reconfiguration and masking of the loss of the common law from liberal theory. In the suffragists' narrative, the abolition of coverture was not a radical break with the past but a proto-feminist intervention into the tensions and inconsistencies within American principles. Woman suffragists pointed to the presence of vestiges of a dark age that America wanted to leave behind. Their project was one of harmonizing American principles and making them consistent with their own internal logic. Bringing America's feudalism to the surface was not an indictment of Americans but a reminder that Americans should be horrified by the feudalism in their midst. Woman suffragists could refer to core American principles to present women's rights as an issue that would continue the advancement of liberal doctrine and render it consistent.

Liberalism was the doctrine that could sweep away the feudal past. Speaking of liberalism, the woman suffragists said, "Once in a great while God blesses us with a mind which is like a sweeping machine, and whose vision is so clear, that it can see the dust and mould which have accumulated for years over the moral condition of society."[98] Liberal theory would provide the eagle eye for discerning in appropriate traditions, and liberal rights would serve as the broom for sweeping away the mold of an old, musty tradition.

References to liberalism are ubiquitous in woman suffragist literature of the mid to late nineteenth century. The writers employed *liberal* as an attribute of individuals or education, *liberal* as a description of interpretive methods of scripture or legislation, and *liberalism* as an animating cultural and political force and as a political doctrine.[99] Liberal ideas were crucial in the progress of human development that the suffragists relied on:

> In gathering up the threads of history in the last century, and weaving its facts and philosophy together, one can trace the liberal social ideas, growing out of the political and religious revolutions in France, Germany, Italy, and America; and their tendency to substitute for the divine right of kings, priests, and orders of nobility, the higher and broader one of individual conscience and judgment in all matters pertaining to this life and that which is to come. It is not surprising that in so marked a transition period from

the old to the new, as seen in the eighteenth century, that women, trained to think and write and speak, should have discovered that they, too, had some share in the new-born liberties suddenly announced to the world.[100]

Woman suffragists noted that liberal-minded people of their day tended to be maligned as revolutionaries, but advised, "Take courage ye whom the world stigmatizes as Liberalists, Reformers and Free Thinkers; it is a crown ye wear. Man may not see it, but the angels do and glory in its brightness—a little while and the thorns will lacerate no more."[101] They had truth on their side and had only to endure the oppressions and social pressures of their contemporaries until the truths of liberalism came to fruition. In this, the martyrdom complex they suggested for women's rights workers was modeled on the abolitionists.

Woman suffragists were not simply relying on liberalism to address the feudal past. They were engaged in construction, both of a feudal common law and of a liberalism shorn of the common law. They made use of the available derision of the common law and contrasted it to the notion of progress. They then called this doctrine of progress liberalism, attaching it to the commitment to rights to be traced back the Declaration of Independence. Rather than relying on the Lockean idea of the Declaration as a theory of political authority, they lauded it as the recognition of natural rights, and they construed liberalism as a doctrine committed to natural rights and destined to overcome the impediments of hierarchy. This liberalism was intended to be sweeping in its effects. Despite the early reformist arguments that it was only the hierarchy of the marital relation that needed to be reformed, the invocation of liberal principles promised to sweep away oppressive tradition completely.

With liberalism so defined, the individual could be conceived as it was in the theory of Angelina Grimké. Ernestine Rose could claim that women should be included in the promises of the Declaration of Independence because the tenets of liberty presumed equality for all, including women: "Humanity recognizes no sex—mind recognizes no sex—virtue recognizes no sex—life and death, pleasure and pain, happiness and misery recognize no sex."[102] The concept of an individual abstracted from all social status was becoming the ideal individual rights bearer.

With the common law construed as a system separate from and opposite to liberalism, rights could be conceived as universal human rights, without recourse to any social status or social context. In casting the common law as barbaric, this argument also cast liberalism as a political doctrine that had no relation to the common law and its institutional arrangements. Liberalism was now defined simply by its abstract principles. It had no apparent relation to common-law relations, and the common law was certainly not a source of rights. In reshaping liberalism and its expectations for reform, the woman suffragists offered it as a source of rights that would recognize the rights of the individual without recourse to that individual's social status or conditions. In so doing, they began to delegitimize the derivation of rights within social circumstances. The organic derivation of rights of freedom of speech, or Lydia Maria Child's situated self finding her freedom, were becoming less desirable. Instead, the woman suffragists offered a theory of freedom that they situated in a liberalism that was freed from, rather than accommodating of, social relations and obligations. Despite their identification of a pervasive barbarism in America, woman suffragists found a means of easily dispensing with it. In contrast to the defenders of coverture, who saw it as the foundation of society, they were able to imagine this relic of barbarism as the flotsam and jetsam of development, which had risen to the surface and was now mere garbage that should be disposed of.

It was a persuasive strategy. It allowed them to look backward to the founding Declaration of Independence, claim recognition under its natural rights philosophy, and proceed forward with a theory of freedom to guide the reform of laws and traditions to liberate women. It was a self-fulfilling narrative. The liberalism constructed by the woman suffragists was remarkably effective. They considered that it did not take much to get the ball rolling toward liberal reform. In assessing the married women's property acts, they were not discouraged by the limited reach of the statutes in New York because most of the "Western states copied the advance legislation of New York and some are now even more liberal."[103] Their narrative would prove illustrative in later years, when the trajectory of events did seem to point toward progress, and the tendency seemed to be toward the expansion of women's rights. It was politically salient and morally persuasive. Even if the married women's property acts were not intended to liberate women at the time of their passage, when viewed in retrospect, they seemed to have that effect. Such a retrospective evaluation is displayed in *Adkins v. Children's Hospital*, in which Justice Sutherland found, following ratification of the Nineteenth Amendment, that the inequality of the sexes was diminishing to a vanishing point. For him, to recognize different capacities of men and women under the law "would be to ignore all the implications to be drawn from the present day trend of legislation, as well as that of common thought and usage, by which woman is accorded emancipation from the old doctrine that she must be given special protection or be subjected to special restraint in her contractual and civil relationships."[104]

In *Adkins*, Justice Sutherland displayed the art of the retrospective narrative of women's progress. Even if reforms were not passed in order to emancipate women, and even if those reforms did little to change women's condition at the time of their passage, reforms of women's status could be viewed cumulatively to reveal a pattern

of diminishing difference and inequality. This was the trope of the woman suffragists, who declared married women's property acts to be the deathblow to coverture.
Although not intended in this way, the waves of reform statutes could be so interpreted retrospectively.

THE REMAINING COMMON LAW

In treating the common law as a mere relic that would simply yield to liberal principles, the woman suffragists underestimated the role of the common law in social
ordering in the United States. The common-law domestic relations had served important functions in Locke's theory, and they served purposes in American law. Judge
Herttell recognized that the domestic relations played a role in fixing the status of
men and women and provided for obligations in the home to be met. The woman
suffragists knew this too. They did not oppose marriage; they simply opposed the subjection of women within it. Nevertheless, in disparaging the common law in its en-
tirety, they cast doubt on the legitimacy of the common law and on social relations
as playing a role in the derivation and allocation of rights.

This was not the first time, of course, that the charge of barbarism had been leveled against the common law. William Sampson was just as vociferous as the woman
suffragists, but the radical potential of his arguments fell flat among an audience
of lawyers who found multiple interpretations of the common law possible. The
woman suffragists were able to render their synthesis of theories persuasive because
they struck at the nexus of the common law and liberal theory. The gendered means
of social ordering were in tension with theories of individual freedom as emancipated from status. By declaring the primacy of rights to be a central American value,
woman suffragists urged America to live up to its own aspirations. There was a structural reason for the domestic relations, consistent with the contextualized derivation
of rights that was part of common-law liberty and institutional maintenance. Woman
suffragists had to obscure this reason and instead play up the hierarchy of the common law. They pointed to the subjugation of women upon which these status relations rested and cast the marital relation, and the common law as a whole for that
matter, as an outdated system that should embarrass Americans. If they obscured the
structural reasons for the domestic relations, then the only remaining reasons for
their existence had to be unenlightened views about women's capacities and nature.

In the woman suffragists' capture of the narrative of progress the common law fell
into disrepute. It had long been associated with and accommodated by liberalism,
but now the two doctrines were wrested apart and juxtaposed. Liberalism would now
work upon the common law rather than relying on it to meet its social needs. Lib-

eralism lost its system for ordering citizens on the basis of their sex as it lost the legitimacy for erecting hierarchy in the domestic sphere. A liberalism defined only by its abstract principles is not one that offers much guidance in the social practices or maintenance of liberalism. This is precisely the liberalism fostered by the woman suffragists, which attests to its persuasiveness. The reform movements recounted in the earlier chapters were met with resistance, and the woman suffragists met that resistance as well, yet their theory has emerged as the basis for contemporary liberalisms. In the codification debates, common lawyers could muster defenses of the common law's feudal and barbaric origins and give them a positive spin. When the issue was women's subjection under coverture, it was more difficult to argue for the common law's suitability for moderns. Thus, the gendered component of the common law proved to be more susceptible to the negative connotations of barbarism than did the methods of the common law in the codification debates. In adopting derogatory language, woman suffragists cast aspersions on the common law as a whole, not simply on its domestic relations, casting the common law as a whole into aspersion, and destined it to fall against the power of liberalism.

The woman suffragists' innovations have certainly benefited American women by enabling them to gain broader rights and civic status. To call these advances into question would seem to express a wish to return to the days of women's subjugation or to risk women's equality.[105] But it is not necessary to respond to the suffragist narrative with a nostalgia for the conservative. One can assume a feminist stance and assert that, in too hastily identifying progress, the woman suffragist narrative was not progressive enough. The narrative was an overstatement of liberal possibilities and an understatement of the tenacity of the common-law domestic relations. There is good reason to be wary of the suffragist narrative, not because narratives obscure reality but, rather, because narratives can constitute reality and the formation of community.[106] The woman suffragist narrative would come to be highly persuasive. Its recourse to American principles allowed the suffragists to refer to familiar concepts and to situate themselves as community members of equal standing as they constructed a new narrative of community. Powerful in its ideas, this story nevertheless provided only a partial account of the common law in America. Its hopeful account of reforming the common-law domestic relations underscored the anachronism of those domestic relations. To hear the woman suffragists tell it, the domestic relations were a thing of the past. If they survived into the present, it was only because of prejudice. Such a narrative obscured the reasons why nineteenth-century American laws continued to include the domestic relations.

When the woman suffragists wrote and acted, the common-law domestic relations were not poised to succumb to the sweep of liberal principles. Those who supported women's rights were perfectly capable of retaining the rules of coverture, because rights had always been attached to contextualized subjects, whether as "Englishmen" or as married men or women. Despite the woman suffragists' construction of a new and liberalized liberalism, the common-law institutions continued to operate upon women's lives. Woman's rights activists did not succeed in dismantling coverture but only in obscuring its purposes and its legitimacy. Because coverture continued and adapted to declining legitimacy for its rules, the woman suffragist version of liberalism fails to explain why coverture persisted, offering only the machinations of a misogynist culture. Such explanations fail to provide the analysis of practices and institutions that can grasp the needs and practices of liberalism.[107]

The common law lived up—or, down—to its expectations. The increasing illegitimacy of the common-law domestic relations in political culture made it more difficult for common law's defenders to justify them. With the passage of more and more married women's reform statutes, the common-law rules lay in disarray, and common-law defenders, particularly those who were removed from the state-level courts where this battle was being played out, turned to outside traditions to justify and reassert those common-law rules of coverture. This made the woman suffragist narrative self-fulfilling. To look at the champions of coverture in the late nineteenth century is to witness nearly boorish defenders of the status quo, whose very outlandishness contributed to the legitimacy of the woman suffragist narrative, attesting as it did to the inappropriateness of such sentiments for a modern polity.

The woman suffragist narrative as liberal triumph over the common law would be the end of the story, except for its lapses. Detaching the common-law domestic relations from liberalism would seem to be a triumph as well, except that it did not solve the problem of coverture. The woman suffragist narrative obscured the institutional commitments that sustained coverture, and women's condition continued to be determined by rules of coverture well into the twentieth century. Furthermore, the loss of the common law from liberalism caused a shift in rights derivation. The separation of common-law institutions from liberalism also meant a rejection of common-law methods of rights derivation. The woman suffragist theory of rights was moving toward the abstraction of the political subject developed by the Grimké sisters. Just as Lydia Maria Child hesitated to endorse these methods of rights derivation, we can now ask whether the woman suffragist shift toward abstraction was realistic or desirable. This is a difficult question to pose, as the outcome of the suffragist narrative—acceptance of the assumption that women deserve rights—is so appealing. How does one go about constructing the reluctant response to the woman suffragists without denying the merits of their project? That is the task of Part Two.

Lingering Status

CHAPTER FOUR

The Married Women's Property Acts

Collaborating for Coverture

Despite the woman suffragists' pronouncement that the married women's property acts inflicted the deathblow to coverture, the rules of coverture and married women's status persisted. Married women gained the right to own property, that linchpin of liberal theory, and even subsidiary rights to acquire, use, dispose of, and contract for that property, but often within limits. The civic capacity recognized in these property rights was not extended to married women's other civil disabilities, which were left untouched by statute, so a married woman might be able to run her own business and support her family but have no say in where her family lived. The woman suffragist narrative of the married women's property acts provided a model of aspiration for women's rights, but it hinders understanding of the maintenance of coverture in the late nineteenth century.

Because the married women's property acts were passed state by state, some regional patterns emerged in their timing and extent. Joan Hoff has identified the Northeast, the Mid-Atlantic, and the Midwestern states as providing the most protection of women's rights. She identifies six categories of reform legislation—debt-free estates, separate estates, wills, access to personal estate, *feme sole* status, and earnings acts.[1] Although Western states were leaders in granting suffrage to women, they fell behind in extending property rights to married women, most likely because women were not inheriting the large ranches and farms in the West.[2] By 1900, western states had caught up to their peers. Although the first to grant property rights, the South was the last to pass significant reform legislation. Despite these regional differences in the passage of the acts, Sara Zeigler has identified a uniformity in the effects of the acts, noting that household hierarchy continued across the country because of the continued judicial control of married women's status: "Courts insisted upon conformity to the feudal dependencies embodied in the rules of the common law, even in the face of legislative efforts to reform the marriage law in favor of women's rights."[3]

The simultaneous presence of rights and status is indeed puzzling, and it would seem that the only explanation for the maintenance of the remaining rules of coverture was a resistance to change, and judges emerge as the likely culprit. The inability of the married women's property acts to bring about women's emancipation is commonly attributed to the conservatism of judges who, out of ideological or institutional imperatives, refused to construe married women's property acts liberally and thwarted a potential revolution in women's rights.[4] Judges employed the rule of statutory interpretation that dictated that statutes passed in derogation of the common law were to be construed narrowly so as not to alter the common law further than expressed in the statute.[5]

Institutional analyses that posit courts acting as the depository of a feudal common law and legislatures as the location of a reformist liberal commitment to rights mirror the woman's rights activists' conceptual distinction between liberalism and the common law.[6] The dichotomy closes off consideration of the role that the common law played in the development of liberalism and in Americans' derivation of rights. Karen Orren does locate a function for the common law in American political development in recognizing that the master-servant relation maintained stability in the economic order so that American industrialization and capital could develop, but she does not consider the relation between the common law and liberalism itself.[7] Attention to gender opens up the opportunity to consider the relation between the common law and liberalism in institutional analysis and to solve some of the remaining puzzles of the married women's property acts.

Because institutional explanations of the survival of coverture fall short of explaining why the fiction of marital unity and the contradiction between rights and status had such staying power, the most likely explanation becomes the one offered by the woman suffragists—coverture's retention was due to old-fashioned prejudice or to misogyny. This explanation discourages the opportunity and imperative to inquire into the institutional commitments of liberalism, to the social practices upon which liberal polities rely for the maintenance of principles, and into the ways in which those principles act upon liberal subjects.[8]

The woman suffragist narrative, furthermore, proves to be a foil in studying the married women's property acts. Dichotomizing the common law and liberalism, with the consequent normative assessments, produced the dynamic of a bad, oppressive common-law doctrine pitted against a beneficial, ameliorative, reformist doctrine of liberalism. Given that the woman suffragist dichotomy was the product of a particular political strategy, there remain other possibilities for interpreting the married women's property acts; the alternative rights discourses in the previous chapters provide a model. Common-law liberty provided a model for deriving rights affixed to status and adapting to circumstances, such as changes in political culture and imperatives, and for ameliorating conditions through the equitable adjustment of common-law rules. The married women's property acts altered the common-law rules of coverture in conferring property rights to married women, but they retained the common-law status of married women. That both courts and legislatures were careful to retain this status suggests a collusion of, rather than a conflict between, institutions. Both legislatures and courts in the late nineteenth century operated with a view of rights and status that cannot be captured, or hardly recognized, by the woman suffragist version of liberalism. This chapter demonstrates this collaboration by examining the legislation and judicial interpretation of married women's property acts in Massachusetts, Indiana, and Kentucky.[9]

MASSACHUSETTS

Massachusetts was a state with a strong activist tradition of both abolition and woman's rights, so it would seem that the conferral of property rights to married women recognized women's autonomy and liberation from coverture. While women's activism has been cited as influential in the passage of the earnings statutes in the 1860s and beyond,[10] its influence in the passage of the property statutes should not be overstated. The account of events in *History of Woman Suffrage* details the activities of both men and women who sought relief from coverture, and it presents the statutes as passed under the pressure that they applied. While there is some evidence that some liberal statutes were passed during the brief period in which the Know-Nothing party gained a majority in the Massachusetts legislature, the Massachusetts married women's property acts were not intended to emancipate women from coverture. Rather than replacing common-law status with rights, they balanced status with rights by attaching conditions to the conferral of property rights.

Massachusetts passed some early property statutes that codified equitable procedures, enabling a married woman to own her separate property in trust and allowing a husband and wife to make antenuptial agreements. In 1853, the state constitutional convention confronted issues of women's rights, primarily because an active, vocal, organized woman's rights contingent pressured the convention. The activists inundated the convention with petitions asking to have the word *male* struck from the state constitution and requesting that women be able to vote on the proposed amendments.[11] They also asked the convention to consider an amendment that would allow married women to own property. The question was sent to the Committee on the Frame of Government, which reported back to the convention that married women were indeed in need of more protection of their property. It nevertheless recommended that this matter be left to the legislature, because it had already begun passing reform statutes and because "the Committee believes that the remedy can be most safely and beneficially applied by the action of the legislature, adjusting, in detail, the somewhat complicated relations, which result from the marriage contract. They therefore report that it is inexpedient for the Convention to act thereon."[12]

The committee's report suggests that committee members were not unsympathetic to the concerns of woman's rights advocates, but deferring to the legislature was a means of ensuring that reform would be implemented in a different way. Had married women's property rights been added as a constitutional amendment, it could have trumped any reliance on married women's status. In deferring to the legislature, the committee—and the convention, implicitly, in its approval—recognized that these relations were "complicated." The committee determined that the relations should be preserved even as rights were conferred. This complicated procedure was best enacted by the incremental, specific process of legislation.

The legislature did pass laws conferring property rights to married women after the convention, and the laws reflect the complications that the committee perceived. The legislature gave women the right to own property and, later, to make contracts regarding that property, but these rights were limited. In the General Statutes of 1859, the rights of a married woman to own property looked much as they did in other states, allowing her to retain both real and personal property as her sole and separate property, which would not be attached to her husband's debts.[13] In 1859, a married woman could bargain, sell, or convey only her separate property. The ability to contract was not a broad recognition of an individual capable of consent but was limited to those contracts pertaining to her separate property.

Married women were not recognized as autonomous individuals capable and entitled to contract but, rather, as married women with a few contractual rights. Subsequent reform statutes reflected the same conditional character of these new rights, so that a married woman could hold an insurance policy as separate property, *but* she needed a trustee or judge to intervene on her behalf. A married woman could be an administrator, *but* as a probate court deemed fit. A married woman or minor who was to appear in court as witness could send someone else in her stead. A married woman could run her own business, *but* she needed to file a certificate, and she could not enter into a co-partnership. A married woman could contract to purchase

or pay for necessaries, *but* that did not relieve her husband from his marital obligation to support the family. A married woman could contract, *but* a husband and wife
could not contract with each other. A married woman could sue and be sued, *but*
a husband and wife could not sue each other.[14] The married women's property
statutes did not effect this transition from status to contract; instead, they positioned
women between status and contract.

The conditions attached to the reform statutes suggest that women were accorded
this transitional status out of fear that they would be unable to exercise their rights.
It was not that married women were incapable but that they lacked experience, and
others could take advantage of them. As the committee's report indicated at the convention, this was part of the complicated nature of rights. It was not that Massachusetts was hostile to women's rights, but it did not deem married women ready to exercise them as autonomous individuals. If the court readings were conservative, it is
because the statutes themselves were ambivalent.

INDIANA

In Indiana the married women's property statutes were limited in their conferral
of rights, and the courts respected those limits. The Indiana legislature was not committed to married women's rights in the 1840s, but after married women's property
rights became a heated topic at the state's constitutional convention in 1850, reform
statutes began to appear in the next legislative session. The first few years of statutes
were modest in scope. Given that married women could now own their separate
property, the statutes set the terms by which married women could acquire, use, and
convey property, usually requiring that the husband join the wife in any business
transaction regarding the wife's property.[15] Other statutes made provisions for married women whose husbands were insane or had deserted them.[16] It was not until
1879 that the Indiana legislature passed a major reform statute, bringing Indiana up
to date with other states.[17] Under the 1879 act, a married woman could bargain, sell,
assign, and transfer her separate property as if she were *feme sole*, thus eliminating
the role of the husband in her transactions. Section Two of the act allowed a married woman to retain her own earnings, a trend that was observable in other states.
Furthermore, a married woman could now enter into any contract in reference to
her separate estate. In 1881, Indiana abolished all legal disabilities of a married
woman to make contracts, with some exceptions: restrictions on her ability to contract for her real property were retained; she was prohibited from entering any contract as surety for another's debt; and, although she would be liable for torts committed in the presence of her husband, they would be jointly liable.[18] Even though

the language of the statutes suggests that these reforms were revolutionary in women's status, the exceptions revealed the ongoing presumption that married women needed to be protected when making contracts and the presumption of co-ercion when women exercised rights in the presence of their husbands. As in Massachusetts, the Indiana legislature conferred rights but retained status, presenting married women as incapable of exercising the full rights of the contracting individual.

The Indiana courts' interpretations of the legislation of 1879 and 1881 indicate just how much of the common law survived the statutes. In an 1883 case in which a widow tried to sue her husband's estate for the rents he had collected off her land for many years, the court denied her request on two grounds. First, the husband had begun the practice of managing his wife's property before the statute of 1852, which allowed a married woman to keep the rents derived from her own property, and since he continued to do so afterwards, the court could presume that husband and wife had implicitly agreed to the ongoing arrangement. The court also considered the family situation; he had used the rent money to provide a dwelling house and to maintain the family. This family obligation, secured by the husband's status under the common law, could be retained even under reform. Furthermore, the court, fearing the "evil" that would result if a wife could make a claim against her deceased husband's estate, would not let the new rights of married women disrupt the family relations.[19]

The court also pointed out that, notwithstanding the expansive language of the 1879 and 1881 statutes, the legislative reforms left many of the common-law relations unchanged. The 1879 statutes did not abrogate the 1852 statutory provision that the husband must join his wife when he is party to the suit.[20] While the 1879 statute allowed her to make contracts in reference to her separate trade or business, apart from the conferral of those limited rights, "the statute left such married woman precisely as she had been prior to its enactment."[21] The court pointed to Massachusetts and New York as states that had arrived at similar positions.

The Indiana court's narrow reading of the married women's property statutes found many of the common-law rules of coverture to have survived legislative reform. It would be misleading, however, to see the court in the role of conservative seeking to limit the potential of the statutes, because the legislature had tried to confer rights within limits and to retain the status of married women and the protection that status provided.

In the case of suretyship for debts, the court was more progressive than the legislature. It was common in many states to forbid a wife to use her separate property as surety for her husband's loans, because this would put her in the position of using her property to pay his debts, a situation that the early property statutes wanted to avoid, as it invited the opportunity for the husband to coerce the wife. In 1885 the Indiana supreme court reviewed the married woman's ongoing ability to sign a contract as surety for another's debt. It found that in 1852 the legislature had passed an act saying that a wife's land was not liable for the debts of her husband, but the court subsequently recognized that a mortgage held by husband and wife for the husband's debt was valid. The legislature then declared that a wife could not mortgage for a husband's debt, but the court nevertheless held that a joint mortgage for the husband's debt was valid. Finally, the legislature passed an act that expressly stated that a married woman could not make a contract of suretyship in any manner. The court now complied, acknowledging the legislative purpose of protecting a married woman's property and preventing her from entering into "burdensome obligations from which neither she nor her property would be benefited."[22]

The misunderstandings regarding suretyship confound the charge that courts were hindering the liberal efforts of legislatures. The court was willing to allow a married woman to live with the consequences of her contract. It recognized her citizenship in terms not only of her rights but also of her capacity to accept responsibility for the exercise of those rights. The court demonstrated that she was capable of upholding the obligations that stand as the corollary of rights.[23] In putting an end to such recognition, the legislature may have aided women's short-term interests of protecting their property, but it hindered their status as rights-bearing citizens.

The experience in Indiana suggests that one cannot assign blame to the courts for inhibiting the potential of the statutes. Rather than seeing one institution as more conservative than another, it helps to see such episodes as reflective of the uncertainty involved in the balancing of status with new rights for married women. Neither the legislature nor the courts could anticipate all the questions that would arise, and the development of dual purposes invited uncertainty and experimentation. The relation between the institutions was one of collaboration; it was not a conflict between a progressive legislature and a conservative court.

KENTUCKY

Reform in Kentucky began with a few modest changes in married women's property-holding. In the 1840s the legislature made provisions for married women to own property if their husbands abandoned them. This reform was not significant in content, as married women could receive the same relief under the common law,[24] but it demonstrates recourse to legislation in the area of marital status. Kentucky held a constitutional convention in 1849–50. The "big questions" to face the convention involved slavery, elections, the inhibition of the use of credit by the state for internal improvements, the composition of state courts, representation in the legislature, and the public school system.[25] Married women's property and even women's issues do not appear on this list, yet in the legislative session following the convention there was an outpouring of legislation regarding marriage, including married women's property rights and rules regarding the marriage contract and divorce.

Despite the increase in legislative activity, the laws regarding married women's property rights continued to have only slight effects on the common law. The law in 1851 acknowledged that married women could own real estate or slaves and that this property was not liable for their husbands' debts. It also stated that despite the married woman's ability to own property, the husband was still liable to provide her and the family with necessaries.[26] Statutes passed over the next few years clarified issues regarding the sale of a married woman's property, allowing her to sell her land or slaves if joined by her husband or "next friend."[27] It was not until 1866 that a broader reform statute was passed, allowing a married woman to act as *feme sole* in regard to her separate property provided she submit a joint petition with her husband before a court of chancery.[28]

Of these three states, the legislature in Kentucky meted out married women's property rights at the slowest pace, removing civil disabilities only a few at a time. The Kentucky court actually emerges as more generous toward married women's property rights; in looking to relieve married women from common-law disabilities it looked not just to those statutes that abrogated common-law principles but also to equity. The court did continue to uphold the marital obligations and, therefore, married women's status. Hence, the husband remained the head of the household, as evidenced by the court's acknowledgment that he chose the domicile, provided the necessaries, and could act in his wife's defense.[29] Despite upholding these common-law obligations, the court was willing to turn to equity. The court acknowledged that the common law forbade contracts between husband and wife because it considered them to be one person; but, the court determined, "the rule is otherwise in equity. For many purposes equity treats them as distinct persons, capable of contracting with each other, and their contracts will sometimes be enforced, even against the creditors of the husband."[30] Specifically, "such contracts, when advantageous to the wife, will be upheld in equity for her benefit and protection."[31] The court indicated that it would recur to equitable principles, especially when the outcome would favor the married woman, that is, when it would protect her. The court combined this construal of equity with its rendering of the statutes emerging from the legislature. The purpose of the statutes was to protect the married woman from her husband's creditors and even from her husband, who might try to place his earnings beyond her reach.[32]

The Kentucky supreme court, in its use of equity, indicated that it was aware that married women might need relief of their common-law disabilities, but this is a position distinct from abolishing the doctrine of coverture from which those disabilities arose. The accounts of the statutes in all three of these states indicates that legislatures, too, sought to relieve disabilities while retaining the status relations.

JUDICIAL INTERPRETATION AND POWER

Theories of institutional power presume that state courts were conservative because they would jealously guard the power of discerning the common-law rules from legislative encroachment. Hence, we would expect state courts to interpret the married women's property statutes narrowly so as to cede as little power as possible. Because of these presumptions, narrow interpretation by the courts has been cited as the reason for the limited extent of married women's property reform.[33] The foregoing examples, however, demonstrate that there was no vast potential that the courts could inhibit because the statutes themselves were narrowly drawn, in their content and in the conditions they attached to the rights they conferred. The description of the legislature-court relation as legislative enactments limited by conservative courts does not obtain. This was not a situation in which courts guarded coverture while legislatures sought to abolish it. Rather, there was collaboration between the branches to work out the inconsistencies between coverture and married women's rights. Instead of abolishing the tension between rights and status, courts and legislatures sought a means of reconciling them.

Theories of conservative courts obscure the limited purposes of the married women's property statutes. They also skew the activities of the courts, which carved out institutional power by adhering to the statutes rather than resisting them. Courts found a space from which to remain involved in married women's status by faithfully upholding the purposes of the statutes. The conditional features of the statutes conveyed the idea that women could have rights but that they were incapable of fully exercising those rights. The courts could serve as one of the paternalistic actors remaining in place to guide married women in these early exercises of rights. State courts closely monitored married women in their practice of new rights, thus ensuring continued judicial involvement in the altered status of married women.

In the shift from judicial common-law methods to legislative enactments, courts retained their role in the production of married women's status by drawing a new portrait of the family. The common-law fiction of marital unity gave way to the recognition of a family of individuals who possessed the human characteristics of greed and deceit. The courts acknowledged fraud and division within families and used that recognition to insist on the need for courts to continue to protect vulnerable women. By thoroughly scrutinizing married women's actions in the use of their newly gained rights, the courts carved out a new role for themselves.[34]

The few recognized Supreme Court cases that address the family tend to rely on romanticized ideas of woman and family to justify the denial of rights to married women.[35] State courts, however, were quite willing to recognize the family as a site of deceit and disharmony. Fraud was a concern after passage of the married women's property acts. Husbands could take advantage of their wives' new rights to own property by putting property in their wives' names, effectively shielding it from creditors. State-level courts refrained from issuing elegies on the sanctity of the family and instead acknowledged the financial machinations wrought by family members after the reform statutes. For example, a married woman held title to a piece of land, but the land had been paid for by her husband. When he subsequently fell into debt, he had a house built on his wife's land, an investment that increased its value from $500 to $3,500. A Kentucky court found that this building, which was not used to house the husband and his family, served instead as a pretense for him to transfer his property out of his name in order to defraud his creditors.[36]

In *Virgie v. Stetson*, the Maine court reviewed the development of reform legislation to show that the legislature, fully aware of frauds perpetuated by husbands, responded with further statutes. When married women in Maine were initially given the right to own separate property, their use of that property was left to their own discretion. The legislature then had to confront "a custom which had arisen where, 'in numerous instances, the title of real estate of married men in embarrassed circumstances was transferred to their respective wives, and thence to third persons, thereby clogging the proof of fraudulent conveyances by this other remove from the original fraudulent grantor.'"[37] The reform statute of 1856 limited the wife's ability to convey property received from her husband. Thus the Maine legislature addressed fraud by limiting the married woman's uses of property received from her husband. Husbands sometimes carried out these fraudulent schemes without the knowledge of the wife. When Mrs. Bennett's husband proposed to her, he offered to give her land; she was not aware that he was in debt when she accepted the deed.[38]

Courts met legislative provisions regarding fraud with a posture of protectionism, both toward creditors and toward married women who might be duped out of their property ownership and enjoyment by their husbands. Protecting married women invited scrutiny of their situations, a maneuver that ensured that judges would not be absent from the exercise of rights by married women. When a statute stated that a married woman could make a contract, but only in regard to her separate property, the courts needed to be sure that the married woman's exercise of her right was in compliance with the statute. When Mrs. Robinson and her trustee bought her husband's land at a creditor's auction, the Kentucky court declared the purchase void, not because of the allegations that she had fraudulently recovered the land her husband lost to creditors, but because, as a married woman, she was not capable of making such a contract. "The contract of a *feme covert*, unless in regard to her separate estate, is not only voidable, but absolutely void."[39] Courts wanted to be sure that the married woman used her right to contract only within the enumerated limits.

State courts found additional reasons to scrutinize the exercise of rights by married women. Courts closely examined married women's applications to acquire separate property or separate businesses to be assured that they were capable of meeting the responsibilities entailed by such ventures. Elizabeth Franklin owned seventy-two acres of land she had inherited from her grandfather, and she and her husband jointly petitioned the circuit court to empower her to act as *feme sole* in regard to that property. Before conferring the power, the court needed to be persuaded that she possessed the capacity to manage it.[40] In this case, the court's role appears to have been paternalistic, putting another hurdle in place to assess the abilities of women before according them property rights. In other cases, however, women who were incapable were applying for extended property rights as a part of their husbands' fraudulent schemes. When Mrs. Gross applied for a license to act as a *feme sole* in keeping a tavern, the court found that she had no means of her own to undertake a business, that she was not qualified to run a business, that she bought no supplies, made no sales, handled none of the money, and spent her time taking care of her children. The court suspected that this was the husband's business venture and that he was placing ownership in the wife's name to keep it beyond the reach of creditors.[41]

Despite the conferral of rights to married women, courts were careful to make sure that husbands retained their obligations to the family, sustaining the fiction of the husband as head of the household, even in the face of evidence to the contrary. Although Elnora Thomas owned separate property she could not use it to pay for the services of a physician because her right to contract was limited to the right to deed, mortgage, or improve her separate property. The court knew that Mr. Thomas was "notoriously insolvent and worthless," and the doctor, knowing this, too, would not accept his credit. Promising to pay out of her own pocket was the only way that Mrs. Thomas could get an appointment with the doctor. Nevertheless, the court determined that it was up to the legislature to change the laws if they were problematic.

Until that happened, the court would limit a married woman's contractual rights and turn to the common-law rules, under which the husband was responsible for paying the physician.[42]

The husband would also be shirking his marital obligations if his wife were to use her separate property to pay off his debts. In *Bidwell v. Robinson* the court acknowledged that women in Kentucky had been given the right to contract and to sue but that these abilities were limited to the control and management of their separate property. The court refused to enlarge these abilities beyond those stated in the statute, especially when it came to wives trying to hold themselves liable for their husbands' debts.[43] Even in the civil-law system of Louisiana, courts would scrutinize in order to be sure that the wife's contract was made free from her husband's influence. A wife who acted as surety for her husband's debts was likely to be performing "under marital influence." Owing to this possibility, the court stated, "whatever the form of the contract, its true character may be inquired into and laid bare."[44]

Whatever the reasons for scrutiny, the state courts assumed a paternalistic stance, keeping judges closely involved in married women's transactions. Institutionally, the involvement of state courts in marital relations did not diminish after passage of the reform statutes.

MARRIED WOMEN'S ALTERED STATUS
AND THE COVERTURE DEFENSE

The courts' scrutiny of the statutes had an effect on married women's status during the transitional period in which married women held rights while retaining the disabilities of coverture. Scrutiny itself was not new; prior to the statutes, when married women sought relief from the civil disabilities of coverture in courts of equity, courts were involved in a similar level of scrutiny. In the colonial era and the early American republics, courts established a private examination procedure to protect wives from conveying property out of concerns of the husbands' coercion. If a married woman wanted to convey real property, she and a judge would go alone to a separate room, where he would read the contents of the deed and assure himself that she understood the meaning of the transaction.[45]

Equitable procedures, which required protective procedures and presumptions of husbands' coercion and wives' vulnerability, were the means of recognizing married women's property ownership within coverture. The status of married women after the reform statutes was not much altered. The conditional features of some of the statutes indicate the continuation of the limitations and invitations to scrutiny occasioned by the statutes. Married women were given enumerated rights, but these did not confer full legal autonomy. They continued to hold the status of wives who were able to exercise a few limited rights, with courts serving as guardians of these rights.

Some married women were complicit in the generation of their new status. Married women who found themselves the object of a lawsuit found coverture to be an available defense. The could claim that they were not liable by presenting themselves as feeble, incompetent, or coerced, in any case, as incapable of standing as an individual against whom suit could be brought. One novel claim raised in defense was that a married woman who had been made *feme sole* was ignorant of what it meant. Mrs. Sypert had been made a *feme sole* through proper court procedures in 1874 but in 1889 claimed ignorance of her responsibilities when a creditor tried to recover money from her. The Kentucky court was not persuaded. After all, she had made no complaint during all her years as a *feme sole*, when she enjoyed the privileges and benefits that accompanied that status.[46] Mrs. Sypert also claimed that her husband coerced her into applying for *feme sole* status in the first place, thus invoking marital coercion, one of the most popular defenses brought by married women.

Married women could rescind a contract by claiming that they had signed it under duress. The source of this defense lay not in contract doctrine but in the common-law presumption that a married woman acted under the coercion of her husband. A common complaint was that wives mortgaged their separate property in order to pay off their husband's debts. The presumption, however, could be waived by evidence to the contrary, and courts tended to be persuaded by the evidence. Thus, when Mrs. Rush claimed that she was so feeble after the birth of her child that she needed help to sit up to sign the mortgage urged upon her by her husband, the court was not moved. Although her sister, nephew, and nurse supported her version of the story, the testimony of her doctor and a factor from the lending agency indicated that she was physically and mentally capable of signing the contract. Added to this was the information that a few years earlier she had taken over debt-collection from her husband and had extorted money from a man who owed her husband's company. The court saw a shrewd, aggressive businesswoman hiding behind the disabilities of coverture.[47]

A Louisiana case reveals the similarities and differences between the common-law and civil-law systems. Mrs. Myers obtained the services of an attorney while her husband was in jail, and the attorney sought action against her for payment. The court did not accept her argument that she had signed for their services under marital coercion. As in the other states, there was a presumption of coercion available for defense and the opportunity for it to be rebutted by evidence. Then the Louisiana court said that under civil law, the wife was obligated to her husband at such times:

"The fees thus earned by these attorneys formed a personal debt of the wife, which she had full power under our laws to contract, in discharge of a duty imposed on her by the law which provides that 'the husband and wife owe to each other mutually, fidelity, support and assistance.' C.C. Art. 199."[48] The Louisiana Civil Code required mutual obligations of husbands and wives. In common-law states, husbands and wives each had their respective obligations. A husband was obligated to support his wife, but this was not expected to be reciprocated by the wife.

The common-law obligations of husbands were ripe for manipulation by married women when suit was brought against them. Married women could escape liability for their crimes or contractual obligations by reverting to legalities, although they were not always successful. Mrs. Darling wanted to back out of a sale of her property, claiming that her agent was not authorized to make the sale because she had never received proper authorization from the district judge to borrow money and mortgage her property. The court found that the sale did have marital authorization, so her argument failed.[49]

A more common resort to legality was to recover the common-law rules that placed the husband at the head of the household. In Massachusetts, particularly, owing to the laws regarding the sale of liquor from the home, there are a number of cases in which married women were prosecuted for selling intoxicating liquor. For these women, the ready defense was to claim that they were carrying out the business in the home of their husbands, and in the presence of their husbands, and were thus acting under marital coercion. As head of the household, the husband was responsible for controlling the members of the family, so the husband was liable for actions of the wife. These cases represent an intersection between the married woman acting as businesswoman, running her own separate business, and the common-law arrangement of husband as head of the household. The courts determined that the statutes conferring rights to run a business would not interfere with the common-law arrangements. The Massachusetts supreme judicial court found the following instructions of a lower court judge to be correct: "The statutes which give a married woman the right to carry on business on her separate account do not deprive a husband of his common law right to control his own household; he has the power to prevent his wife from using his house for an illegal purpose; . . . the fact that his wife owned the house did not abridge the husband's right to control its use while occupied as their home."[50] Those married women who were held liable for selling intoxicating liquors from the home during this period were either at home alone while their husbands were at sea or had husbands who were sick in bed.[51]

A married woman who ran a business from her own home could make her husband liable for all debts because he was the head of the household. The Indiana court wrestled with the case of a married woman who ran a milliner's shop from the front of the family home. When suit was brought against her to recover for payment of goods sold to her, she claimed coverture as a defense, which would transfer liability to her husband, but her husband claimed that she had made the transaction without his knowledge. To have believed both of them would have meant that neither was liable, and the creditors would have been unable to recover their debt, leading to an economically unstable situation that the reform statutes were supposed to alleviate. The Indiana supreme court admitted that it did not know how to rule and affirmed the holding for the couple "after some hesitation, and without any firm conviction that we are right."[52]

The Indiana court's uncertainty is understandable. In trying to balance the married woman's new rights with the obligations of husband and wife within the marital relation, courts had to confront the capacity of the married woman. At times it appeared that she was an individual, capable of making and fulfilling her own contracts and standing trial for her own crimes. At other times, courts reverted to the common law and the presumption that a married women who was in the presence of her husband acted under his coercion; the husband was expected to be coercive because he was responsible for his wife's behavior.

In cases such as these, married women rationally claimed their common-law status, and husbands appeared willing to escape liability by renouncing their privileges and obligations as head of household. To be deprived of obligations is a short-term exemption and benefit in that one escapes liability, but one also loses recognition by the state. Women's citizenship status can be identified not by tracing the denial of rights but by locating their inability to uphold obligations.[53] Such civic duties as voting, jury service, and military service were historically limited to men, and what this has meant for women depends on one's perspective. At the time, it could be seen as women's privilege that they were exempt from these duties, but these exemptions also reflected a lack of confidence in a woman's ability to perform those duties. The coverture defense in the midst of reform of married women's rights invited a similar dynamic.

THE MODERNIZATION OF THE COMMON LAW

The intermediary status of married women after the reform statutes is consistent with the modernization of status law,[54] a phenomenon in which status regimes are reformed but not entirely abolished, leaving relationships based on status to survive in modernized forms. State-level courts served to modernize and preserve the common-law domestic relations, not by resisting reform but by embracing it and reconciling common-law status with the rights of the married woman. The courts modernized the common law by coming to grips with change and establishing a means of staying involved with the marital relations.

In an Indiana case, the court ruled that, although some disabilities of coverture still existed, enough of them had been eliminated by statute that married women no longer fell into the category of the legally disabled, namely, children, criminals, and lunatics.[55] The result of such a stance was that women were not classed as disabled, but this made their remaining civil disabilities less obvious. The Kentucky court declared itself to be construing statutes liberally to enlarge the rights of married women. In the same case it recognized the need for a court of chancery to declare a married woman to be *feme sole*.[56] Hence it failed to acknowledge that women still needed the participation of the state in order to carry out their individual rights. Furthermore, this development was nothing new; there had always been a common-law remedy for married women whose husbands had abandoned them. So the court's strategy was a matter of sustaining the common law but calling it modern.

In adhering to the statutes, courts recharacterized what it meant to be to be a married woman by formulating new justifications for their statutes. Before the statutes, there was little reason to justify married women's status or civil disabilities, because one had only to refer to the common-law rules. After the reform statutes, courts had to balance the status of the married woman with her newly acquired rights and had to have a reason for sustaining both traditions. They chose the paternalistic stance.

Some of the old practices of the common law needed no explanation. The court provided no justification for the domicile of the wife being that of the husband, the Kentucky court citing only "the general rule."[57] Other practices were more carefully considered and accepted. Indiana recovered the common-law property-ownership rule of tenants by entireties. This was an ownership reserved specifically for married couples that was similar to, but markedly different from, joint ownership in that the former included obligations incurred by the marital relation. After allowing married women to own separate estates, the legislature had to grapple with the manner in which these women could receive and dispose of property. There was "too much machinery" involved in the equitable practice of holding a married woman's property in trust and allowing husbands and fathers to deed property directly to her; the practice "was attended with baneful and disastrous consequences. It disturbed the peace and harmony of families."[58] The solution lay in reverting to the little-known common-law construction of tenants by entireties, by which husband and wife held property jointly. This provided a middle ground between the husband owning all of the family property and the wife owning and having full control over her separate property.

This was Indiana's way of reconciling the shift from common-law status relations to the property-holding wife; it recovered and updated the purposes of a common-law rule.

FAMILY UNITY

Judges retained status, and with it the respective obligations of husband and wife. Despite the acquisition of rights by married women, the family was left intact with a family-unity thesis that replaced the common-law unity of the husband and wife. This is reflected in those rights that, no matter how liberally they were conferred, were not allowed to be exercised within the marital relation. No matter how extensive a married woman's right to contract was, she could not contract with her husband, not because they were still one person but because it would "introduce the disturbing influences of bargain and sale into the marital relation."[59] A wife could not use her new ability to sue alone to sue her husband because this ability to sue alone was intended to give the married woman the option of excluding her husband from the suit in order to be free of his influence. Thus, the right to sue alone was not a recognition of her independence but rather a mechanism to protect the wife from her husband.[60] Despite the understood purposes, the end result of this prohibition against husband and wife suing each other contributed to the family- unity thesis by keeping litigious and economic transactions outside the home.

Family harmony was also protected in Massachusetts by protecting the family from the effects of alcohol abuse. Massachusetts passed a law that allowed family members to sue the supplier of alcohol for injury to the family. In so doing, the statute rewrote the family relations into law. In 1879 Massachusetts passed "an act to provide for the recovery of damages for injuries caused by the use of intoxicating liquors."[61] If a person was injured by an intoxicated person, his or her husband, wife, child, parent, guardian, or employer had a right of action for the injury. The Massachusetts court acknowledged the reliance on the domestic relations in the statutes: "We think the language itself imports that the relations of husband and wife, parent and child, guardian and ward, employer and employed, are valuable relations; that they are themselves the subject of injury; that those relations themselves may be so affected by the excessive use of intoxicating liquors as to constitute a substantial injury. That is, that drunkenness of a husband may be of substantial injury to the wife; of the wife, to the husband; . . . the Legislature regarded as capable of injury the family and social relations."[62]

Laws and judicial interpretation therefore reconstructed a narrative of family harmony which did not preclude hierarchy in the family. Within this unified family, the status of husband as head of the household remained. A husband was justified in killing a wife's attacker as an extension of his own self-defense, a vestige of the unity of the husband and wife as one person.[63] Louisiana's community property cases made it clear that family property belonged to both the husband and the wife, but it made this arrangement look much more like the common law when it declared the husband to be the head of that community, with the wife having no claim to it until he died. Until then, she could only hope that he not squander it.[64]

Given the widespread concern to maintain the marital relations, the persistence of coverture following the married women's property acts becomes less puzzling. Coverture survived not only because the statutes were never designed to abolish it but also because different institutions collaborated to retain the social orderings of the domestic relations. Married women held a status that fell short of full recognition as contracting individuals, but their status had nevertheless changed. No longer was a married woman simply the *feme covert* under the common law. In recognizing the obstacles of power they faced in the exercise of their new rights, courts contributed to the construction of a new status for married women. This new identity invited courts to scrutinize the exercise of married women's property rights and thus to retain an institutional role in these reformed rights. Statutory reform therefore did not see a transfer in power from courts to legislatures.

Recognizing this narrative calls into question the progressive potential of the married women's property acts. The rights conferred by the acts were not a liberal alternative to the common law but a working out of liberalism's relation with the domestic relations of the common law. The transition did not transfer power from courts to legislatures in a corresponding development from common law to liberalism. Instead, institutions collaborated to reconcile the common law with liberal developments, to retain status even as the rights of married women were being expanded. Far from ushering in liberal reform, the property statutes occasioned a modernization of the civil disabilities of the common-law domestic relations, making the common-law rules less apparent. Coverture persisted not because of judges' conservative attachment to it, ideologically and institutionally, but because it was reformulated in light of statutory change.

The woman suffragist narrative fails to appreciate the measures to balance rights with status and fails to recognize the reconfiguration of women's subjugation. In pronouncing the married women's property acts to be a commitment to progress, they invited a retrospective narrative that would ultimately support the rights of women, but it would then operate under false pretenses. The woman suffragist narrative suggested that liberal principles simply had to strike at prejudices in order to be realized. Meanwhile, coverture was being retrenched, updated, and modernized and was operating upon married women as courts and legislatures collaborated to modernize the status regime. The woman suffragist narrative obscured these processes and the continuing source of women's oppression.

CHAPTER FIVE

The Domesticity of the Domestic Relations

In interpreting the married women's property acts, state supreme courts acted in collaboration with legislatures to retain the status of the common law and the legal construction of the household. The household remained a viable concept in law because of changes in the domestic relations themselves. Historically one of the domestic relations, the master-servant relation was increasingly coming to be considered as public, rendering the remaining domestic relations more properly familial. The new legal household provided an updated basis for retaining married women's status and the remaining rules of coverture.

MASTERS AND SERVANTS

The master-servant relation was a contractual relation that, like the husband-wife relation, incurred status and obligations for each party. The master-servant relation had traditionally been considered a domestic relation along with the other relations that were more obviously domestic—husband-wife, parent-child, guardian-ward—and the servant was considered to be part of the household, even though he or she could have been any worker who worked for wages, including a clerk or a secretary. Workers who today would be considered employees were, under the common law, servants. Legally, they were part of the household, subservient to the same head of household as the married woman. Certain characteristics of the master-servant relation resembled a family relationship. The master owed the servant certain obligations, including such necessaries as food, clothing, housing, and medical assistance, just as a husband and father owed them to his family members. Like a husband or father, the master was responsible for the conduct of his servant, for whom he would have to answer in court.

Despite the familial features of the master-servant relation, this was not a relation of benevolence. Before there was public transportation, for example, it was more convenient to house one's servant than to send him home each night.[1] The care-taking of the master was born of paternalism rather than good will. As the treatise writer James Schouler explained, the master-servant relation was one in which the parties stood on unequal footing, thereby making the master's obligation morally binding: "A moral obligation resting upon every master whose connection with his servant is a very close one, the latter being manifestly on an inferior footing, is to ex-ert a good influence, to regard the servant's mental and spiritual well-being."[2]

In the late nineteenth century, labor relations in the United States became in-creasingly antagonistic. In the face of labor unrest, strikes, and increases in labor as-sociations, members of Congress grew alarmed at the disharmony in labor relations. They held a hearing on the relations between labor and capital in 1883, inviting the testimony of workers, industrialists, labor organizers, and foremen in order to assess the animosity among different classes. They asked workers such questions as, "How do you workingmen feel towards the people who employ you and pay you?" to which they received such direct responses as "They hate the bosses and the foremen more than the bosses, and that feeling is deep."[3]

The antagonism of the workplace could be regarded with nostalgia for a more peaceful time of personal relations. As one witness testified, employer-employee re-lations were mediated by a foreman. An employee was unlikely to know his em-ployer.[4] The master-servant relation could be recalled fondly and nostalgically as personal relations in which masters and servants cared for one another in a common household. The loss of personal ties was seen as the cause of labor problems.[5] Whether the recollection of happier times was accurate or not, its invocation pointed to the household as an important counterbalance and corrective to the ills of the market.[6]

The household itself was seen to be in jeopardy, as well. Senators were curious about the physical condition of workers' homes. They asked detailed questions of people who had visited the homes of coal miners and other workers, wanting to know the size of homes, their layouts, the type of furniture, the health of the families of workers, and whether workers could support families on their wages.[7] The commit-tee had a tour of a tenement. They were worried that the poor working conditions and wages of paid workers were affecting the conditions of homes. Rather than be-ing sites of intimacy and refuge, homes were afflicted with the disharmony and ills of the market.

The judiciary proved responsive to absorbing this anxiety over economic and social change. Homes had to be protected from the corrupting influences of the market. If this could not be carried out in actuality, it could be accomplished in legal fiction. Courts could effect a reconstruction of the home. State courts had the opportunity to rescue the home from harsh economic conditions because the master-servant relation was undergoing change. A significant development in the domestic relations in the late nineteenth century was the departure of many so-called servants from the categories of the master-servant relation. At that time, judges and treatise writers expressed increasing uneasiness about counting the master-servant relation as a domestic one, and they began to replace the household model of paid labor that had governed the master-servant relation with a contractual model of agreements made between individual employers and employees. This had little material consequence for workers, whose conditions would not undergo significant change until the New Deal.[8] It had greater impact on the status of those workers whose status continued to be considered properly domestic.

A CHANGING LEGAL HOUSEHOLD: TREATISES

The notion of the household as distinctly domestic did not originate in the late nineteenth century. Separate-spheres ideology had appeared earlier in the century, with salience in culture and politics.[9] Such separation had not obtained in the common law, however, because male servants remained part of the domestic relations through the late nineteenth century. The progression of the master-servant relation outside the household was predicated upon the traditional distinctions among servants. The term *servant* had always encompassed varying categories of occupations, distinguished by their activities, location, and nature. In the late nineteenth century, those servants whose work occurred outside the physical house ceased to be seen as properly belonging to the domestic sphere. Treatments of the master-servant relation in legal treatises over the course of the late nineteenth century present a progression in tone from one that is unquestioning of the inclusion of the master-servant relation in the domestic relations to one that complains about including workers as domestic, and, finally, to one that drops public-sphere employment from the domestic relations.

In Blackstone's *Commentaries,* the master-servant relation was listed as first of "the three great relations in private life," along with the husband-wife and parent-child relations. Whereas the other domestic relations had their origins in nature, the master-servant relation was "founded in convenience, whereby a man is directed to call in the assistance of others, where his own skill and labour will not be sufficient to answer the cares incumbent upon him."[10] Blackstone conveyed little discomfort with the relation of authority and subordination between master and servant, contrasting the servant to the slave, a status that was "repugnant to reason, and the principles of natural law."[11] The disabilities of the servant were benign in comparison.

Blackstone listed four categories of servant, the first being menial servants, the name deriving from *inter moenia* ("within the walls"), otherwise known as domestic servants. The common-law rule for the hiring contract was one year, unless the parties agreed otherwise. Apprentices, the second category, were indentured for a predetermined number of years. This relation was established so that a minor could learn a trade, and Blackstone's comments suggest a background story of social management in which town overseers apprenticed out the children of the poor. The third class, laborers, hired themselves out for service by the day or week and did not reside in the household. Blackstone admitted of hesitancy in adding the final category: "There is yet a fourth species of servants, if they may be so called, being rather in a superior, a ministerial, capacity; such as stewards, factors, and bailiffs."[12] Although Blackstone considered the master-servant relation to be primary among the domestic relations, he had qualms about including these more prestigious occupations with other servants. He interchanged "master" with "employer," suggesting that, even though servants worked with their masters, they did not occupy the same positions of subordination as other servants.

American treatises of the mid-nineteenth century did not seriously question the placement of the master-servant relation as a domestic relation. In his *Commentaries*, James Kent assumed the more customary ordering by listing the master-servant relation last among the domestic relations. Kent classified servants by three broad categories: slaves, hired servants, and apprentices.[13] The suitability of the master-servant relation as a domestic relation was, likewise, not an issue in Tapping Reeve's treatise. In his categorization Reeve reverted to Blackstone's classifications, listing slaves, apprentices, menial servants, day laborers, and a final category that included the more prestigious positions of agent, factor, and attorney.

In the 1880s treatise writers began to complain about having to include servants, specifically, the more professional occupations, in their works on domestic relations. In 1882 James Schouler began his chapter on master and servant by stating that it was "not strictly a domestic relation" because "the relation of master and servant presupposes two parties who stand on unequal footing in their mutual dealings, yet not naturally so, as in other domestic relations."[14] The putative difference in origin between the master-servant relation and other domestic relations began to influence the tolerance of hierarchy in the relations. Hierarchy was tolerable in the husband-wife relation because it was deemed natural, but the master-servant relation was, after all, only founded in convenience. Schouler was thus selectively disturbed by the hierarchy of the domestic relations, reserving his consternation for the master-servant relation: "This relation is, in theory, hostile to the genius of free institutions. It bears the mark of social caste. Hence it may be pronounced as a relation of a more general importance in ancient than in modern times."[15]

Despite Schouler's disapproval of the master-servant relation as domestic, he continued to discuss it as a domestic relation, revealing that only some of the categories of the master-servant relation were repugnant to modern mores. This is evident in his treatment of the categories of servants: "Not only cooks, butlers, and housemaids are thus brought within the scope of this relation, but farm-hands, plantation laborers, stewards, bailiffs, factors, family chaplains, and legal advisers."[16] Those workers of higher prestige did not belong with the lower grades, who also happened to be menial servants. Schouler presented this not as a class issue but as a legal issue rooted in the concept of contract, explained by the theory that "the common law, under the head of master and servant, discusses principles which, in this day, belong more justly to the relation of principal and agent; and that we constantly find an offensive term used in court to denote duties and obligations which rest upon the pure contract of hiring. Clerks, salaried officers, brokers, commission merchants, all are designated as servants; and our topic in this broad sense is not, if words mean anything, within the influence of domestic law at all."[17] After the Civil War, the ability to contract served as the touchstone for freedom.[18] Within the domestic relations, however, the contract model did not erase feudal status.[19] Nevertheless, contract theory could serve to distinguish categories of servants from one another.

The distinctions among servants was maintained in later treatises. In 1883, Irving Browne considered who should be counted as a servant for the purposes of his treatise. "Strictly speaking, so far as this subject comes with Domestic Relations, it should be confined to menial service, but usage has brought under this title many other relations, particularly that of employer and employee."[20] Walter Tiffany expressed similar sentiments in 1896: "The relation of master and servant has from a very early period been classed . . . as one of the domestic relations; and it is still so treated in modern text-books, and in some of the modern codes. This classification is accurate enough when applied to slaves, apprentices, and domestic servants, but it is not accurate when applied to other servants, like clerks in stores and offices, laborers, employés of railroad companies, and many other employés who are subject to the law governing the relation of master and servant."[21] In 1899, W. C. Rodgers' discussion reflected modern changes. He would not talk of slavery or indentured servitude: "Nor will that wide branch of the law of master and servant pertaining to the service of employees in the large business and public as well as *quasi*-public enterprises and undertakings of the present day be discussed at exhaustive length."[22]

Whereas the distinction had been made earlier according to the location of the service or the duration of the contract, Rodgers introduced a new categorization. Some classes of service "require very high attainments and accomplishments in the particular duty, and the performance of the service may be attended with the most gigantic and solemn responsibilities," in contrast to others, of which "the service may be of such a nature as to require little intelligence and perhaps only medium physical strength."[23] By 1911, the master-servant relation was largely absent from Edward Spencer's treatise on the domestic relations.[24]

These treatises reflect the gradual removal of the master-servant relation from its placement in the domestic relations. Because of the customary distinctions among servants, it was possible for only some of the categories of servant to cease to be domestic, while others could remain. The term *employee* was increasingly replacing *servant*, but only for those classes of servants that were on the brink of leaving the domestic sphere.

Employer and *employee* were not new terms. Blackstone had used *employer* interchangeably with *master*. American judges, however, were treating it as a novel concept. "The word employé, or employee, . . . is not a legal term, nor is it an English word, but a word imported with its native pronunciation from the French language, which is frequently used by English speaking people as a convenient common-place term to designate the relation or situation of a class of persons who are not precisely menial servants, but whose whole time and services are employed and paid for by another person or persons, or by a corporation, or by the government."[25] When a servant engaged in a contract for hire, he contracted into a subordinate status. When an employee contracted, he contracted as an individual and would remain an individual. The employee simply worked for wages. The attendant obligations and status were absent from the concept of employee. Domestic servants, however, continued to fall under the master-servant relation. Domestics came to be known as menial servants, not only to describe their work "within the walls" but connoting work that was degraded. The "word 'servant' is losing the connotation it had in earlier days and older decisions, possible because as a word of usage rather than a word of art it connoted a menial and its use was distasteful."[26]

A CHANGING LEGAL HOUSEHOLD: JUDICIAL DECISIONS

Not only did domestic servants remain in the home, but their representation in judicial decisions became increasingly intimate. In judicial decisions of the 1830s in which domestic servants appeared as parties or in the facts of a case, they tended to be mentioned in passing. By the 1870s and 1880s, there was an increase in references to servants in the midst of the family. A marital squabble might be noted as occur-ring in front of the children and the servants.[27] Or servants might have "stormy" fights with their masters.[28] Testimony of a mistress in a case involving her maid in-dicated that each knew the comings and goings of the other.[29]

The servant as member of the household appeared earlier in the South. While the language of familiarity did not become notable in Illinois, Indiana, Massachu-setts, and Maine until the 1870s (with one exception, discussed below), it was pres-ent in Louisiana in the 1850s and in Kentucky even earlier.[30] Domesticity and heads of household played an important role in constructing the identity of the slaveholder as patriarch. The South preceded the North in presenting the patriarchal family while waxing romantic about it. The southern slave was considered to be a member of the slaveholding household. As Elizabeth Fox-Genovese documented, the house-hold was not home—it was a unit of production—and the family was easily demar-cated into "my family—white and black."[31] Yet southern slaveholders were master-ful at presenting these racial and hierarchical arrangements as familial. Robert Jeffrey Young pointed to the slaveholders' responses to growing critiques of slavery in the 1830s. Slaveholders modernized their defense of slavery by acknowledging the slave as a human being, then claiming that the slaveholder treated the slave as a member of the family.[32]

The southern patriarchal family is often presented in contrast to the bourgeois northern family,[33] yet even the bourgeois family, valuing individual rights, was not immune from patriarchy. Young points out that slaveholders justified slavery by ap-pealing to bourgeois ideals rather than by fleeing from them. Similarly, Carole Pate-man demonstrated that social contract theory can rest on gender hierarchy.[34] The appeal to modernity coexisted quite easily with patriarchy and hierarchy. Imbuing this balance with the language of intimacy would only obscure it more.

The South served as a model for the modernization of the status of servant. The legal fiction of the household of family and servants as kin anticipated the notion of an intimate home, including domestic servants, that would emerge in the late nine-teenth century, made possible by the exit of nonhousehold laborers from the do-mestic relations. The growing notions of familiarity and intimacy that could then de-scribe the home included the remaining domestic relations, and intimacy was not incompatible with hierarchy.

Servants' appearances as witnesses occasioned a view of the extent of familiarity between masters and servants. In Kentucky in 1839, a son who was excluded from his father's will questioned the validity of the will itself, claiming that his father was insane. In considering the family's situation, the court was struck by a father's sud-den change in feelings toward his son. The court was inclined to pronounce the father, Mr. Singleton, insane because he suddenly excluded his son from the church, banished him from the house, and refused to allow his wife to visit him. In accepting proof of Mr. Singleton's insanity, the court relied upon the testimony of the man's wife, close friends, and acquaintances. These were the people the court determined were best suited to speak to his condition. As for those who attested to his soundness of mind, "it may be remarked that the witnesses generally, who deposed for the defendants, had not the same opportunities afforded them, as the complainants' witnesses, to arrive at a true knowledge of his condition. They were, for the most part, mere general acquaintances who met with him occasionally."[35]

Upon rehearing of the case, however, the court reversed its position on Mr. Singleton's insanity and on the reliability of the witnesses, as well, because it had gained some new facts about the family. It found that Mr. Singleton's reason for disinheriting his son was that the son, William, had engaged in "illicit cohabitation" with one of his slaves. Mr. Singleton's behavior was now seen as natural, the paternal duty a father owed his son after attempts at reform had failed. This new evidence altered the court's interpretation of the witnesses' reliability as well. Those who testified on behalf of Mr. Singleton's sanity were now noted as being distinguished men of the town who had done business with Singleton. One of the most influential witnesses was the overseer, who had actually been a witness for William, but who hurt his case: "Here is their own witness, who lived as an overseer with the testator, during the year '33; slept in the same house, eat [sic] at the same table, and labored in the fields with him, received orders every day from him, and almost every hour communicated with him, was placed in a situation which above all others enabled him to ascertain the state of his mind, his qualities and properties of character, yet he 'did not think he was deranged.'"[36]

The overseer's testimony was considered reliable. Unlike other domestic servants, his knowledge of Singleton was not limited to personal matters; he could attest to his capacity to carry out his work. Thus the overseer could be portrayed as a fellow professional rather than as an intimate within the home. Those who were intimates, on the other hand, whether family or servant, lacked credibility in the rehearing. The court saw them as being too interested in the outcome of the case: The court was skeptical about the nephew of the widow who testified about Mr. Singleton's insanity, noting that "the Court will not forget that Ben Taylor is the full nephew of Mrs. Singleton, and palpably betrays all the predilections and aversions of his aunt in the foregoing deposition."[37] Immediate family members, likewise, came to be seen as compromised. Whereas the court deferred to the wife's testimony in the first hearing, referring to her as "an aged matron, the simplicity and candor of whose details, carries with it intrinsic evidence of its truth,"[38] in the rehearing it found that she "was further in the wane of life, than her husband. She was a year older. She was subject to all the imperfections and infirmities of age."[39] Over the course of these two hearings, her characterization was transformed from that of a gentle, doting helpmate to that of a confused old woman incapable of offering valid legal testimony.

In the first hearing, the court respected the testimony of household members, while in the second hearing it questioned their motives and capacities. The familiarity with Mr. Singleton that earned them credibility in the first hearing rendered them unreliable in the second. Those business associates and colleagues now proved to be more trustworthy precisely because of their personal distance from Mr. Singleton. Falling in the middle was the overseer. He was a servant, but not a mere domestic servant, so he could attest to Mr. Singleton's professional, not merely personal, behavior.

In other cases the domestic servants were clearly lodged in the home. A similar set of witnesses was brought by both parties in an 1859 Illinois case in which a married woman signed away her trust property to her husband's creditors. At first the court treated the matter as one of simple technicality—the law provided that a married woman could dispose of separate property only as explicated in the marriage settlement. Since she used other means, the conveyance of property was void. In a separate opinion, however, one of the judges introduced the matter of coercion. He found the conveyance void because he presumed that the husband had coerced the wife into turning her property over to him. This presumption of coercion was rooted in the common law and became relevant as married women owned and used their separate property. Mrs. Castle's property had been held in trust for her and managed by a third party, a traditionally equitable means of shielding property from husbands. When a married woman signed her property over to her husband, courts presumed that she was coerced.[40] This presumption of coercion could be refuted with evidence, however, so the Illinois court examined the trial records more closely, and when it did, it altered its views on the facts. The court found that Mrs. Castle's testimony of fraud, duress, and coercion was "made up of her own declarations, detailed by her relatives and familiars sympathizing with her, and disposed to magnify small circumstances into great matters."[41] Those whom she had called forward to attest to her husband's coercion were the children's music teacher (who lived with the family), the family doctor, a hardware merchant, a baggage master who was a friend of Mrs. Castle, Mr. Castle's clerk, her friend, her sister, and her brother-in-law. In this list of intimate acquaintances were servants who lived in the household and friends who were not domestic servants but were in the lower grades of service.[42] As in *Singleton's Will*, the witnesses' very proximity to the parties rendered them unreliable.

In 1883, a Louisiana case involved a will that was questioned for the testator's mental capacity. Edward Burke, whose forced heir under Louisiana's civil law was a grown daughter from his first marriage, had rewritten his will in the last days of his life, when his brother visited from Ireland. Burke changed his will to make his brother his universal legatee. Burke committed suicide days later. In determining whether Burke was of sound mind in those final days, the court initially drew upon its first impressions. There was something "strange and unnatural" about "the father of an only child" abandoning that child, the "fruit of his first love," in that manner in order to sign his estate over to a brother who had rushed in from a foreign country and had likely exercised undue influence over him.[43] The only explanation for this behavior, the court determined, was that Burke lacked his full mental capacity.

In ruling Burke to be insane, the court reviewed the testimony of witnesses for both parties, and there were many of them—the testimony of fifty witnesses filled a transcript of more than 1,000 pages. Those witnesses who testified that Burke was insane included his longtime friends, his clerks and employees, and his wife and two house servants. Those testifying against insanity included a bank president, bank clerks, the druggist, a store clerk, and his priest. The court was particularly moved by the "loud and violent denunciations made of the wife, of the servants, and of the clerks" and recounted their testimony in great detail.[44] Those who lived within Burke's household were witness to his bizarre behaviors, and it was particularly owing to their anecdotes that the court found him to be insane: "He could not distinguish meat from potatoes or from fish, salt from sugar, brandy from water; that he would try to put on pillow cases and pocket handkerchiefs for shirts; would go around the room in the night drilling, militia drilling; speaking about fighting, having a great battle, fighting dogs; that he would buy cotton shirts unnecessarily when he had a quantity of the finest linen shirts at home; that he would chalk his shoes all around and then cut them; . . . that he would have black alpaca sewed on his socks."[45]

The court saw this same behavior in a new light, however, when it reheard the case. In the second decision, the court reassessed the reliability of the witnesses who had produced these stories, finding that "the attention is arrested by the fact that all the witnesses of intelligence and good judgment are on one side, and those of ignorance and passion on the other."[46] In the rehearing, one's being an intimate meant that he or she had an interest in the outcome of the case and was not to be trusted. To be distant from this intimacy was to know Burke but with a clearer judgment of his capacity—not to mention that those in this category were more likely to be distinguished men.

In the rehearing, rather than focusing on Burke's behavior in the home, the court examined his public behavior. It found that he continued to attend to the management of his business in the last days of his life. These large affairs included depositing money in the bank, drawing checks, and pursuing his debtors. In these dealings he "had been in almost daily intercourse with persons of intelligence and observation."[47]

In the rehearing the court waxed romantic about Burke's manliness. When the court looked more closely at Burke's relation with his daughter, who had been referred to in the first hearing as "fruit of his first love," it found that she lived in New Jersey and had such little contact with her father that some of his associates were unaware that he even had a daughter. His brother, on the other hand, had apparently remained close, even though he lived in Ireland, Burke's birthplace. This was significant to the court because "there can be no doubt that laws mould individual and national character. They exert their influence silently and to the individual unconsciously, but the spirit of independence, of self-reliance, of robust manhood" remain indelible.[48] The Louisiana court presumed that Burke would have had difficulty accepting Louisiana's law of the forced heir, and the court assumed that it was natural that, with this assault on his "manly independence," his thoughts had "reverted to the old country and the kindred that were there."[49]

The court found explanations for the servants' testimony about Burke's bizarre behavior. It produced a new context for the socks incident:

> His feet hurt him. He called for lighted candles one evening, and a piece of chalk. Putting the candles on the floor and standing up, he made one of the women of the house chalk his shoes where he wished to cut them, and seating himself, cut the uppers and transformed them into low quarter shoes. Then his white socks became visible, and this offended his taste. He sent his wife out the next day to buy black silk socks. It will be a cause for alarm if a *penchant* for that article of dress shall be judicially pronounced a badge of insanity. His wife could not find any, and then the tidy old gentleman had black alpaca sewed over his socks to conceal the glare of their whiteness. The incident is at once tender and delightful, and warms one's heart to the punctilious old man.[50]

Changing categories of servant appear in each of these cases. Those higher classes of servant, who in the legal treatises were ceasing to be thought of as domestic, appear in their fluctuating positions, sometimes as familiars and sometimes as professionals. The courts also shared some confusion over how to view the family. All these cases involved a revision in the courts' initial rulings, and they attested to a decreasing legitimacy of the family when objectivity was called for. Those who were becoming known as employees were seen to possess the virtues of the public citizen. Those in the home—friends, family, and servants—were cast as intimates with private machinations and familiar mores.

Because domestic servants were not making the transition to employee, they remained bound within the household as the household itself grew distant from the public sphere. They came to be seen not just as servants in the household but as members of the family. In an Illinois case in which a widow's dower was called into question, the court had to determine how much the widow was allowed in a statutory provision allowing for "such bed, bedsteads, bedding and household and kitchen furniture as may be necessary for herself and family, and provisions for a year for herself and family."[51] The court included grown children and servants in the definition of family; since this was the way the family had been constituted when the husband was alive, this was the widow's family after his death.

To be considered a family member under the law was not to enjoy the privileges and intimacy of immediate family members, however. The domestic relations were relations of hierarchy, within each relation and also between relations. As the household was being reconfigured as consisting of immediate family and domestic servants, distinctions between family and servants were parsed, as is seen in a seduction case. Under the common law, when a woman was "seduced," it was not she who brought suit but, rather, her husband or father. The reasoning behind this rule was that the husband or father was suing for injury to his wife or daughter, he having lost her services. In an 1881 Massachusetts case in which a woman was raped by her husband's boss, the husband brought suit against his superior. The Massachusetts court did not see this as a case of seduction, explaining that "the plaintiff cannot maintain this action for an injury to the wife only; he must prove that some right of his own in the person or conduct of his wife has been violated. A husband is not the master of his wife, and can maintain no action for the loss of her services as his servant."[52] While this might seem to signal recognition of a woman's right to bring assault cases in her own name, this was not where the court's reasoning led. Instead, it recovered the common-law doctrine of loss of consortium, finding that the employer's sexual assault upon his wife had robbed the husband of his wife's company, cooperation, and aid. In acknowledging that a wife was not a servant, the court did not liberate married women. Instead, it reasserted the rules of coverture, insisting that a wife remained a wife, just as she had been under the common law.

The Illinois courts reconsidered common-law rules. In its seduction cases involving servants, the Illinois supreme court questioned the rule of a father having to show loss of services.[53] The loss of menial services was an "old" idea that was fast giving way to the "more enlightened views" of the times: "In this class of cases, the loss of services may be the alleged injury, but the injury to the character of the family is the real ground of recovery when the cause of action relates to the wife or daughter. The degradation which ensues, the distress and mental anguish which necessarily follow, are he real causes of recovery."[54] Just as the court looked as if it was going to abandon the old rules of coverture, it found new reasons to retain them. Replacing the loss of services with protection of family, the court managed to modernize the rules of coverture.

The status of family members was likewise retained, even when it was clear that the husband had fewer financial resources than the wife. In a case in which a husband performed the agricultural work on land that belonged to his wife, it was unclear who could claim ownership of the products raised on the farm. The court conveyed its perplexity. By statute, a husband could not interfere with or control the separate property of his wife, and the court knew it had to "proceed cautiously."[55] It finally determined that the materials produced from the husband's labor on the land were his property, notwithstanding the Married Women's Property Act of 1881, because he occupied the land for the benefit of the family.

In that case, it was clear that a husband working on his wife's land was not a servant, but differences between a wife and a servant, and a child and a servant, were less clear. Such distinctions were raised in a number of intriguing cases in which women came forward to claim that, even though they were nominally daughters, they did the work of servants, felt treated like servants, and hence demanded compensation for their housework.[56] The courts consistently found that these complainants were all members of the family, but in a peculiar way. The court did not find household service to classify one as a servant; all family members contributed labor to the home. This labor did not destroy the notion of household intimacy, however, because the courts were able to distinguish between labor practices.[57]

SERVANTS AND CHILDREN

These challenges to the family structure gave courts the opportunity to refine what it meant to be a member of a family. One way in which this situation would arise was if a child remained with the family after coming of age. If no express contract had been made, then the services of that adult child were performed as a member of the family, and she could not expect compensation. This rule was questioned by an adult woman whose position in the family was marked by her being a child from her father's first marriage.[58] She remained living with her father and his second wife and family until she was thirty-six years old and sought compensation for having served as the family's domestic servant. The court found, however, that she was a member of the family and thus should offer those services for free. There was an expectation that such service arose naturally out of the family relation, but the court did not look simply to this. It also weighed evidence of how she was treated and whether she had been treated differently from the other daughters of the family.

Finding that her father furnished her clothing and that she ate with the family indicated that she was, indeed, treated as a member of the family. Rather than merely applying common-law rules of parent and child, courts were constructing new grounds for how family members were expected to treat one another.

A similar case in which a child had been taken into her grandmother's family and remained there until she was twenty-seven years old relied on evidence that the grandmother had clothed and nurtured her and sent her to school. She was treated like family rather than like a servant.[59] Another woman sought to recover $965 from the estate of her father-in-law for nursing him in his final illness. She won the jury trial, but the appellate court ordered a retrial, which would allow evidence of the things the father-in-law had provided: He furnished a home for her and her husband on his farm, bought all the groceries, furnished household servants, provisions, and furniture, and he had bestowed gifts, including a sixty-dollar silk dress. The reason for allowing this evidence into the retrial was not to show that the daughter-in-law had already been paid but to show that she and her father-in-law had lived as family, and as such, he had fulfilled his obligations toward her and she should reciprocate.[60]

A child who had been taken into her aunt's family and "made visits at her pleasure, using the horse and buggy of the family, was well dressed, had pin money, and went into general society in the neighborhood" was a member of the family, not a servant.[61] She had also essentially been paid, having been left $200 when her aunt died and having lived rent-free on the farm owned by her uncle, who subsequently conveyed the land, worth $1,000, to her and her husband for $1.

Quasi-children and servants had much in common. Each performed labor for the household, and each received some form of compensation. They were distinguished by the kind of compensation they received. Servants earned a wage, while children were supported by guardians and could expect advancement in their education and social prospects. Supporting a child was done in a different spirit from paying a servants' wages, and it was that spirit that the courts saw as setting the family apart from mere contractual relations. Indeed, services were present in all the domestic relations, but judges did not reduce any family relation to this service. What distinguished a child from a servant was not that the servant performed household service, for none of the courts questioned that the children in these cases had actually performed services. The question was whether they were treated as members of the family. To be a child was to not be a servant, despite the feelings—whether alienation or opportunistic enterprise—that brought these children to claim that they did not feel like children of their respective families.

This distinction between wives and children and servants indicates that, even though domestic servants were part of the shrinking household, there were limits to the extent to which they were part of the family. Social historians have demonstrated how the ambiguity of the servant's position was manifested in the architectural trends of the middle-class nineteenth-century household. With the growth of large family fortunes and the rise of the middle class, beginning in the 1840s, those with new money sought to acquire servants as a sign of prestige and to distinguish themselves from those servants. Mistresses might dole out small or inferior portions of food, which would be eaten on plates reserved for servants. Whereas earlier in the century, household help may have eaten with the family, by the late century, servants were not welcome at the family table. Housing design of the day tended to separate the home by class distinction, insulating servants and workplaces from the family living areas, with back bedrooms, back stairways, and back entrances making the household help invisible.[62] Servants lived in, but did not feel part of, the family or of the home.[63] This came at a time when domestic service was becoming increasingly racialized, and servants suffered long-term consequences. Because they were not considered to be part of the family but were considered to be part of the home, they would fail to be categorized under protective labor legislation during the Progressive Era or as eligible for Social Security benefits under the New Deal.[64]

The wife and child of the family enjoyed privileges over their household servants, but these were maintained by continuing to mark the common-law status of wife and child. In insisting that the wife and child were not servants, the courts reasserted their status as married women and children under the common law. As a companion to the consideration of married women's status after the enactment of the married women's property acts, the rearranging of the domestic relations, with the departure of many servants from the master-servant relation, contextualizes the process, helping to explain why it was felt to be so important to retain married women's status. The family was being split off from public relations, and distinctions within the family were being reinforced. This all served to strengthen the intimacy of the family against the perceived hostility and impersonal transactions in the public sphere. Intimacy, of course, did not preclude hierarchy and did not guarantee happiness. It could foster particularistic and biased behavior. One might feel that one's services to the family were drudgery, not dutiful obligation. Nevertheless, the setting apart of the household in the law provided a welcome respite for those who were anxious about changes in the economic and social spheres.

PROTECTING THE HOUSEHOLD

The background conditions and anxiety that necessitated protection of the home, which in turn reasserted the remaining rules of coverture to sustain married women's status, makes it hard to attribute the limits of the married women's property acts to the conservatism of judges, whether ideologically or institutionally. The domestic relations were a resource for larger social dynamics and responses to altered conditions. This certainly was no progressive project, but it was certainly not a knee-jerk response to the reform statutes. Judges and legislators were engaged in a balancing of rights and status, and they saw the domestic relations as serving purposes that responded to and benefited society.

The change in domestic relations also demonstrates that the woman suffragist narrative is of limited use in explaining the acts and their interpretation because it overstates the prejudices against women and underestimates the extent to which the domestic relations persisted. The setting apart of the remaining domestic relations had long-term consequences for those in the subservient position in each relation. When employees finally did benefit from the contract model in the New Deal, those who were still considered servants and farm workers were left out and did not enjoy the benefits of labor laws and Social Security.[65] To accept the suffragist narrative and its expectations is to miss the developments that resulted in the modernization of a status regime. With new justifications produced and new arrangements constituting a new, modern home, coverture was able to survive. Equality was not the most effective means of emancipation for married women and other subordinates in the domestic relations. The polity had to consider why the domestic relations still persisted, what role they served, and why they were so important, not just to discrete families but to the constitutional order.

CHAPTER SIX

Common Law Lost

Coverture survived the passage of the married women's property acts, and it even found a place for itself in the new regime of married women's reformed status. Modern society could not complete the transition from status to contract while coverture proved so tenacious. Over the course of the nineteenth century, as the common-law doctrine of coverture increasingly became a political topic, rather than an issue internal to law, a new public narrative of the common law emerged. As the gendered social ordering of the common law came into focus, common lawyers reacted by becoming apologists for coverture. Faced with the loss of the old theories of unity of husband and wife, they sought new justifications for coverture, turning to other traditions that were legitimate at the time—scripture, natural law, tradition, nature—and used these to justify the status of married women under coverture. Rather than finding resources in the adaptability of the common law, as had been done in the earlier codification debates, they staunchly defended the status quo. Judges were equipped to discern the rules of the common law. Those who defended the common law in the political sphere, on the other hand, knew that there were important reasons to maintain married women's status, but they lacked the capacity to explicate them. Woman suffragists had been arguing that married women's subjugation was due to simple backward views, and these narrative constructions affirmed that. More than ever, it appeared that women continued to be oppressed only because of outdated stereotypes.

INDIANA, 1850

In mid-century Indiana, the battle lines over coverture were still forming when the constitutional convention of 1850 addressed the marital relation of the common law. Robert Dale Owen introduced a measure to add married women's property rights to the constitution. His proposal would be defeated at the convention, but not before it set off a protracted debate over the status of married women. The defenses of the common law differed significantly from those of the earlier codification debates.

Owen was already a familiar figure to his fellow delegates. The son of Robert Owen, founder of the socialist utopian community New Harmony, Owen had spent his early career founding a community for former slaves, serving in both the Indiana and United States House of Representatives, and editing a free-thought newspaper, the *Free Enquirer*, with Frances Wright in New York. In his newspaper he had advocated for woman's rights and had published tracts on birth control and divorce reform.

He was a familiar figure to the woman suffragists as well, for both his activism and that of his wife, Mary Robinson Owen.[1] While a member of the Indiana House of Representatives in 1837, Owen had introduced a married women's reform bill. It failed, but at the time he suggested that Indiana adopt Louisiana's civil-law system of marital relation and property. This suggestion was not forgotten by the convention delegates, and they were prepared to defend the common law against Owen's proposal in 1850. In 1847 the Indiana legislature passed a law allowing married women to own separate real property and to control real estate. Wealthy women benefited the most from this reform, so Owen sought to extend the opportunities to all women by allowing married women to control their personal property, as well.[2]

During the convention Owen headed the Committee on the Rights and Privileges of the Inhabitants of the State, and he used that position to advocate for the extension of the property rights of married women. On October 29, 1850, he introduced a provision that would allow married women to acquire and possess property for their sole use and disposal. It was defeated two weeks later. Owen and other reformers then endorsed a more conservative provision, which was passed on November 27. On December 11, however, another delegate moved to reconsider that vote, and the reform was defeated. On January 16, Owen came forward with a third proposal, which was defeated on January 29. A week before final adjournment he presented a fourth proposal (met with exasperated cries of "no, no, no"). It initially passed, but that afternoon, the vote was reconsidered and defeated.[3] The responses to Owen's proposals may have been ad hominem, with delegates aware of Owen's larger political activism and reacting not so much to the issue of married women's property rights as to him personally.[4] Regardless, the ongoing drama generated by these repeated proposals resulted in extended debate over the status and disabilities of married women, and it provides a glimpse into the ways in which coverture and the common law were perceived by both reformers and defenders of the status quo.

Owen's initial proposal at the 1850 constitutional convention addressed the plight of widows. Under Indiana's common-law rules, a widow was not entitled to inherit her husband's real estate, and she was only entitled to one-third of the rents and profits of his estate during her lifetime. This policy resulted in many widows living in poverty. Selecting this issue was a clever tactic on Owen's part because the cause of widows was sympathetic and did not immediately threaten the marital relations.[5] There were a few elements of his argument, however, that worried convention delegates. He framed the proposal as an issue of women's rights, noting that the protection of property is a right that is natural, inalienable, and inherent, yet denied to women. By the time he finished presenting his proposal, he had identified the common law as the source of women's deprivation and suggested altering it. He knew his audience, and he anticipated the reactions to his proposal. He and other reformers expected to hear the familiar arguments of domestic harmony, attributing the peace and stability of the home to the roles of husband and wife, and Owen did not dispute them. Instead, he questioned whether domestic felicity required that the woman be financially dependent upon her husband.[6] He also pointed out that the common-law domestic relations rested on the benevolence of the husband; a rascal of a husband could leave a wife with no protection.

While the protection of wives from unscrupulous husbands was a fairly safe position, Owen went on to suggest that Indiana introduce principles of civil law into the regressive features of the common law. This suggestion raised alarms and brought on the eventual defeat of every proposal that Owen endorsed. The debate over women's rights at the convention became a debate over the intact survival of the common law. Opponents to Owen's proposals did not protest the extension of rights to women so much as they sought to protect what they perceived to be the foundation of society.

Owen never suggested dismantling the common law; he only wanted to introduce some principles of the civil law into those areas in which the common law had proven insufficient to protect the rights of women. Owen pointed out that the common law was the best system for protecting civil and political rights: "The Civil Law cannot be compared with the free spirit of the English and American Common Law system."[7] When it came to private rights and personal contracts, on the other hand, the civil law offered greater protection. Owen pointed out that when one looked at other states, civil-law states were not adopting common-law rules, but common-law states were adopting civil-law principles.

What Owen saw as timely reform was perceived as an assault on a way of life by other delegates. They issued vigorous defenses of the common law and pointed to the vagaries of civil-law societies. One delegate relied on history to remind Owen of "the many evils which the Roman civil law entailed upon the Romans themselves," such as debauchery and producing women who were haughty and insulting toward their husbands once they had as much money as they did.[8] As proof, he invoked "the immortal Jefferson, writing in reference to the then state of society in France . . . permitting the wife to hold, acquire, and own property separate and distinct from the husband."[9] Another urged his fellow delegates to compare the common-law countries of England and the United States with the civil-law countries of France, Spain, Italy, Portugal, Holland, South American states, and Mexico: "Why is there less enjoyment, less happiness, and less prosperity in these countries than in those where the common law prevails? By their fruits ye shall know principles; it is an intrinsic defect in the system."[10] The civil law system in Louisiana offered a familiar illustration. Owen claimed that things were going well in Louisiana and that he enjoyed fair trade with dealers there, while an opponent claimed that the community partnership of husband and wife under Louisiana's civil law opened the door for fraud.[11] Another opponent added that "in Louisiana . . . [it is] a sickening fact that a large portion of the litigation in that State is by wives against their husbands."[12]

Delegates revealed their organic understanding of a good society by tying a stable economy and social life to peaceful homes in which husband and wife were not at odds, not litigious, and not in economic competition with each other. The liberal appreciation of individual rights ended at the home, for unsettling the home would risk affecting larger social structures. Many Indiana delegates saw the common-law system as maintaining this stability and the civil-law system as undermining it. Thus, when an opponent declared that "there are no homes in Paris,"[13] this statement was fraught with meaning and anxiety.

Opponents to reform mustered contemporary reasons for the marital relation. Coverture provided useful services. Delegates recalled their republican mothers: "When a boy, from the lips of a mother I first heard the doctrines of righteousness and sobriety," and "It is from woman that man in his prime receives the consolation and sympathy and love that nerves him to the faithful performance of the part he has to play in the great theater of life."[14] They transferred the virtue and sacrifice of the iconic republican mother to the wife, who would provide support for her husband, because, delegates argued, the marital relations helped men to develop themselves as fully human. Unsettling the common law threatened to damage the project of achieving full personhood. Opponents continually referred to the idea that the feminine nature completed the masculine, that women's presence in a man's life softened his masculine harshness. This was seen as beneficial for each partner: "Woman was given to man to make up for his deficiencies, . . . to teach him to love everything around him. . . . Has she not modified the natural ferocity and roughness of man?"[15] In short, "The more we can unite the male and the female, the better it will be for both."[16] This unity was derived not simply out of natural conditions but also by securing it with the domestic relations. That this relation of the masculine and feminine was symbiotic was summed up in the imagery familiar at the time: "While the vine clings to and is supported by the oak it is loaded with fruit, . . . but independent of the oak, it trails upon the ground, losing all its beauty."[17] The use of vine-and-oak imagery to describe relations between the sexes was fairly common, but it fell short of symbiosis: The clinging vine may have been dependent on the oak, but there was no indication that the oak needed the vine.

In distinguishing the wife as a clinging vine that flourished in her relation with her husband, the Indiana delegates acknowledged the separate personalities of the husband and wife. This did not necessarily lead to women's emancipation, but, instead, to new justifications for coverture.[18] These delegates were not simply relying on the domestic relations but were updating them. Coverture was premised on the notion that the husband and wife were one person in the eyes of the law. The new justifications articulated in Indiana included men's own human development. The delegates feared that men's character would be denuded as public citizens. To enjoy all the benefits of society and to engage in public pursuits was not to lead a complete life. There is something in the home that could complete the man and make him fully human. The home was a refuge from the anxieties of the day, and the delegates would make sure that the home was retained by retaining the status, obligations, and civil disabilities of the domestic relations.

Using women's subjection instrumentally to achieve other purposes was nothing new, yet the Indiana delegates offer a stark contrast to the reasoning of those state supreme court judges who also retained coverture to serve larger purposes. The delegates' statements bordered on the bombastic. For them, protecting the domestic relations from reform was not a matter of retaining an epistemological standpoint, as it was for the common lawyers in the codification debates, or of balancing rights and status, as it was for state supreme courts. Rather, the delegates resisted change and stubbornly retained the status quo. The common law was losing its intellectual champions, and these were the kinds of arguments that were now issued to justify it.

"I knew, sir, that we should have to meet the old and stereotyped arguments," complained one of the convention's reformers.[19] He turned the tables on all the talk of maintaining the common law to protect women and complete men by declaring, "Shame, shame, on the manhood of the nation that tolerates so foul an outrage."[20] Reformers knew what to expect from their political adversaries, but they did not turn to the burgeoning rights discourse to produce equality as a trump against those stereotypes. Instead, they took seriously the concern that the marital relation served some purpose, and they argued that reform was a better way to protect women. In doing so, they issued a theory of reform that ameliorated, rather than eliminated, status relations and that acknowledged underlying need for those relations.

Some reformers underplayed their agenda, insisting that they were not determined to give women political rights or to "enlist and equip an army of female Amazons."[21] They claimed that they were only trying to protect women's welfare in an area in which the common law had failed to secure adequate protection. Pointing to the opportunities for husbands to abuse the power given to them by the common law, they were concerned that wives be given adequate protection from their husbands.[22] It was in the "wrongful acts of an improvident or dissolute husband" that the tranquility of the home was threatened,[23] not reforms of the common law. The state could provide property rights and still retain the home—even make it better, they urged.

Owen, too, made it clear that the granting of property rights to married women would not damage the marital relation. He agreed that domestic harmony was important, but he doubted that it required a woman to be financially dependent upon her husband, asking, "Is, then, the secret of domestic felicity to be found in pecuniary dependence?"[24] He did not dispute that there would be some inequality between husband and wife in financial matters, but he did object to wives being divested of all property rights: "Dependent, to some extent the relation of a wife to her husband, is and always must be. Men have monopolized all the most profitable occupations of life; custom sanctions this; and even if it did not, women would be, in a measure, shut out from these, by the engrossing character of their maternal cares and duties. There is great danger that this dependence, natural and necessary as it is, should give birth, on the one hand, in coarse and overbearing natures, to tyranny, and on the other, in timid and yielding natures, to abject fear."[25]

He also considered that men and women had respective duties in the home. Thus he did not object to status relations, but he did object to that status serving to deny rights and to fully define that person: "Household cares properly claim the wife's— the mother's attention; no true woman neglects these. So is it the husband's and father's first and bounden duty to provide support for the family. But it no more follows that a man of commanding talents shall tie down every energy of his soul to the one task of accumulating dollars and cents, than that the influence of a woman, fitted to aid in the civilization of her race, should be restricted to her parlor or her kitchen."[26]

Owen shared with the opponents to reform a concern for the importance of the home. He objected to the hierarchy of the marital relation and the denial of property rights. He pointed to Indiana's 1847 law allowing married women to own real estate, noting that this change had not resulted in husbands and wives living less harmoniously.[27] He pointed out a dozen states that had passed married women's property acts without destroying marriages. England, too, provided exceptions to common-law rules by resorting to equity to allow married women to own property through trusts, and he did not find domestic harmony to have been sacrificed in England, either.

Owen found a way to argue for women's rights that did not attack the premises of the common law. Instead, he pointed out the gaps and oversights of the common law that could be ameliorated through reform, a method that resembled equity more than equality. He was not opposed to the status of the marital relation; he only wanted to question why subjection and total immersion were so critical to maintaining it. Thus, when faced with a statement such as, "How cheering to the husband . . . when returning from his daily toil to . . . the kind greetings of his beloved partner,"[28] Owen responded not by refuting the dynamic of a wife greeting her husband but asking why she had to give up everything to do it: "I ask, whether, instead of devoting the glorious talents God has given them, to improve, to instruct, to delight mankind, their highest ambition, their noblest avocation through life should be, — to make pies and puddings for the gentleman from Laporte and the rest of his high-minded and most generous sex!"[29]

Owen represents an alternative reformist theory, one that called upon egalitarian sentiments not to abolish coverture but to modify it, to recognize its material consequences and to alter the traditional rules. It was a position that was possible because he was aware of the conditions of women's subjection. Women attended the constitutional convention and later that year a group of women describing themselves as the "Women of Indiana" presented Owen with a silver pitcher to thank him for his efforts. In his acceptance speech, Owen reflected more candidly on the debates of the past months. He was disappointed, not in the opponents' invocation of the common law as a tradition, but in the unassailability they assigned to it. He compared his opponents to the Tories of the revolutionary generation (and, by implication, reformers such as himself to the American revolutionaries), equating the defense of coverture with the defense of the divine right of kings.[30] As for their invocation of nature to justify coverture, Owen remarked, "Ah! poor Nature! how many sins, what thousand abuses, are loaded on thy shoulders! How eagerly is thy sanction suborned, to justify heartless oppression, to legalize cold blooded injustice!"[31]

He knew that the maudlin justifications were being constructed in an effort to retain coverture. He knew, though, to look past them to appreciate why they were so important to the defenders of the common law and to meet their perceived needs while ameliorating women's condition. This kind of equity argument would become less salient as the rules of coverture increasingly came to be justified, as they did in Indiana in 1850. The language of equity was difficult to sustain politically because discussion of women's rights was prone to polarization. There were fairly reasonable justifications for retaining the status of the marital relation, but in relying on such conservative justifications, such as God, nature, and unexamined tradition, common lawyers distinguished the common law as the barbaric doctrine that woman suffragists charged it to be. The enthusiasm is puzzling, considering that the state legislature passed its first married women's property act the next year.

BRADWELL V. ILLINOIS

The U.S. Supreme Court did not deal with coverture or the property rights of married women very often. Cases tended to remain in state appellate courts, since marriage is an issue left to the states. State courts therefore dealt with the reform of married women's property rights regularly, and the Supreme Court lacked their experience. When the Supreme Court did encounter a case regarding married women's status in the late nineteenth century, its justices looked much more like the Indiana convention delegates than jurists of the common-law tradition.

When Myra Bradwell was denied a license to practice law in Illinois, she appealed her case to the Supreme Court, testing the meaning of the relatively new Fourteenth Amendment by claiming the right to practice law as a privilege of citizenship under the Fourteenth Amendment's privileges and immunities clause. The Supreme Court denied her claim in *Bradwell v. Illionois*,[32] based on the limited reading of the privileges and immunities clause that had just been issued in *The Slaughter-House Cases*.[33]

The *Bradwell* decision is notorious for its concurring opinion, in which Justice Bradley muses on the role of wife and mother. This is the opinion that is sure to be included in any constitutional law or sex discrimination textbook, and it was referenced as evidence of treatment toward women by the Supreme Court in the twentieth century.[34] To read it is to be outraged, stunned, and a bit fascinated at the portrait of women drawn by a Supreme Court justice. "Civil law, as well as nature herself, has always recognized a wide difference in the respective spheres and destinies of man and woman. Man is, or should be, woman's protector and defender. The natural and proper timidity and delicacy which belongs to the female sex evidently unfits if for many of the occupations of civil life. The constitution of the family organization, which is founded in the divine ordinance, as well as in the nature of things, indicates the domestic sphere as that which properly belongs to the domain and functions of womanhood."[35]

If stereotypes could justify women's subjugation, then the expected recourse would be to strip those stereotypes of any legal power by recurring to equality between men and women. Women need only be imagined as worthy individuals, and their rights will fall into place, just as the woman suffragist narrative instructs. The problem with this strategy is that women's subjugation was not owing to mere stereotype. It was institutionally entrenched and, after the passage of reform statutes, obscured in judicial strategies and new family unity rhetoric. Banishing stereotypes is insufficient for identifying and dismantling these institutional arrangements. In passing down these dicta as a sensationalist tale of women's oppression, the role of the common law in Myra Bradwell's status has been lost from view.

Bradwell, already editor of the *Chicago Legal News*, received a recommendation to practice law after being examined by a state circuit court judge and the state's attorney.[36] When she then appealed to the supreme court of Illinois to apply for a law license, she provided them with some guidance on the question of whether it could issue a law license to a woman. She offered an interpretation of the Revised Statutes' provision relating to the practice of law by remarking that reference to "he" in the statute was gender-neutral. To support this, she cited Section 90 of the Revised Statutes, which offered a guide to phrases and words and stated, "When any party or person is described or referred to by words importing the masculine gender, females as well as males may be deemed to be included."[37]

The Illinois supreme court denied Bradwell's application because her condition as a married woman imposed disabilities (despite the absence of any reference to her marital status in her initial appeal). The court conceded that it could not grant her application until the legislature had changed the rules.[38] Bradwell responded with an additional brief in which she pointed out reform legislation that had granted married women property rights and further rights that allowed them to transact their separate property and to employ agents to carry out her separate business. Married women's property acts had increasingly held married women responsible for their actions, required women to be held responsible for their torts (unless committed under coercion of the husband) and to be sued as if they were *feme sole*. The state supreme court again refused Bradwell's application, pointing out that, despite the amount of legislation the state had passed, it had not granted married women the right to make contracts. Statutes in abrogation of the common law were to be strictly construed, and the court followed this rule of statutory construction, recognizing married women's rights as explicated in the statutes but recognizing no expressed or intended right to contract. Thus the common-law rules obtained, and the common law had never recognized the right of a married woman to be an attorney. The court admitted that these practices may have been in error, that women were fully capable of being attorneys, and that it would be desirable to see such statutes passed, but the proper place for such recognition, it found, was in the legislature.[39] Consistent with other judicial interpretations of the married women's property acts, the Illinois supreme court recognized the likelihood of the capacity of a married woman to own property, but it left the conferral of that right to the state legislature. The state supreme court held this position even as it cast doubt on the reasoning behind married women's civil disabilities: "That God designed the sexes to occupy different spheres of action, and that it belonged to men to make, apply, and execute the laws, was regarded as an almost axiomatic truth. It may have been a radical error, and we are by no means certain it was not, but that this was the universal belief certainly admits of no denial."[40]

Bradwell appealed her case to the U.S. Supreme Court with a writ of error filed by her lawyer, Matthew Hale Carpenter, complaining that she had been denied admission to the bar for the sole reason that she was a married woman. Carpenter argued for a more expansive reading of the privileges and immunities clause and for women's rights when representing Bradwell. In his oral argument, Carpenter proclaimed that the time for status was over: "Commencing with the barbarism of the East and journeying through the nations toward the bright light of civilization in the West, it will everywhere be found that, just in proportion to the equality of women with men in the enjoyment of social and civil rights and privileges, both sexes are proportionately advanced in refinement and all that ennobles human nature."[41]

Bradwell lost her appeal, notoriously, in *Bradwell v. Illinois*. In the majority opinion, Justice Miller avoided the issue of married women's rights by refusing to categorize law practice as a privilege of national citizenship under the Fourteenth Amendment. A companion to *The Slaughter-House Cases*, *Bradwell* is not a case about women's rights but about the limitations of the powers of the federal government over the states, and Bradley's concurrence is, after all, only a concurrence.[42] Nevertheless, the presence of the *Bradwell* holding and Bradley's concurring opinion contribute to the narrative that has accompanied and informed Supreme Court jurisprudence on women.

In the areas in which it did address women's issues in *Bradwell*, Justice Miller demonstrated that he was largely unconcerned with the law concerning married women. Miller's opinion begins with the statement that "the record in this case is not very perfect," but it was able to determine her residency.[43] Because he was framing the issue as one of the limited privileges and immunities of national citizenship, Miller made questions of residency the leading ones. Bradwell complained that the irregularities lay in her status as a married woman. When it denied her application for a license, the Illinois supreme court made its decision on facts it did not have, as it assumed (or knew) that she was a married woman. Under the common law, it was only the *feme covert* whose property and contract rights were denied. The *feme sole* was free to own property and contract for it as she pleased. Miller avoided review of any this irregularity by restricting the legal question to the limits of the privileges of national citizenship.

Justice Bradley conflated the civil disabilities of the *feme sole* and *feme covert*. He explained that the limitation of the right to practice law in Illinois was predicated on the rules of the common law, noting that only men were admitted to the bar in the common-law tradition.[44] The common-law doctrine of coverture affixed civil disabilities upon women once they entered into marriage, but Justice Bradley dismissed the distinction by noting that the rights of single women were exceptions to the rule.[45] In treating the common law as a system of sex classification, Bradley provided an ill-informed account of the common law that, because of his opinion's visibility, threatened to provide the definitive description of the common law in its defense against reform.

Bradley recognized that the state supreme court found itself bound because the legislation was not designed to alter married women's inability to contract or to practice law. Although this summarizes the Illinois state supreme court opinion, it leaves out the lower court's rules of statutory interpretation. The Illinois supreme court expressed an ideological aversion to the common law but upheld it nevertheless in following the rules of statutory construction, and it avoided reflecting on the larger social justifications. Bradley relished the common-law status of married women, summoning additional reasons for married women's status, referring to time immemorial, civil law, nature herself, natural disposition, the family, and divine ordinance. The U.S. Supreme Court rarely addressed the property rights of married women, and in retaining the status and civil disabilities of married women, it either did not know or refused to rely upon the reasoning of state courts. Instead, Bradley relied on external traditions to justify and reassert married women's status. The Illinois supreme court refused to act as a champion of women's rights, but it did not embrace the common law, either. Bradley, on the other hand, not only upheld the common law; he derived new justifications for it.

The Bradley concurrence tends to be the version of *Bradwell* that is passed down, thus producing a misleading account of tensions concerning women's rights in the nineteenth century. Merely recalling Bradley's concurrence both overstates the prejudice and understates the institutional basis for women's civil and political disabilities. The prejudice in 1873 was not as bad as Bradley's opinion indicates: although the Supreme Court denied her claim, Bradwell subsequently heeded the advice of the state supreme court and soon saw passage of state legislation that recognized women's right to practice law, a piece of legislation introduced by her husband. The prejudice that characterizes Bradley's concurrence was not a uniform description of women's condition but the musings of a U.S. Supreme Court justice who was groping for justification of the rules of the common-law domestic relations. The reform of rules of coverture required judges to balance new rights with the remaining rules of coverture. Without the experience of the lower-court judges, Bradley appealed to bombastic reasons to justify women's subjection. Because Bradley's concurring opinion is better known than the more measured considerations of state-level courts, the common law as the source of anachronistic views on women has been made central to the narrative of women's subjugation.

CODIFICATION REDUX

New justifications for married women's status were likewise reproduced in the codification debates. When codification was debated once again in the 1870s and 1880s, the issue of woman's rights became a dividing wedge and shifted the content of the debate. Codifiers and common lawyers continued to debate the merits of simple rules accessible in a legislative code, but they also took positions on the merits of social reform. The legal reform was much more politicized than it had been earlier in the century. In defending the common law, common lawyers were now willing to defend the rules of coverture, regardless of the civil disabilities they incurred for women.

Interest in codification had decreased by the 1840s, but it was revived by the New York lawyer David Dudley Field.[46] In 1846, the New York state constitution called for a code commission, to which Field was appointed in 1857. Field committed his late career to the codification of New York state law, and he drafted a set of codes—a penal code, a political code, and a civil code.[47] The drafts lay dormant in the New York legislature for years but circulated throughout the United States and were adopted, partially or fully, primarily in western states and territories. By the mid-1860s, interest in codification had once again waned as states grew preoccupied with the Civil War, but Field persisted in his efforts to see the codes passed in New York.[48] When he proposed his codes once again in 1879, he lobbied the legislature persistently over the next ten years.[49] He was continually beset by his political opponents in New York, primarily the members of the Bar Association of New York City. They defended the common law against Field's civil code, which was the most radical of Field's codes, with its statement that, where the code applies, there would be no common law.[50]

The science of the law was in vogue by the 1880s, with the popularity of the German historical school of legal science, which posited law as the expression of the consciousness of a people that grows from its culture organically over time. Imported from the German legal thinker Friedrich Karl von Savigny, the historical school modernized the common-law methods of Blackstone, and even Kent and Story, who were now viewed as insufficiently scientific.[51] The historical school of legal science is often mistaken for mere conservatism when, in fact, it was quite capable of reform and its ideas more sophisticated than its critics allow.[52] James C. Carter, in particular, has emerged as an intellectual thinker of the historical school. He demonstrated a commitment to morality, to reform of political corruption, to a flexible and contextualized understanding of law in the service of justice.[53] Unwilling to sacrifice justice to scientific certainty, he evoked the earlier common lawyers, who balked at the introduction of positivism into American law. Nevertheless, later historians have tended to portray Carter and his cohorts as elitist mugwumps resisting social change.[54] While more recent scholarship has recovered the sophistication present in the historical school, the derogatory conclusion is not unfounded, for the common lawyers of the 1880s did, indeed, present themselves as resistant to reform and committed to conserving the status and hierarchy of the common law when the issue of women's rights was broached.

As married women's property rights legislation increased across the country, members of the legal community could take a stand on codification through their stance of the rights of married women. Codifiers could define themselves as social reformers. Common lawyers' organic understanding of law as emerging from a particular community translated into political conservatism. In defending married women's status common lawyers positioned themselves as apologists for the hardships of the common law and staunchly defended the status quo. Their defense of married woman's status encouraged them to embrace conservatism for conservatism's sake. In so doing, they contributed to an association of the common law with traditionalism, obscuring the progressive capacity of the common law in rights discourse. They also lost the common law's critical voice in the reform being undertaken in law, politics, and society. Codification could now attach itself to notions of progress. Without a learned, critical common-law voice, the implications of the form that progress took were lost.

In the annual address of the American Bar Association meeting in 1880, Benjamin Bristow urged lawyers to overcome their reluctance to accept New York's Field's Code of Civil Procedure, noting that it was not easy for lawyers in practice to accept change (and new codes to master), but, once they did, they would find the code beneficial.[55] The Field Code had not received such endorsement from the New York City Bar Association. The "Committee on the Amendment of the Law," on which bar member Frederic Coudert sat, found Field's Code to be unacceptable. If a committee of representatives could not intelligently grasp the code, he complained, then "what becomes of the chief argument of Mr. FIELD and his friends if a proper understanding of this Law is so difficult?"[56] The animosity and accusations between Field and the New York City bar association were out in the open, longstanding, and embittered. The debates between them were not polite and were exchanged as invectives more than as studied disagreement.

There were some strong defenses of the common law in the 1880s. Lawyers argued that the common law could keep pace with social progress, and, as common lawyers had done in an earlier generation, they questioned whether the purported certainty of a code was a quality to be desired in law.[57] In editing Coudert's testimony, John Ruggles Strong included a preface that collected historic arguments against codification, including the earlier treatments by Chancellor Kent and Joseph Story. These arguments were eclipsed by the defense of the status quo urged by the changes in the marital relation. In the earlier codification movement, radical codifiers had introduced doubts about the hierarchy of the marital relation in the earlier codification debates.[58] At the time, however, common lawyers largely avoided the gender challenge. They instead addressed the structural and interpretive aspects of the common law and were able to offer a defense of the common law as suitably modern. In the 1880s, it was more difficult to avoid the issue of married women's status, and common lawyers responded by defending the rules of coverture. When they could not rely on old principles, such as the unity of husband and wife, they made up new ones.

Field's Civil Code threatened to abolish the status of the marital relation, and it upset long-settled rules about marriage and family relations. When the Association of the Bar of the City of New York issued an early report in its debates with Field, it pointed to the "sweeping changes" in the rights of married women and in the rules for adopting children as particularly egregious.[59] Field's designation of an area of law called "Personal Relations" to replace domestic relations was a poor substitute, as it would treat husbands and wives as individuals rather than through their respective statuses.

Writing for the Association of the Bar of the City of New York, Frederic Coudert complained that he was disturbed by the code's provision that the father of an illegitimate child could publicly claim the child as his own and include it in his family, thereby legitimating the child from birth.[60] This practice would be at odds with British common-law tradition, morality, and the mores of New York: "I say that our people, who would probably not tolerate this tampering with the sanctity of the marriage relation, even by legitimating offspring as in some other States: that our people, who have always objected to that, will be utterly appalled when they see the immorality of the proposed law; immorality, and confusion, and injustice, and wrong."[61] Coudert referred to an adoption provision that required the mutual consent of the husband and wife as "an artificial interfering with the laws of nature."[62] J. Bleeker Miller associated the tradition of common-law rules with the natural law. If legislatures began tinkering with these rules, therefore, they would not only unsettle standing rules but would destroy their connection with the natural order of things.[63]

John Ruggles Strong was disturbed by Field's provisions for the husband-wife relation, especially by the section that allowed a husband and wife to transact with each other. To buttress his case he turned not to the law but to King Solomon in Proverbs, proclaiming that "Mr. Field's proposition is a barbaric assault upon the more beautiful forms and ceremonies in the Temple of Justice."[64] Strong feared that when Field's code took effect, a married woman would be able to transact with her husband, and he would coerce her in her use of her separate property. The rules of coverture were, therefore, the best protection for a married woman with property rights.[65] Jonathon Smith invoked the standard fear of domestic discord when a man and women were seen as distinct persons.[66] Henry Hitchcock referred to divine design, which endowed a man with "greater strength, cooler judgment, broader foresight."[67]

Codification was now touching upon the remaining rules of the domestic relations and social ordering. To resist this, common lawyers tended to muster defenses of the common-law rules by recourse to natural law or morality, thus raising the stakes of the debate while reducing its quality. In this later wave of the codification debates, common lawyers, in the face of reform of the domestic relation, became stalwart defenders of the status quo. John Ruggles Strong addressed the Field Code's effects on the husband-wife relation by noting that, though it was an issue that interested the people, discussion of it could already be found in "thousands of cases, and, as I may add, in systematic text books founded on actual decisions and written by earnest, able and celebrated lawyers."[68] That is, the common law's method of judicial decisions had already produced treatment of the husband and wife relation. Field's Code, on the other hand, contained a collection of newly sprung provisions for the marital relation, inviting Strong to reflect, "If any more injurious, flimsy, pretentious, and useless book can be thought of, I am unable to imagine it."[69]

Field's provisions for the husband and wife relation, however, were not a radical assault on the common law. He retained the husband as head of the family, with the power to choose domicile. He retained the separation of property that had developed in judicial decisions after enactment of the married women's property acts. Field's primary challenge lay in his introduction of reciprocity into the common-law marital obligations. The obligations of respect, fidelity, and support were now mutual. Husband and wife could contract with each other and could mutually agree to separate.

Field claimed that a code was preferable because it would lay out law simply and remain accessible to the people. As the earlier wave of common lawyers had done, Strong pointed out that the simplicity of a code was deceptive. Strong went on to claim that the common law could achieve the goal of simplicity because it was based on principles of natural justice and common sense. It incorporated principles of justice and so, to conform with the natural order of things, a state merely had to continue relying on the common law. For common lawyers, it was enough to refer to natural law without further explication or justification. Common lawyers were becoming content with the status quo without regard for keeping up social changes. In these politicized debates they were losing their ability or willingness to test the adaptability of the common law when it came to women's rights. Blackstone located natural law in the common law in order to claim its commitment to freedom. These common lawyers were invoking natural law in order to adhere to the past and resist change.

The perceived need to protect the marital relation through reference to external traditions extended to defenses of the common law as a system. "What is law?" Albert Matthews asked, "In its primary and highest sense, considered in the abstract, it might be defined simply as the expressed will of God."[70] That being the case, the common-law system was in accordance with the harmony of the universe. Such matters would never be fully grasped or explained by human beings, so it was best not to tinker with them. As Joel Prentiss Bishop noted, the universe works according to a plan, but the actors in this plan can hardly explain why they do what they do. "We see around us a universe, upon every part of which the Creator has made the impress of law. . . . In the loudest voice ask the earth why it moves thus, it can give you no answer. It does not know."[71] Despite man's capacity to reason, it was best to leave these rules alone and let them operate according to their own internal design. While Blackstone's identification of "manliness" in the common law was not itself a progressive notion, it did value the activity and engagement of legal interpretation. These common lawyers, on the other hand, were beginning to treat the law as a system that lay beyond their understanding and themselves as subjects to the law rather than as active interpreters.

Codifiers were able to revive the old argument that the common law was antithetical to freedom. With the husband-wife relation a prominent component of the codification debates, Robert Ludlow Foster could point to its "repressive tendency" as the primary defect of the common law for modern society.[72] George Hoadly could say that it was absurd to locate freedom in the common law.[73] With the common law no longer a viable source of freedom, the amelioration for past hierarchy could be found in progress, and codifiers saw law as playing a special role in social progress. Early in his codification efforts, Field addressed the graduating class of Albany Law School and asserted that "justice is attainable only through lawyers."[74] Law could take the lead in social progress.[75]

The connection between codification and social reform was not as strong as it could have been. Lawyers who advocated codification of coverture could nevertheless be heard distancing themselves from woman's rights activists. The political reforms of the woman suffragists were far too radical for lawyers. The *Albany Law Journal* poked fun at leading woman suffragists, calling Matilda Joslyn Gage a "goose" for her radical ideas.[76] In their own self-understanding, however, they did see a reformist tendency in their capacities as lawyers, seeing themselves as working for reform, but with quieter measures.

This time, the promise of codification could be issued without common lawyers responding with evidence of common law's modernity. Blackstone carved out a place for the common law as a legal system for moderns. Earlier in the century, common law's defenders had pointed to its freedom and adaptability in the face of codification proposals. In the 1880s, however, common lawyers largely abandoned this assertion of modern suitability and instead recovered common law's tradition, staunchly defending it in the face of reform and change. Not only that, they justified tradition as a legitimate resource by recurring to external doctrines of natural law and nature, not to protect freedom, but to resist change. The common law in rights discourse and in legal theory was only as strong as its defenders. And the understanding of reform was only as good as those defenders. In the earlier codification debates, codifiers had introduced notions of reform without full consideration of the implications for the source of authority and interpretation of law. Common lawyers, in their rigorous defense of the common law, provided that consideration. In the 1880s, with little legal theory being debated, the common law became associated with allegiance to tradition, regardless of its political implications, and codification could now be accepted as timely reform. The common law was losing those defenders who would ensure that it kept pace with modernity; they now touted the common law not for its adaptability but for its adherence to the status quo in the face of change. With this view of the common law becoming more popular, reformers found their best strategy in opposing this old tradition—a source of hierarchy, justified with stereotypes of women's natures and calling-with the abstract principle of equality.

SOLITUDE OF SELF

With the common-law voice eroding in rights discourse, and the common law serving as the restraint on liberty rather than as an alternative source of liberty, the woman suffragists' rights theory was ready to serve as the likely version of rights theory. Woman suffragists were ready to provide the model. Having lambasted the common law as a source of freedom or even a legitimate legal system for the United States, they continued to develop their theory of rights of the individual. Elizabeth Cady Stanton provided the culmination of the woman suffragists' development in rights discourse in her speech "Solitude of Self."

"Solitude of Self" was Stanton's farewell address as she stepped down from leadership of the National American Woman Suffrage Association. She reprised the speech in both the U.S. House of Representatives and the U.S. Senate, and the House printing office reproduced 10,000 copies. "Solitude of Self" is a rumination on the ontology and opportunities of the individual and, as such, serves as the culmination of the woman abolitionist theories of individualism and human rights. The task of deriding the common law is largely absent from this speech, and Stanton no longer needed to dwell on it; few could do a better job of demonstrating the oppression of the common law than the Supreme Court justices and lawyers who were stalwartly defending it. With the common law sufficiently delegitimized as a liberal project or companion, she could now dwell on the individual, who bore claim to the tenets of liberalism.

The individual envisioned by Stanton in "Solitude of Self" is an individual considered prior to any rights or obligations based on status. This essay captures the aspirations that the Frances Wright, the Grimkés, Ernestine Rose, and other woman rights activists. At the same time that Stanton presented this abstracted individual, however, she exposed its fictions. The soul that Stanton sought to abstract from repressive social conditions was not as detached as she indicated. She references Robinson Crusoe, who, of course, was not alone but with his companion, Friday. Stanton, too, in describing this individual soul, describes her as "arbiter of her own destiny, an imaginary Robinson Crusoe, with her woman, Friday, on a solitary island."[77] Has the woman citizen liberated herself only at the expense of another servant to meet her physical needs so that she may enjoy her own freedom? The very invocation of Friday, while a timely literary reference, reveals the lapses in this powerful speech. The notion of a solitary self-sufficiency is a fiction, but Stanton was perpetuating it as an effective way to argue for more political and civil rights for women. Its consequences would be felt not in Stanton's generation but in the development of liberal theory, as this fiction came to be seen as definitive of the liberal subject. Stanton had the opportunity to argue that a woman deserved rights even though, and because, she was a wife and mother. Had she inserted a married woman's status into the calculation, she could have issued a form of rights doctrine in which the situated self is recognized as a rights-bearing individual whose rights would be effective in her status as individual. Instead, the fiction of the solitary self produces rights that are expansive yet may not be effective in their application. Furthermore, they further obscure the tensions that had existed within liberalism all along—women were subjugated, in part, to serve the needs of others. In emancipating herself, and others like herself, Stanton was shunting the work off on another Friday (likely racialized), who would assume the obligations and civil disabilities that she dispensed with in her own liberation.[78]

Similarly, she describes all individuals as, centrally, alone: "We come into the world alone, unlike all who have gone before us, we leave it alone, under circumstances peculiar to ourselves."[79] Of course, no one comes into the world alone—at birth, the child is physically attached to the mother. Furthermore, being born provides one with immediate status, as the child of that mother. Our entry into this world is fundamentally tied to another. Stanton wrested a fiction out of birth when she could have highlighted those relations to make the case that relations must be recognized on a more egalitarian basis.

The point of the speech, she explained, was to acknowledge the "individuality of each human soul."[80] Faced with a woman's multiple statuses as citizen, woman, wife, mother, sister, or daughter, all of which informed her political rights, her civil disabilities, and her social standing and behavior, Stanton referred to the abstracted soul to argue that a woman was deserving of rights before any of these status indicators. This is a moving speech, the product of Stanton's half century of political activism and leadership. She was not denying that women would become wives or mothers but asserting that their rights should not be based on the duties that arose from these relations. Men's rights were not denied on the basis of their reciprocal statuses as husbands and fathers, and women should be treated accordingly. To deny a woman rights because she might become a wife and mother was to strip her of the opportunity to develop herself as an individual at the expense of this temporary station in her life. Women needed equal rights and educational opportunities so that they could acquire the skills to be their own masters: "To guide our own craft, we must be captain, pilot, engineer; with chart and compass to stand at the wheel; to watch the winds and waves, and know when to take in the sail, and to read the signs in the firmament over all."[81] Women needed skills to be their own captains, even if their occupation would be as wife and mother. Here Stanton indicated that she was not plotting a social revolution. She was not endorsing an exodus from the home and domestic duties; rather, she was appealing to the government to stop denying women rights because of those duties.

The acceptance of women's domestic role might appear to be evidence that Stanton retained a social context, but in abstracting the subject to a solitary soul, she was altering the method of rights derivation. She attached rights to an abstracted subject without knowledge of that individual's social or political status. "Solitude of Self" conveys the development of suffragist thought and the tension it produced. Suffragist theorizing sought to deliver women from repressive social conditions by seeking to transcend them, pretending that those conditions were irrelevant for viewing the individual. "Solitude of Self" betrays the myth of this endeavor, with the social context and relations slipping in the very essay in which Stanton sought to overcome them. The woman suffragist theory thus did not provide a means of overcoming society but a method of suppressing and ignoring it. With this method, "Solitude of the Self" is the culmination of the libertarian theory of the abolitionists. The abolitionists had formulated an incipient libertarian theory in response to a repressive social context. Stanton further abstracted the subject while obscuring the relevance of the social context. The social context now became the site wherein rights would be exercised rather than the site from which rights emerged.

While the solitary self captures Stanton's longing for recognition as a rights-bearing individual prior to her gendered and marital status, the lapses apparent in her speech have come to haunt feminist theory and rights-discourse in general. The "Girl Friday" is now recognizable as the subjugated woman upon whom the freedom of the liberated woman rests, repeating the dynamic of patriarchal subordination of women in social contract theory.[82] Theories of freedom abstracted from social conditions can produce such results. The resources of the common law allow for theories of equality to be applied to the lived conditions of status, but the degeneration of the common-law theory of liberty into a defense of the status quo has obscured them.

Conclusion

When American liberalism lost its association with the common-law domestic relations, it became a doctrine defined by its abstract principles and understood outside the context in which it operated. Rights had always been contextualized. Property rights, freedom of speech, and equity had all offered the possibility of protective rights theories rooted in context. Even the abolitionists' most abstracted rights theories were responses to context in a political construction of the Constitution — the more abolitionists were affected by regulatory laws and social norms, the more abstract their rights theories became. When women's rights activists sought their own liberation by tearing at the domestic relations at the foundation of the constitutional order, they relied on abstraction to overcome their oppression, and they encouraged future generations to think of rights and the constitutional order in opposition to that context.

Liberal analyses have tended to cast institutions for family arrangements as illiberal because they have taken on illiberal form historically. In doing so, liberal analyses have overlooked the institutions upon which a liberal society rests. The liberal lens has not been trained on the progressive possibilities of the common law. When studies use the liberal lens to view married women's property rights or rights in general in studies of American political development, they scour the statutes and their interpretation for signs of rights and their limits. This lens has obscured the reassertion of married women's status, with the result that the heuristic of liberalism in American political development poses a hindrance to explanation and understanding. Even after passage of the married women's property acts, the reassertion of common-law rules was made possible by the continuation of the traditional common-law rules. In mistaking the passage of the statutes for progress, the liberal lens obscures the source of coverture's survival and attributes it to illiberal prejudice rather than analyzing its role in institutional maintenance.

The common law was a source of women's subordination, but it also contained a progressive capacity in its methods and in its rules. James Madison's consideration of the rights that the polity needs to govern itself, Lydia Maria Child's engagement within forms, and Robert Dale Owen's application of equality to the marital relation all provide examples of progressive use of common-law methods. As the common lawyers attested when they defended the common law against codification, the common law could adapt, and it is possible that it could have adapted to the growing recognition of women's capacities. Common-law methods were equipped to ameliorate women's condition in a way that more formal equality doctrine cannot, by acknowledging the context in which their oppression persisted.

The activism of the woman suffragists encouraged a theory of equality that has benefited women in giving them recognition and opportunities, but the loss of context in rights discourse brought on a loss of the situated self in that discourse. Even reformers such as Judge Herttell and Robert Dale Owen did not seek to eliminate the marital relation or the obligations within it; they only questioned why a woman had to be subjugated to achieve the purposes that the household served. It was quite possible to recognize both men's and women's obligations within the home, but to distribute them fairly and without undue burden on either's political or civil rights. This would be equitable, and this was the direction in which state legislatures and courts could have taken married women's property reform. In effecting the juxtaposition of liberal principles against the common law, however, woman suffragists shut off equity as a response, because status became illegitimate in the acknowledgment of rights. As the treatment of women's rights largely shifted from state court treatment of the common-law rules to constitutional considerations of equality, the alternative was set aside.

The woman suffragist narrative was not immediately persuasive. Schisms within the suffrage movement itself divided woman suffragists' thoughts on the proper rights claims of women. After ratification of the Nineteenth Amendment, American feminism faced another division between equality feminists and labor feminists, who feared that formal equality would make it harder to recognize material differences between citizens and would harm efforts to pass protective labor laws. The labor legislation of the New Deal reduced the difference between equality feminists and labor feminists in the 1960s and, by the 1970s, *"everyone* was on the formal equality bandwagon."[1] This is not to say that feminists have agreed on the meaning or merits of equality but, rather, to point out that equality came to serve as an animating principle.

In Supreme Court doctrine, the woman suffragist narrative came to dominate judicial narratives of women's oppression. Justice Brennan cited some of the more provocative lines of Bradley's *Bradwell* opinion as a demonstration of the stereotypes that have justified women's oppression in the United States.[2] Supreme Court equal protection jurisprudence was based upon this misleading reference to stereotypes. Equality was invoked to attack those stereotypes, while the more durable institu-

tional sources of women's inequality remained unaddressed.[3] The legacy of inequality did not go away; it only became more difficult to see continued social ordering under the formula of equality doctrine.

Recent scholarship has contended with the merits of bringing context back in.
James Stoner laments that benefits of the common-law status relations have been obscured by the notoriety of the *Bradwell* opinion, including obligations that ensured
that the husband would protect the family and that the wife would nurture the children (and husband).[4] The common law tended to the physical and material needs
of its citizens. The useful allocation for meeting these needs was the gendered division of men and women in the family. Stoner would like to restore the gender roles.
Mary Shanley, on the other hand, locates a feminist theory of justice through recognition of this status. The state's recognition of the marital relation provides for acknowledgment of the ways in which citizens forego the presumptions of individualism. Contract theory does not capture the contingencies and irrational choices made
by people as members of families.[5] An ethos of care remains obscured beneath the
prevailing doctrine of individual rights.[6] The status relations of the common law may
contain a history of oppression, but they also contain the reflection (and production)
of the way that citizens live, the relations they forge, and the labor they perform.
When rights abstract from hierarchy, they also grow distant from this experience and
may fail to adequately address the protections that these situated selves require.
Shanley demonstrates that there is a feminist potential in recovering the history and
experience of status.

Martha Fineman illustrates what such a transition would look like in her incorporation of dependency against the fictions of autonomy in American law and policy. The common law retained a hierarchical family and relied on that family to serve
social needs. The relationship between family and state can be reconceived, with
the work of an egalitarian family recognized by the state. Fineman's vision provides
a means of getting at the hierarchy of the traditional family, not only in its patriarchy
but in its heteronormative arrangements as well, thus protecting individual freedom
while retaining the importance of the family to the state.[7]

The common-law method allows for a recognition of power that liberal rights theories overlook. Wendy Brown has charged rights discourse with substituting an abstract subject and abstract rights for actual injury claims. The injured must couch
her experience in the framework and dictates of existing rights talk, getting her story
right in order to demonstrate the violation of a right. When she wins, she is ideally
emancipated, but practically subordinated, because she has taken on a preexisting
subject position and failed to express her own experience.[8]

The struggle for women's rights pointed to past discriminations and the justice of recognizing women's status as individuals in according them their due rights. This reform rests on certainty in past discrimination and certainty in the measure of relief. Brown's work suggests that the very certainty closes off the possibilities for questioning the rightness of those methods, discourages the questioning of existing forms and encourages the injured to make use of them, a situation that closes off alternative methods that could emancipate the individual.

Under the common-law methods, the injured can voice her claim, and the institution can assess her situation against the committed principles of the polity. The differences between a constitutional-rights process and an equitable correction is that the latter allows the injured to tell her own narrative rather than couching it in existent rights doctrine. She can introduce the context of her condition. The judge (or other arbiter) can assess the points at which her experience is out of place with the principles valued by that polity. The injured need not identify herself according to her race, national origin, sex, or other established category, but can articulate her own identity as it plays out in her experience. Under the common-law methods, the decision maker employs discretion in narrowing the gap between principles and experience, making adjustment to rules or issuing exceptions. There is a flexibility at play here and a recognition of experience. The arbiter hears the experience of the injured and gauges how much that experience demonstrates a failing of principle commitments. The arbiter can then ask whether the polity would allow for a lapse in principles or whether this people would find it legitimate to seek a corrective. Hence the act of ameliorating the condition of the injured involves and produces a constitutive process that invites reflection upon the values of the polity. Constitutional understanding emerges through practice rather than through recourse to authoritative documents and ideas.

Today's debates over constitutional interpretation reflect the turn toward certainty and authority. The experience of women's rights assists in understanding why and appreciating what was gained and lost. Woman suffragists relied on the natural rights tradition to unmoor liberalism from its grounding in the domestic relations of the common law, effecting a distrust of context in rights discourse. The development of American constitutionalism occurred during a period of expanding liberal principles as well as the rise of technocratic knowledge of the truth of women's historic oppression. By relying on trends in both legal and political reform in their efforts to liberate themselves, woman suffragists introduced a constitution that aspired to include more citizens in its promises while keeping them removed from the endeavor of constitutionalism. In opting for a constitution of aspiration,[9] these political reformers closed off the resources of the common-law methods, which were too particular, too uncertain, too ridden with status to be suitable for modern law and political regimes.

While expertise and detachment in interpretation bring certainty and authoritative meaning, the early codification debates demonstrate the cost. As the common lawyers pointed out, greater certainty emerges when more authority is exerted in the enterprise. Uncertainty in meaning, on the other hand, invites new interpreters to the project of constitutional construction. The activity of the woman suffragists is exemplary of the expansion of the interpretive enterprise under conditions of uncertainty. When the status of married women was rendered indeterminate after the passage of married women's property acts, and judges and treatise writers struggled to make sense of the acts, woman suffragists took advantage of the opportunity to provide their own version. Uncertainty in meaning called authority into question and made it possible for a disenfranchised group to take part.

While the women's rights efforts point out the opportunities for political constitutionalism, they also point to the perils that face the participants. The muted debate between the Grimké sisters and Lydia Maria Child suggest that when the costs are too high for the political cause, participants will not make their case public. Without the public engagement, the political process of constitutionalism loses important voices and challenges to emergent theories. The democratic possibilities are limited by the deployment of political strategies in the larger political arena. Theories of multiple interpreters should be cognizant of the presence of power and privilege in the arena of interpretation.

The great irony in this history is that the groups that were so moved by their experience — abolitionists by the existence of slavery, women's rights activists by women's subordination — passed down theories that abstracted from context and that encouraged reference to truth and certainty rather than an acceptance of the indefinite project of common-law constitutionalism. Common-law constitutionalism is not lost; David Strauss makes the case that we practice it but refuse to come to terms with it.[10] Recovering common-law constitutionalism invites a change in posture rather than a change in practice. The uncertainty of the common law opens up the opportunity for engagement in constitutional matters from the place of one's status so that one can be sure that reform acts upon that status rather than upon a fictionalized subject. The interpreter must be modest in seeking the truth, resisting the claim to certainty and giving in to the doubt and open-ended questions, with the faith that they offer the invitation to engagement. This alternative rights derivation is fraught with its own difficulties, and it does not offer a solution, only a disposition to engage in ongoing constitutionalism.

Notes

INTRODUCTION

1. See Sanford Levinson, *Constitutional Faith* (Princeton, NJ: Princeton University Press, 1988); Daniel Farber and Suzanna Sherry, *Desperately Seeking Certainty: The Misguided Quest for Constitutional Foundations* (Chicago: University of Chicago Press, 2002).

2. William Harris, *The Interpretable Constitution* (Baltimore: Johns Hopkins University Press, 1993).

3. Stephen Griffin, *American Constitutionalism: From Theory to Politics* (Princeton, NJ: Princeton University Press, 1996).

4. Cornell Clayton and Howard Gillman, eds., *Supreme Court Decision-Making: New Institutionalist Approaches* (Chicago: University of Chicago Press, 1999); Sotirios Barber and Robert George, eds., *Constitutional Politics: Essays on Constitution Making, Maintenance, and Change* (Princeton, NJ: Princeton University Press, 2001); David Strauss, "Common Law Constitutional Interpretation," *University of Chicago Law Review* 63 (Summer 1996): 877–935; Antonin Scalia, *A Matter of Interpretation: Federal Courts and the Law* (Princeton, NJ: Princeton University Press, 1997).

5. Rogers Smith, "Beyond Tocqueville, Myrdal, and Hartz: The Multiple Traditions in America," *American Political Science Review* 87 (Sept. 1993): 549–66.

6. Michael Kent Curtis, *Free Speech, 'The People's Darling Privilege': Struggles for Freedom of Expression in American History* (Durham, NC: Duke University Press, 2000); David Rabban, *Free Speech in Its Forgotten Years* (New York: Cambridge University Press, 1997).

7. Daniel T. Rodgers, *Contested Truths: Keywords in American Politics Since Independence* (New York: Basic Books, 1987).

8. William Novak, *The People's Welfare: Law and Regulation in Nineteenth-Century America* (Chapel Hill: University of North Carolina Press, 1996), 37.

9. Leonard Levy, "The Law of the Commonwealth and Chief Justice Shaw," in *American Law and the Constitutional Order: Historical Perspectives*, ed. Lawrence M. Friedman and Harry N. Scheiber (Cambridge, MA: Harvard University Press, 1978), 151–61.

10. Michael McCann, "How the Supreme Court Matters in American Politics: New Institutionalist Perspectives," in *The Supreme Court in American Politics: New Institutionalist Interpretations*, ed. Howard Gillman and Cornell Clayton (Lawrence: University Press of Kansas, 1999), 63–97; Michael McCann and William Haltom, *Distorting the Law: Politics, Media, and the Litigation Crisis* (Chicago: University of Chicago Press, 2004); Ronald Kahn, "Insti-

tutional Norms and the Historical Development of Supreme Court Politics: Changing 'Social Facts' and Doctrinal Development," in Gillman and Clayton, *Supreme Court in American Politics*, 43–59; Ronald Kahn, *The Supreme Court and Constitutional Theory, 1953–1993* (Lawrence: University Press of Kansas, 1994).

11. Keith Whittington, *Constitutional Construction: Divided Powers and Constitutional Meaning* (Cambridge, MA: Harvard University Press, 1999).

12. Julie Novkov, *Constituting Workers, Protecting Women: Gender, Law, and Labor in the Progressive Era and New Deal Years* (Ann Arbor: University of Michigan Press, 2001).

13. Levy, "Chief Justice Shaw"; J. R. Pole, "Reflections on American Law and the American Revolution," *William and Mary Quarterly* 50 (Jan. 1993): 123–59; William E. Nelson, *Americanization of the Common Law: The Impact of Legal Change on Massachusetts Society, 1780–1860* (Cambridge, MA: Harvard University Press, 1975); Morton Horwitz, *The Transformation of American Law: 1780–1860* (Cambridge, MA: Harvard University Press, 1977).

14. See Gerald Berk, *Alternative Tracks: The Constitution of American Industrial Order, 1865–1917* (Baltimore: Johns Hopkins University Press, 1994); Gretchen Ritter, *Goldbugs and Greenbacks: The Antimonopoly Tradition and the Politics of Finance in America* (New York: Cambridge University Press, 1997).

15. Elizabeth Clark, "Matrimonial Bonds: Slavery and Divorce in Nineteenth-Century America," *Law and History Review* 8 (Spring 1990): 25.

16. "Declaration of Sentiments," in *History of Woman Suffrage*, vol. 1, *1848–1861*, ed. Elizabeth Cady Stanton et al. (1881; Salem, NH: Ayer Co., 1985), 70–71.

17. J. David Greenstone, "Political Culture and American Political Development: Liberty, Union, and the Liberal Bipolarity," *Studies in American Political Development* 1 (1986): 1–49.

18. The Lockean origins of the Declaration of Independence are contested. Some see the document as upholding the natural rights theory of Locke. See Scott Douglas Gerber, *To Secure These Rights: The Declaration of Independence and Constitutional Interpretation* (New York: New York University Press, 1995); Michael Zuckert, *The Natural Rights Republic: Studies in the Foundation of the American Political Tradition* (Notre Dame, IN: University of Notre Dame Press, 1996). Others see it as "mere rhetoric." See John Phillip Reid, *The Concept of Liberty in the Age of the American Revolution* (Chicago: University of Chicago Press, 1988); Rodgers, *Contested Truths*.

19. Carole Pateman, *The Sexual Contract* (Stanford, CA: Stanford University Press, 1988).

20. Lawrence M. Friedman, *A History of American Law* (New York: Simon & Schuster, 1985), 108–10; Charles Cook, *The American Codification Movement: A Study of Antebellum Legal Reform* (Westport, CT: Greenwood Press, 1981), 3.

21. Edmund Burke, *Reflections on the Revolution in France*, ed. Conor Cruise O'Brien (New York: Penguin Books, 1986); Harvey Mansfield, "Gentlemen's Gentleman," *Times Literary Supplement*, July 11, 1997, 15.

22. Benjamin Cardozo, *The Nature of the Judicial Process* (New Haven, CT: Yale University Press, 1921); Strauss, "Common Law Constitutional Interpretation," 888; Ernest Young, "Rediscovering Conservatism: Burkean Political Theory and Constitutional Interpretation," *North Carolina Law Review* 72 (Mar. 1994): 653.

23. Cass Sunstein, *One Case at a Time: Judicial Minimalism on the Supreme Court* (Cambridge, MA: Harvard University Press, 1999).

24. Civil libertarian theories of free speech prove to be limited in addressing economic inequalities. See Mark Graber, *Transforming Free Speech: The Ambiguous Legacy of Civil Libertarianism* (Berkeley: University of California Press, 1991). For the polarized positions on pornography and free speech, see Catharine MacKinnon, *Only Words* (Cambridge, MA: Harvard University Press, 1993), and Nadine Strossen, *Defending Pornography: Free Speech, Sex, and the Fight for Women's Rights* (New York: New York University Press, 2000).

25. Uday Mehta, *Liberalism and Empire: A Study in Nineteenth-Century British Liberal Thought* (Chicago: University of Chicago Press, 1999), 22–23.

26. R. Kent Newmyer, "Harvard Law School, New England Culture, and the Antebellum Origins of American Jurisprudence," *Journal of American History* 74 (Dec. 1987): 814–35.

27. Strauss, "Common Law Constitutional Interpretation."

28. Griffin, *American Constitutionalism*, 19–26.

29. See Martha Minow, "'Forming Underneath Everything That Grows': Toward a History of Family Law," *Wisconsin Law Review* 1985 (July 1985): 819–97; Reva Siegel, "She the People: The Nineteenth Amendment, Sex Equality, Federalism, and the Family," *Harvard Law Review* 115 (Feb. 2002): 947–1046.

30. Hendrik Hartog, *Man and Wife in America: A History* (Cambridge, MA: Harvard University Press, 2000).

31. Henry S. Maine, *Ancient Law: Its Connection with the Early History of Society, and Its Relation to Modern Ideas*, 3rd American ed. (1885; Tucson: University of Arizona Press, 1986).

32. Some rules, such as the requirement that wives follow the domicile chosen by their husbands, were retained well into the twentieth century. See Burnita Shelton Matthews, "Legal Discriminations against Women Existing in the U.S. Today," *Congressional Digest* 3 (Mar. 1924): 195–96.

33. Hendrik Hartog, "Wives as Favorites," in *Law as Culture and Culture in Law: Essays in Honor of John Phillip Reid*, ed. Hendrik Hartog and William E. Nelson (Madison, WI: Madison House Publishers, 2000), 292–321.

34. Elizabeth Warbasse, *The Changing Legal Rights of Married Women, 1800–1861* (New York: Garland, 1987).

35. Peggy Rabkin, *Fathers to Daughters: The Legal Foundations of Female Emancipation* (Westport, CT: Greenwood Press, 1980).

36. See Linda Kerber, "Separate Spheres, Female Worlds, Woman's Place: The Rhetoric of Women's History," *Journal of American History* 75 (June 1988): 9–39.

37. Richard Chused, "Married Women's Property Law: 1800–1850," in *Domestic Relations and Law*, ed. Nancy Cott (Westport, CT: Meckler, 1992), 153–219; Joan Hoff, *Law, Gender, and Injustice: A Legal History of U.S. Women* (New York: New York University Press, 1991), 129.

38. Norma Basch, who has identified the nonliberal purposes of the Married Women's Property Acts, nevertheless notes the limited reach of the statutes because they did not usher in a revolution in women's status. She attributes the blame to the piecemeal character of the statutes themselves and to narrow interpretation by courts. See *In the Eyes of the Law: Women, Marriage, and Property in Nineteenth-Century New York* (Ithaca, NY: Cornell University Press, 1982). See also Sara Zeigler, "Uniformity and Conformity: Regionalism and the Adjudication of the Married Women's Property Acts," *Polity* 28 (Summer 1996): 467–96.

39. Ken Kersch, *Constructing Civil Liberties: Discontinuities in the Development of American Constitutional Law* (New York: Cambridge University Press, 2004).

40. Louis Hartz, *The Liberal Tradition in America: An Interpretation of American Political Thought since the Revolution* (San Diego, CA: Harcourt Brace & Co., 1955).

41. Rogers Smith, "Beyond Tocqueville, Myrdal, and Hartz: The Multiple Traditions in America," *American Political Science Review* 87 (Sept. 1993): 549–66; Karen Orren and Steven Skowronek, *The Search for American Political Development* (Cambridge: Cambridge University Press, 2004).

42. Rogers Smith, *Civic Ideals: Conflicting Visions of Citizenship in U.S. History* (New Haven, CT: Yale University Press, 1997).

43. Ibid., 111.

44. Ibid., 67.

45. Kersch, *Constructing Civil Liberties*, 11.

46. Mehta, *Liberalism and Empire*, 200. Rogers Smith points out the futility of dwelling too much on the internal imperatives of liberalism, as liberalism is a heuristic in understanding American political development. "Liberalism and Racism: The Problem of Analyzing Traditions," in *The Liberal Tradition in American Politics: Reassessing the Legacy of American Liberalism*, ed. David F. Ericson and Louisa Bertch Green (New York: Routledge, 1999), 9–27; Carol Horton, "Liberal Equality and the Civic Subject: Identity and Citizenship in Reconstruction America," in Ericson and Green, *The Liberal Tradition*, 115–35.

47. Peter Bardaglio, *Reconstructing the Household: Families, Sex, and the Law in the Nineteenth-Century South* (Chapel Hill: University of North Carolina Press, 1995); Nancy Cott, *Public Vows: A History of Marriage and the Nation* (Cambridge, MA: Harvard University Press, 2000).

48. William Galston, *Liberal Purposes: Goods, Virtues, and Diversity in the Liberal State* (New York: Cambridge University Press, 1991).

49. Stephen Skowronek, "Order and Change," *Polity* 28 (Fall 1995): 91–96; Karen Orren and Stephen Skowronek, "Order and Time in Institutional Study: A Brief for the Historical Approach," in *Political Science in History*, ed. James Farr et al. (New York: Cambridge University Press, 1995), 296–317.

50. Karen Orren and Stephen Skowronek, "In Search of Political Development," in Ericson and Green, *The Liberal Tradition*, 29–41.

51. Karen Orren, *Belated Feudalism: Labor, the Law, and Liberal Development in the United States* (New York: Cambridge University Press, 1991).

52. Smith, "Beyond Tocqueville"; Orren, *Belated Feudalism*.

53. See Wendy Brown, *States of Injury: Power and Freedom in Late Modernity* (Princeton, NJ: Princeton University Press, 1995).

54. Daniel Ernst, "State, Party, and Harold M. Stephens: The Utahn Origins of a New Dealer," *Western Legal History* 14 (Summer/Fall 2001): 133.

55. James Stoner, *Common Law Liberty: Rethinking American Constitutionalism* (Lawrence: University Press of Kansas, 2003); Paul Carrese, *The Cloaking of Power: Montesquieu, Blackstone, and the Rise of Judicial Activism* (Chicago: University of Chicago Press, 2003).

56. Theodore Plucknett, *A Concise History of the Common Law*, 5th ed. (Boston: Little,

Brown & Co., 1956); Arthur Hogue, *Origins of the Common Law* (Indianapolis, IN: Liberty Fund, 1986); Kermit Hall, *The Magic Mirror: Law in American History* (New York: Oxford University Press, 1989).

57. Nelson, *Americanization of the Common Law*; Howard Schweber, *The Creation of American Common Law, 1850–1880: Technology, Politics, and the Construction of Citizenship* (Cambridge: Cambridge University Press, 2004).

58. William Blackstone, *Commentaries on the Laws of England*, vol. 1, *A Facsimile of the First Edition of 1765–1769* (Chicago: University of Chicago Press, 1979).

59. Stanton et al., *History of Woman Suffrage*, 1:64.

60. Marylynn Salmon, *Women and the Law of Property in Early America* (Chapel Hill: University of North Carolina Press, 1986).

61. Although equity was available, it was not widely used and, therefore, did not make a difference in women's lives. See Salmon, *Women and the Law of Property*; Carol Elizabeth Jenson, "The Equity Jurisdiction and Married Women's Property in Ante-Bellum America: A Revisionist View," *International Journal of Women's Studies* 2 (1979): 144–54. While this is true historically, the project here assesses the alternative ways in which the form of rights discourse could have developed in the nineteenth century.

62. Mary Ritter Beard, *Woman as Force in History: A Study in Traditions and Realities* (New York: Macmillan, 1946).

63. Suzanne Lebsock, "Reading Mary Beard," *Reviews in American History* 17 (June 1989): 324–39; Berenice Carroll, "Mary Beard's *Woman as Force in History: A Critique*," in *Liberating Women's History: Theoretical and Critical Essays*, ed. Berenice Carroll (Urbana: University of Illinois Press, 1976), 26–41; Carl Degler, "*Woman as Force in History*, by Mary Ritter Beard," *Daedalus* 103 (1974): 67–73; Basch, *In the Eyes of the Law*.

64. Norma Basch, "Equity vs. Equality: Emerging Concepts of Women's Political Status in the Age of Jackson," *Journal of the Early Republic* 3 (Autumn 1983): 297–318.

65. Orren, *Belated Feudalism*; Sara Zeigler, "Wifely Duties: Marriage, Labor, and the Common Law in Late Nineteenth-Century America," *Social Science History* 20 (Spring 1996): 63–96.

66. Siegel, "The Modernization of Marital Status Law: Adjudicating Wives' Rights to Earnings, 1860–1930," *Georgetown Law Journal* 82 (Sept. 1994): 2127–211; Joan Williams, "Is Coverture Dead? Beyond a New Theory of Alimony," *Georgetown Law Journal* 82 (Sept. 1994): 2227–90.

CHAPTER 1: CODIFICATION OF THE COMMON LAW CONSIDERED

1. Lawrence M. Friedman, *A History of American Law* (New York: Simon & Schuster, 1985), 109–10.

2. Theodore Plucknett, *A Concise History of the Common Law*, 5th ed. (Boston: Little, Brown & Co., 1956), 23–25; Ralph Turner, *Magna Carta: Through the Ages* (Harlow: Pearson Longman, 2003), 2; James Stoner, *Common Law Liberty: Rethinking American Constitutionalism* (Lawrence: University Press of Kansas, 2003), 1. Cf. Michael Kent Curtis, who points out that this reading of liberties of the ancient constitution is a revision of an agreement between members of the nobility and not about the rights of the people. *Free Speech, 'The People's Dar-*

ling Privilege': Struggles for Freedom of Expression in American History (Durham, NC: Duke University Press, 2000), 26.

3. Plucknett, *Concise History*; Arthur Hogue, *Origins of the Common Law* (Indianapolis, IN: Liberty Fund, 1986); Kermit Hall, *The Magic Mirror: Law in American History* (New York: Oxford University Press, 1989).

4. Stoner, *Common Law Liberty*, 13.

5. William Novak, *The People's Welfare: Law and Regulation in Nineteenth-Century America* (Chapel Hill: University of North Carolina Press, 1996), 25.

6. Perry Miller, *The Life of the Mind in America: From the Revolution to the Civil War* (New York: Harcourt, Brace & World, 1965).

7. As new states entered the Union, they tended to adopt the common law. The exceptions were those states with a history of French or Spanish colonization — Texas, California, Louisiana — which used a civil law system or a combination of common law and civil law.

8. Friedman, *History of American Law*, 21.

9. Charles Cook, *The American Codification Movement: A Study of Antebellum Legal Reform* (Westport, CT: Greenwood Press, 1981), 53.

10. Morton Horwitz, *The Transformation of American Law, 1780–1860* (Cambridge, MA: Harvard University Press, 1977).

11. Robert Gordon, "Book Review: The American Codification Movement," *Vanderbilt Law Review* 36 (1983): 431.

12. Maxwell Bloomfield, *American Lawyers in a Changing Society, 1776–1876* (Cambridge, MA: Harvard University Press, 1976), 138; Friedman, *History of American Law*, 94–97; Cook, *American Codification Movement*, 14.

13. Bloomfield, *American Lawyers*, 40; Friedman, *History of American Law*, 113.

14. Novak, *People's Welfare*, 26.

15. William E. Nelson, *Americanization of the Common Law: The Impact of Legal Change on Massachusetts Society, 1760–1830* (Cambridge, MA: Harvard University Press, 1975); Howard Schweber, *The Creation of American Common Law, 1850–1880: Technology, Politics, and the Construction of Citizenship* (Cambridge: Cambridge University Press, 2004).

16. Thomas Hobbes, *A Dialogue between a Philosopher and a Student of the Common Laws of England*, ed. Joseph Cropsey (Chicago: University of Chicago Press, 1971), 55.

17. Ibid.

18. Thomas Hobbes, *Leviathan*, ed. C. B. MacPherson (New York: Penguin, 1985), 317; see James Stoner, *Common Law and Liberal Theory: Coke, Hobbes, and the Origins of American Constitutionalism* (Lawrence: University Press of Kansas, 1992), 84.

19. Stoner, *Common Law and Liberal Theory*, 119.

20. Commentators have pointed to enough factual errors to question Blackstone's merits as a historian. See William Blackstone, *Commentaries on the Laws of England*, ed. William Carey Jones (San Francisco: Bancroft-Whitney Co., 1916), 29, editor's note 10.

21. While Bentham would criticize Blackstone's identification of common law's modernity, more charitable critiques are found in Daniel Boorstin, *The Mysterious Science of the Law: An Essay on Blackstone's Commentaries* (Boston: Beacon Press, 1958), and Herbert Storing, "William Blackstone," in *History of Political Philosophy*, 3rd ed., ed. Leo Strauss and Joseph Cropsey (Chicago: University of Chicago Press, 1987).

22. Cf. Norman Cantor, *Imagining the Law: Common Law and the Foundations of the American Legal System* (New York: HarperCollins, 1997), 30.

23. William Blackstone, *Commentaries on the Laws of England*, vol. 1, *A Facsimile of the First Edition of 1765–1769* (Chicago: University of Chicago Press, 1979), 18.

24. Ibid., 26.

25. Ibid., 74.

26. Ibid., 126.

27. Ibid., 74.

28. Bentham, *A Comment on the Commentaries: A Criticism of William Blackstone's Commentaries on the Laws of England* (Oxford: Clarendon Press, 1928; Darmstadt: Scientia Verlag Aalen, 1976), 67, 106.

29. Ibid., 157.

30. Ibid., 191.

31. Ibid., 192.

32. Bentham, *The Works of Jeremy Bentham* (New York: Russell & Russell, 1962), 564–81.

33. Ibid., 453.

34. Ibid., 467.

35. Ibid., 475–76.

36. Ibid., 483.

37. Ibid.

38. Marianne Constable, *The Law of the Other: The Mixed Jury and Changing Conceptions of Citizenship, Law, and Knowledge* (Chicago: University of Chicago Press, 1994), 88.

39. Bentham, *Works*, 561.

40. Ibid., 542.

41. Thomas Spragens, *The Irony of Liberal Reason* (Chicago: University of Chicago Press, 1981), 28.

42. Constable, *Law of the Other*, 1–2.

43. Ibid., 88–89.

44. Cook, *American Codification Movement*, 74.

45. Friedman, *History of American Law*, 174.

46. Cook, *American Codification Movement*, 129.

47. Andrew P. Morriss, "Codification and Right Answers," *Chicago-Kent Law Review* 74 (1999): 360–61.

48. Cook, *American Codification Movement*, 136.

49. Morriss, "Right Answers," 363.

50. Cook, *American Codification Movement*, 167; Bloomfield, *American Lawyers*, 87.

51. David Rabban, "The Historiography of Late Nineteenth-Century American Legal History," *Theoretical Inquiries in Law* 4 (July 2003): 541–78.

52. Bloomfield, *American Lawyers*, 85.

53. *"Rationale of Judicial Evidence Specially Applied to English Practice*. From the Manuscripts of Jeremy Bentham, Esq. Bencher of Lincoln's Inn. In 5 vols. 8 vol. London. 1828," *Southern Review* 10 (May 1830): 381.

54. *"Principles of Legislation*. From the MS. of Jeremy Bentham, Bencher of Lincoln's Inn. By M. Dumont," *Southern Review* 14 (Aug. 1831): 261.

55. "Codification, and Reform of the Law-No. 1," *American Jurist* 14 (Oct. 1835): 281.

56. Cook, *American Codification Movement*, 75.

57. Joseph Story, "An Address delivered before the Members of the Suffolk Bar, at their anniversary, on the fourth of September, 1821, at Boston," *American Jurist* 1 (Jan. 1829): 31–32.

58. "Codification and Reform of the Law-No. 1," 281.

59. Bloomfield, *American Lawyers*, 81.

60. "The Greatest Happiness Principle," *American Jurist* 20 (Jan. 1839): 332–62; "Bentham's Theory of Legislation," *American Jurist* 23 (July 1840): 332–38.

61. "Life and Writings of Sir William Blackstone," *American Jurist* 1 (Jan. 1829): 121.

62. Ibid., 126.

63. Ibid., 131.

64. Story, "Address," 13.

65. Spragens, *Irony of Liberal Reason*, 38.

66. "Codification of the Common Law in Massachusetts," *American Jurist* 17 (Apr. 1837): 20.

67. Howard Schweber, "The 'Science' of Legal Science: The Model of the Natural Sciences in Nineteenth-Century American Legal Education," *Law and History Review* 17 (Fall 1999): 421–66.

68. "Necessity of the Common Law," *North American Review* 27 (July 1828): 168.

69. Ibid., 180.

70. "President Quincy's Address on the occasion of the Dedication of Dane Law College," *American Jurist* 9 (Jan. 1833): 49–50.

71. "On the Legal Profession in New England," *American Jurist* 19 (Apr. 1838): 51.

72. "Walker's Introduction to American Law," *American Jurist* 18 (Jan. 1838): 379–80.

73. Ibid., 381.

74. "Written and Unwritten Systems of Law," *American Jurist* 5 (Jan. 1831): 28.

75. Ibid., 31.

76. Ibid., 30.

77. "Written and Unwritten Systems of Law," *American Jurist* 9 (Jan. 1833): 5.

78. Ibid., 11.

79. "On Political Hermeneutics, or On Political Interpretation and Construction, and Also on Precedents. By Francis Lieber," *American Jurist* 18 (Oct. 1837): 37–101; "On Political Hermeneutics — Precedents. By Francis Lieber," *American Jurist* 18 (Jan. 1838): 281–94.

80. "On Political Hermeneutics" (1837), 64.

81. Bloomfield, *American Lawyers*, 69.

82. William Sampson, *Sampson's Discourse and Correspondence with Various Learned Jurists, Upon the History of the Law, with the Addition of Several Essays, Tracts, and Documents, Relating to the Subject* (Washington, DC: Gales & Seaton, 1826), 5–11.

83. Ibid., 12.

84. Ibid., 11.

85. Ibid., 18.

86. Ibid., 28.

87. Ibid., 70.

88. "An Anniversary Discourse delivered before the Historical Society, on Saturday, De-

cember 6, 1823, showing the Origin, Progress, Antiquities, Curiosities, and Nature of the Common Law. By William Sampson," *North American Review* 19 (Oct. 1824): 411.

89. Ibid.

90. Ibid., 414.

91. "Legal Reform," *American Jurist* 9 (Apr. 1833): 289.

92. "On Mistakes of Law," *American Jurist* 23 (Apr. 1840): 156.

93. "The Common Law," *Atlantic Magazine* 1 (May 1824): 26.

94. "The Progress of Society," *North American Review* 36 (Apr. 1833): 428.

95. "On the Legal Profession in New England," 71.

96. "The Customs of the Germans as Described by Tacitus—a Source of the Common Law," *American Jurist* 20 (Oct. 1838): 101–2.

97. Ibid., 102.

98. "On the Substitution of a Written Code, in the Place of the Common Law," *Atlantic Magazine* 1 (Aug. 1824): 285.

99. Ibid., 285.

100. "Necessity of the Common Law," 173.

101. Ibid.

102. "Letter of Charles T. Watts to William Sampson," in Sampson, *Discourse*, 87.

103. Ibid.

104. "Necessity of the Common Law," 172.

105. Ibid., 175.

106. "Written and Unwritten Systems of Law" (1831), 31.

107. "The Common Law," *Atlantic Magazine* 1 (May 1824): 27.

108. "Written and Unwritten Systems of Law" (1831), 29.

109. Ibid., 34.

110. "On the Substitution," 290.

111. "Written and Unwritten Systems of Law" (1831), 30–31.

112. "Common Law Jurisdiction," *North American Review* 21 (July 1825): 108.

113. Ibid., 133.

114. Joseph Story, *The Miscellaneous Writings of Joseph Story*, ed. William Story (New York: Di Capo Press, 1972), 66–67.

115. Ibid., 70.

CHAPTER 2: ABSTRACTING RIGHTS

1. Keith Melder, *The Beginnings of Sisterhood: The American Woman's Rights Movements, 1800–1850* (New York: Schocken, 1977); William O'Neill, *Feminism in America: A History*, 2nd rev. ed. (New Brunswick, NJ: Transaction Publishers, 1989).

2. See James A. Morone, *Hellfire Nation: The Politics of Sin in American History* (New Haven: Yale University Press, 2003); Lawrence J. Friedman, *Gregarious Saints: Self and Community in American Abolitionism, 1830–1870* (Cambridge: Cambridge University Press, 1982).

3. Michael Kent Curtis, *Free Speech, 'The People's Darling Privilege': Struggles for Freedom of Expression in American History* (Durham, NC: Duke University Press, 2000), 134.

4. Curtis, *People's Darling Privilege*; David Rabban, *Free Speech in Its Forgotten Years*

(New York: Cambridge University Press, 1997); Mark Graber, *Transforming Free Speech: The Ambiguous Legacy of Civil Libertarianism* (Berkeley: University of California Press, 1991).

5. See Stanley Elkins, *Slavery: A Problem in American Institutional and Intellectual Life*, 2nd ed. (Chicago: University of Chicago Press, 1968), and Ann Lane, ed., *The Debate over Slavery: Stanley Elkins and His Critics* (Urbana: University of Illinois Press, 1971); Lewis Perry, *Radical Abolitionism: Anarchy and the Government of God in Antislavery Thought* (Ithaca, NY: Cornell University Press, 1973).

6. See Leonard Levy, *Freedom of Speech and Press in Early American History: Legacy of Suppression* (New York: Harper Torchbooks, 1963).

7. Stephen Griffin points out that popular sovereignty was initially used to determine the source of political authority, but over time it has been wielded as an abstract concept that does not yield robust discourse or political results. *American Constitutionalism: From Theory to Politics* (Princeton, NJ: Princeton University Press, 1996).

8. James Madison, "The Virginia Resolution," *The Kentucky-Virginia Resolutions and Mr. Madison's Report* ([Richmond]: Virginia Commission on Constitutional Government, 1960), 15–82.

9. Akhil Amar, *Bill of Rights: Creation and Reconstruction* (New Haven, CT: Yale University Press, 1998).

10. Don L. Smith, *The Right to Petition for Redress of Grievances: Constitutional Development and Interpretations* (Ph.D. diss., Texas Tech University, 1971), 47.

11. Douglas Strong, *Perfectionist Politics: Abolitionism and the Religious Tensions of American Democracy* (Syracuse, NY: Syracuse University Press, 1999), 69; Ronald Walters, *The Antislavery Appeal: American Abolitionism after 1830* (Baltimore: Johns Hopkins University Press, 1976). The charge of fanaticism was liberally dispensed in congressional debates over abolition petitions. See *Appendix to the Congressional Globe*, 24th Cong., 1st sess., 1835, 15, 16.

12. *Appendix to the Congressional Globe*, 24th Cong., 1st sess., 1836, 49, 92, 139, 146, 298.

13. William Lee Miller, *Arguing about Slavery: The Great Battle in the United States Congress* (New York: Alfred A. Knopf, 1996), 108–10.

14. Miller, *Arguing about Slavery*, 32–35.

15. *Register of Debates in Congress*, 24th Cong., 1st sess., 1836, 3757.

16. *Appendix to the Congressional Globe*, 24th Cong., 1st sess., 1836, 53.

17. Ibid., 138, 148.

18. Ibid., 109–10.

19. Ibid., 133.

20. Ibid., 99, 109.

21. Ibid., 99, 133.

22. Ibid., 89.

23. Ibid., 134.

24. Ibid., 215.

25. Ibid.

26. See Peter Bardaglio, *Reconstructing the Household: Families, Sex, and the Law in the Nineteenth-Century South* (Chapel Hill: University of North Carolina Press, 1995).

27. *Appendix to the Congressional Globe*, 24th Cong., 1st sess., 1836, 108.

28. Ibid., 170.

29. Ibid., 185.

30. William Lloyd Garrison, "On the Constitution and the Union," in *William Lloyd Garrison and the Fight against Slavery: Selections from "The Liberator,"* ed. William Cain (Boston: Bedford Books, 1995), 89.

31. *Appendix to the Congressional Globe*, 24th Cong., 1st sess., 1836, 49.

32. Ibid., 117.

33. Ibid., 289.

34. Ibid.

35. See Miller, *Arguing about Slavery.*

36. Aileen Kraditor, *Means and Ends in American Abolitionism: Garrison and His Critics on Strategy and Tactics, 1834–1850* (New York: Pantheon Books, 1969), 7.

37. Editorial, *Philanthropist* (New Richmond, OH), Jan. 1, 1836.

38. Ibid.

39. "The Demand of the Slaveholders," *Philanthropist*, Mar. 4, 1836.

40. "To John C. Wright, Esq.," *Philanthropist*, Feb. 26, 1836, Mar. 4, 1836, Mar. 11, 1836.

41. "To John C. Wright, Esq.," *Philanthropist*, Mar. 11, 1836.

42. "Abolitionists Beware," *Philanthropist*, July 15, 1836.

43. See, e.g., George Bourne, *Slavery Illustrated in Its Effects upon Woman and Domestic Society* (1837; Salem, NH: Ayer Co., 1972).

44. Oliver Johnson, *William Lloyd Garrison and His Times* (London, 1882), 292.

45. Gilbert Hobbs Barnes, *The Antislavery Impulse: 1830–1844* (Gloucester, MA: P. Smith, 1957), 140; Susan Zaeske, *Signatures of Citizenship: Petitioning, Antislavery, and Women's Political Identity* (Chapel Hill: University of North Carolina Press, 2003), 174.

46. Zaeske, *Signatures of Citizenship*; Julie Roy Jeffrey, *The Great Silent Army of Abolitionism: Ordinary Women in the Antislavery Movement* (Chapel Hill: University of North Carolina Press, 1998).

47. Paula Baker, "The Domestication of Politics: Women and American Political Society, 1780–1920," in *Unequal Sisters: A Multicultural Reader in U.S. Women's History*, ed. Ellen Carol DuBois and Vicki L. Ruiz (New York: Routledge, 1990), 66–91.

48. Karlyn Kohrs Campbell, *Man Cannot Speak for Her: A Critical Study of Early Feminist Rhetoric* (Westport, CT: Greenwood Press, 1989), 9–12.

49. Jean Fagan Yellin and John C. Van Horne, eds., *The Abolitionist Sisterhood: Women's Political Culture in Antebellum America* (Ithaca, NY: Cornell University Press, 1994), 4.

50. Paula Giddings, *When and Where I Enter: The Impact of Black Women on Race and Sex in America* (New York: William Morrow & Co., 1984).

51. Angelina Grimké, "To the People of the United States, or to Such Americans as Value Their Rights, and Dare to Maintain Them," *Anti-Slavery Examiner* (New York, NY), Aug. 1836, 3.

52. Frances Wright, *A Few Days in Athens* (Boston: J. P. Mendum, 1850).

53. Gretchen Sween, "Ritual, Riots, Rules, and Rights: The Astor Place Theater Riot of 1849 and the Evolving Limits of Free Speech," *Texas Law Review* 81 (2002): 689.

54. Quoted in Celia Morris Eckhardt, *Fanny Wright: Rebel in America* (Cambridge, MA: Harvard University Press, 1984), 186.

55. Zaeske, *Signatures of Citizenship*, 54.

56. Melder, *Beginnings of Sisterhood*, 50.

57. Rebecca Starr, *A School for Politics: Commercial Lobbying and Political Culture in Early South Carolina* (Baltimore: Johns Hopkins University Press, 1998); Lacy Ford, *Origins of Southern Radicalism: The South Carolina Upcountry, 1800–1860* (New York: Oxford University Press, 1988).

58. Charles Cook, *The American Codification Movement: A Study of Antebellum Legal Reform* (Westport, CT: Greenwood Press, 1981), 130.

59. Gerda Lerner, *The Grimké Sisters from South Carolina: Rebels against Slavery* (Boston: Houghton Mifflin Co., 1967).

60. Stephen Howard Browne, *Angelina Grimké: Rhetoric, Identity, and the Radical Imagination* (East Lansing: Michigan State University Press, 1999), 62.

61. Angelina Grimké, "Letter to Jane Smith, New York, December 17, 1836," in *Women's Rights Emerges within the Antislavery Movement: A Brief History with Documents*, ed. Kathryn Kish Sklar (Boston: Bedford/St. Martin's, 2000), 90.

62. *Turning the World Upside Down: The Anti-Slavery Convention of American Women Held in New York City, May 9–12, 1837*, intro. Dorothy Sterling (New York: Feminist Press, 1987), 13.

63. Angelina Grimké, "Letter to Jane Smith, Boston, May 29, 1837," in Sklar, *Women's Rights Emerges*, 111.

64. Susan Zaeske, "The 'Promiscuous Audience' Controversy and the Emergence of the Early Woman's Rights Movement," *Quarterly Journal of Speech* 81 (1995): 191–207.

65. "Pastoral Letter of the General Association of Massachusetts, July 1837," in Sklar, *Women's Rights Emerges*, 119–21.

66. Sarah Grimké, *Letters on the Equality of the Sexes and Other Essays*, ed. Elizabeth Ann Bartlett (New Haven, CT: Yale University Press, 1988), 37.

67. Ibid.

68. Ibid., 41.

69. Angelina Grimké, "'Human Rights Not Founded on Sex': Letter to Catharine Beecher, August 2, 1837," in Sklar, *Women's Rights Emerges*, 143.

70. Ibid., 144.

71. Angelina Grimké, "Letter to Theodore Dwight Weld and John Greenleaf Whittier, Brookline, Mass., August 20, 1837," in Sklar, *Women's Rights Emerges*, 130.

72. Julie Roy Jeffrey, *The Great Silent Army of Abolitionism: Ordinary Women in the Antislavery Movement* (Chapel Hill: University of North Carolina Press, 1998).

73. See, e.g., Catharine Beecher, *An Essay on Slavery and Abolitionism, with Reference to the Duty of American Females* (1837; New York: Books for Libraries, 1970).

74. Amy Swerdlow, "Abolition's Conservative Sisters: The Ladies' New York City Anti-Slavery Societies, 1834–1840," in Yellin and Van Horne, *Abolitionist Sisterhood*, 31–44.

75. "Letter from Mrs. Child on the present state of the anti-slavery cause," *Liberator*, Sept. 6, 1839, 142.

76. Child was already a well-known author when she published *Philothea* in 1836. *An Appeal in Favor of That Class of Americans Called Africans* (1833) positioned her as a prominent abolitionist early in the abolitionist movement. Her works also included *Juvenile Miscellany*, a children's magazine; *Hobomok* (1824), a romance of the early republic which featured an in-

terracial relationship; *The Frugal Housewife* (1829), a domestic advice treatise; and "A New-England's Boy Song." See Carolyn Karcher, *The First Woman in the Republic* (Durham, NC: Duke University Press, 1994).

77. "Letter from a Lady, concerning Miss Wright," *Massachusetts Weekly Journal*, Aug. 14, 1829, 3.

78. Karcher, *First Woman*, 233.

79. Janice A. Radway, *Reading the Romance: Women, Patriarchy, and Popular Literature* (Chapel Hill: University of North Carolina Press, 1985).

80. L. Maria Child, *Philothea: A Grecian Romance*, new and corrected edition (New York: C. S. Francis, 1845), Preface.

81. Ibid., 16.

82. Ibid., 25.

83. Ibid., 26.

84. Ibid.

85. Karcher, *First Woman*, 234.

86. Child, *Philothea*, 68.

87. Ibid., 93.

88. Ibid.

89. In a 1943 review of *Philothea*, Robert Streeter recognized that *Philothea* was infused with platonic Transcendental ideas of the time, but he did not view Child as contributing to Transcendental thought herself. See Robert E. Streeter, "Mrs. Child's 'Philothea': A Transcendentalist Novel?" *New England Quarterly* 16 (1943): 648–54.

90. Child, *Philothea*, 80.

91. Hildegard Hoeller, "A Quilt for Life: Lydia Maria Child's 'The American Frugal Housewife,'" *American Transcendental Quarterly* 13 (June 1999): 89–104.

92. Pericles was a renowned politician whose power declined; Aspasia did have a reputation for influencing her husband, and she was often parodied in comedic plays; Anaxagoras was exiled; Alcibiades did have a reputation as a handsome rogue.

93. See Cornelius Conway Felton, "Mrs. Child's Philothea," *North American Review* 44 (Jan. 1837): 79; Edgar Allen Poe, "Critical Notices: *Philothea*," *Southern Literary Messenger* 2 (Sept. 1836): 662.

94. Child's artistic license was in keeping with sentimental literature of the time. Such plot contrivances "serve as a means of stating and proposing solutions for social and political predicaments." See Lynne Pearce and Jackie Stacey, *Romance Revisited* (New York: New York University Press, 1995), 15; Jane Tompkins, *Sensational Designs: The Cultural Work of American Fiction, 1790–1860* (New York: Oxford University Press, 1985), xii, xvii.

95. Lydia Maria Child, "Letter to E. Carpenter, March 20, 1838," in *Letters of Lydia Maria Child* (1883; New York: Negro Universities Press, 1969), 26.

96. Lydia Maria Child, *Letters from New York*, 2nd ed., ed. Bruce Mills (New York: C. S. Francis, 1844; Athens: University of Georgia Press, 1998), 155.

97. Karcher, *First Woman*, 224.

98. Jean Fagan Yellin, *Women and Sisters: The Antislavery Feminists in American Culture* (New Haven, CT: Yale University Press, 1989), 54–56.

CHAPTER 3: THE MARRIED WOMEN'S PROPERTY ACTS

1. Law and society approaches point out that formal rules alone do not explain a citizen's experience. Resistance to rules provides space for freedom that is belied by a mere litany of oppressive law. See Hendrik Hartog, *Man and Wife in America: A History* (Cambridge, MA: Harvard University Press, 2000).

2. Sara Zeigler, "Wifely Duties: Marriage, Labor, and the Common Law in Nineteenth-Century America," *Social Science History* 20 (Spring 1996): 63–96.

3. James Schouler, *A Treatise on the Law of Husband and Wife* (Boston: Little, Brown & Co., 1882), 96.

4. Schouler, *Husband and Wife*, 103.

5. Ibid., 105.

6. See *The Young Husband; A Manual of the Duties, Moral, Religious, and Domestic, Imposed by the Relations of Married Life, By the author of "The Young Wife"* (Philadelphia, 1847).

7. Gretchen Ritter, "Jury Service and Women's Citizenship before and after the Nineteenth Amendment," *Law and History Review* 20 (Fall 2002): 479–515.

8. Carol Elizabeth Jenson, "The Equity Jurisdiction and Married Women's Property in Ante-Bellum America: A Revisionist View," *International Journal of Women's Studies* 2 (1979): 144–54.

9. J. R. Pole, "Reflections of American Law and the American Revolution," *William and Mary Quarterly* 50 (Jan. 1993): 145.

10. William E. Nelson, *Americanization of the Common Law: The Impact of Legal Change on Massachusetts Society, 1760–1830* (Cambridge, MA: Harvard University Press, 1975), 46.

11. Ibid., 6.

12. Morton Horwitz, *The Transformation of American Law: 1780–1860* (Cambridge, MA: Harvard University Press, 1977), 31; J. Willard Hurst, *Law and the Conditions of Freedom in Nineteenth-Century United States* (Madison: University of Wisconsin Press, 1956), 113.

13. Nelson, *Americanization of the Common Law*, 120.

14. Ibid., 6; Horwitz, *Transformation of American Law*, 160.

15. Nelson, *Americanization of the Common Law*, 46.

16. Henry Sumner Maine, *Ancient Law: Its Connection with the Early History of Society, and Its Relation to Modern Ideas*, 3rd American ed. (New York: Henry Holt & Co., 1885; Tucson: University of Arizona Press, 1986), lii.

17. Elizabeth Warbasse, *The Changing Legal Rights of Married Women: 1800–1861* (New York: Garland, 1987); Richard Chused, "Married Women's Property Law: 1800–1850," *Georgetown Law Journal* 71 (1983): 1359–1425.

18. Chused, "Married Women's Property Law," 1398.

19. Warbasse, *Changing Legal Rights*, 196.

20. Ibid.

21. Norma Basch, *In the Eyes of the Law: Women, Marriage, and Property in Nineteenth-Century New York* (Ithaca, NY: Cornell University Press, 1982); Peggy Rabkin, *Fathers to Daughters: The Legal Foundations of Female Emancipation* (Westport, CT: Greenwood Press, 1980).

22. Rabkin, *Fathers to Daughters*, 76.

23. Elizabeth Cady Stanton et al., eds., *History of Woman Suffrage*, vol. 1, *1848–1861*; vol. 2, *1861–1866* (1881; Salem, NH: Ayer Co., 1985), 14–15; hereafter cited as *HWS*.

24. *HWS*, 1:64.

25. Lawrence M. Friedman, *A History of American Law* (New York: Simon & Schuster, 1985), 624.

26. Tapping Reeve, *The Law of Baron and Femme, of Parent and Child, Guardian and Ward, Master and Servant, and of the Powers of the Courts of Chancery, with an essay on the terms Heirs, Heirs, Heirs of the Body* 3rd ed., ed. Amasa Parker and Charles Baldwin (1862; New York: Source Book Press, 1970), 49.

27. Melvin Urosfky and Paul Finkelman, *A March of Liberty: A Constitutional History of the United States*, vol. 1, *From the Founding to 1890* (New York: Oxford University Press, 2002), 178.

28. Friedman, *History of American Law*, 333.

29. James Kent, *Commentaries on American Law*, 11th ed., ed. George Comstock (Boston: Little, Brown & Co., 1867), 2:107.

30. Ibid., 108.

31. Ibid., 109.

32. James Schouler, *A Treatise on the Law of Husband and Wife* (Boston: Little, Brown & Co., 1882), 102.

33. Ibid., 104.

34. Reva Siegel, "'The Rule of Love': Wife Beating as Prerogative and Privacy," *Yale Law Journal* 105 (1996): 2117–2207.

35. Jean Soderlund, "Priorities and Power: The Philadelphia Female Anti-Slavery Society," in *The Abolitionist Sisterhood: Women's Political Culture in Antebellum America*, ed. Jean Fagan Yellin and John C. Van Horne (Ithaca, NY: Cornell University Press, 1994), 67–88.

36. *HWS*, 1:50–62; Kathryn Kish Sklar, "Women Who Speak for an Entire Nation: American and British Women Compared at the World Anti-Slavery Convention, London, 1840," in *The Abolitionist Sisterhood: Women's Political Culture in Antebellum America*, ed. Jean Fagan Yellin and John C. Van Horne (Ithaca, NY: Cornell University Press, 1994), 301–33. There are dangers in relying on the woman suffragists' own history. See Rabkin, *Fathers to Daughters*, 4. Because this study analyzes suffragists' rhetoric, however, their rendition of events provides the material for assessing that rhetoric, even if it may not represent events as they actually occurred.

37. *HWS*, 1:68.

38. "Declaration of Sentiments," *HWS*, 1:70.

39. Ibid.

40. Daniel T. Rodgers, *Contested Truths: Keywords in American Politics Since Independence* (New York: Basic Books, 1987).

41. J. R. Pole, *The Pursuit of Equality in American History* (Berkeley: University of California Press, 1978), 55.

42. Pole, *Pursuit of Equality*; John Philip Reid, "The Jurisprudence of Liberty," in *The Roots of Liberty: Magna Carta, Ancient Constitution, and the Anglo-American Tradition of the Rule of Law*, ed. Ellis Sandoz (Columbia: University of Missouri Press, 1993), 147–231.

43. Carole Pateman, *The Sexual Contract* (Stanford, CA: Stanford University Press, 1988).

44. Nathan Tarcov, *Locke's Education for Liberty* (Chicago: University of Chicago Press, 1984), 210.

45. John Locke, *First Treatise,* in *Two Treatises of Government,* ed. Peter Laslett (Cambridge: Cambridge University Press, 1988), 170–71.

46. Locke, *Second Treatise,* in *Two Treatises of Government,* 304.

47. Ibid., 321.

48. Ibid., 319.

49. Tarcov, *Locke's Education,* 79.

50. Locke, *Second Treatise,* 309.

51. John Locke, *An Essay Concerning Human Understanding,* ed. Alexander Fraser (1690; New York: Dover Publications, 1959), 305.

52. John Locke, *Some Thoughts Concerning Education,* ed. Ruth Grant and Nathan Tarcov (Indianapolis, IN: Hackett Publishing Co., 1996), 13.

53. Ibid., 25–26.

54. Ibid., 31.

55. Ibid., 72.

56. Locke, *First Treatise,* 207.

57. David Foster, "Taming the Father: John Locke's Critique of Patriarchal Fatherhood," *Review of Politics* 56 (Fall 1994): 641–70.

58. Locke, *Second Treatise,* 306.

59. Karen Orren, *Belated Feudalism: Labor, the Law, and Liberal Development in the United States* (Cambridge: Cambridge University Press, 1991).

60. Henry Sumner Maine, *Ancient Law: Its Connection with the Early History of Society, and Its Relation to Modern Ideas,* 3rd American ed. (1885; Tucson: University of Arizona Press, 1986), lii.

61. E. H. Heywood, *Uncivil Liberty: An Essay to Show the Injustice and Impolicy of Ruling Woman against Her Consent* (Princeton, NJ: Cooperative Publishing Co., 1871), 10.

62. Maine, *Ancient Law,* xlix. Matilda Joslyn Gage, in particular, confronted the role of the church in women's subjection. See "Woman, Church and State," in *HWS,* 1:753–99.

63. *HWS,* 1:50.

64. Thomas Herttell, *Remarks Comprising in Substance Judge Herttell's Argument in the House of Assembly of the State of New-York in the Session of 1837, in Support of the Bill to Restore to Married Women 'The Right of Property,' as Guaranteed by the Constitution of this State* (New York: Henry Durell, 1839), 7.

65. Ibid.

66. Ibid., 41.

67. Ibid., 50.

68. Sarah Barringer Gordon, *The Mormon Question: Polygamy and Constitutional Conflict in Nineteenth-Century America* (Chapel Hill: University of North Carolina Press, 2002), 55–57.

69. *Proceedings of the First Three Republican National Conventions of 1856, 1860, and 1864, including Proceedings of the Antecedent National Convention Held at Pittsburgh, in February, 1856, as Reported by Horace Greeley* (Minneapolis: Charles Johnson, 1893), 43.

70. *The Barbarism of Slavery: Speech of Hon. Charles Sumner, on the Bill for the Admission of Kansas as a Free State, in the United States Senate, June 4, 1860* (New York, 1863).

71. *Journal of the Senate,* 38th Cong., 1st sess., 1864, 136.

72. *Journal of the House of Representatives,* 33rd Cong., 2nd sess., 1854, 86.

73. *Journal of the Senate,* 40th Cong., 2nd sess., 1867, 15.

74. *Journal of the Senate of the Confederate Congress,* 2nd Cong., 1st sess., 1864, 7.

75. Ibid., 2nd sess., 1865, 517.

76. *Journal of the Senate,* 40th Cong., 2nd sess., 1867, 15.

77. *Journal of the House of Representatives,* 41st Cong., 2nd sess., 1870, 1189.

78. Gretchen Ritter, *The Constitution as Social Design: Gender and Civic Membership in the American Constitutional Order* (Palo Alto, CA: Stanford University Press, 2006).

79. *HWS,* 2:660.

80. *HWS,* 2:224.

81. *HWS,* 2:365.

82. *HWS,* 1:13.

83. *HWS,* 1:20.

84. *HWS,* 1:761–62.

85. *HWS,* 1:622.

86. *HWS,* 1:594.

87. *HWS,* 1:295.

88. Elizabeth Cady Stanton, *Address to the Legislature of New-York, Adopted by the State Woman's Rights Convention, Held at Albany, Tuesday and Wednesday, February 14 & 15, 1854* (Albany, NY: Weed, Parsons & Co., 1854), 8.

89. *HWS,* 1:874.

90. "Woman Wronged," *Revolution,* Apr. 9, 1868, 214.

91. *HWS,* 1:530.

92. *HWS,* 1:340.

93. "Man the Usurper," *Revolution,* Mar. 12, 1868, 152.

94. Ibid.

95. "Woman Wronged," *Revolution,* 215.

96. *HWS,* 2:342

97. *HWS,* 1:227.

98. "Liberalism," *Revolution,* May 7, 1868, 278.

99. *HWS,* 1:98, 35, 36; 17, 52, 76, 220; 171, 256; and elsewhere.

100. *HWS,* 1:50.

101. "Liberalism," *Revolution,* May 7, 1868, 278.

102. Ernestine Rose, "An Address on Woman's Rights, Delivered Before the People's Sunday Meeting, in Cochituate Hall, on Sunday Afternoon, Oct. 19th, 1851" (Boston: J. P. Mendum, 1851), 5.

103. *HWS,* 1:15.

104. *Adkins v. Children's Hospital* 261 U.S. 525 (1923), 553.

105. See James Stoner, *Common Law Liberty: Rethinking American Constitutionalism* (Lawrence: University Press of Kansas, 2003).

106. David Carr, "Narrative and the Real World: An Argument for Continuity," *History and Theory* 25 (May 1986): 117–31.

107. Uday Mehta, *Liberalism and Empire: A Study in Nineteenth-Century British Liberal Thought* (Chicago: University of Chicago Press, 1999), 200.

CHAPTER 4: THE MARRIED WOMEN'S PROPERTY ACTS

1. Joan Hoff, *Law, Gender, and Injustice: A Legal History of U.S. Women* (New York: New York University Press, 1991), 129.

2. Ibid., 130–32.

3. Sara Zeigler, "Uniformity and Conformity: Regionalism and the Adjudication of the Married Women's Property Acts," *Polity* 28 (Summer 1996): 469.

4. Norma Basch, *In the Eyes of the Law: Women, Marriage and Property in Nineteenth-Century New York* (Ithaca, NY: Cornell University Press, 1982); Richard Chused, "Married Women's Property Law: 1800–1850," *Georgetown Law Journal* 71 (1983): 1359–1425; Sara Zeigler, "Wifely Duties: Marriage, Labor and the Common Law in Nineteenth-Century America," *Social Science History* 20 (Spring 1996): 63–96.

5. Theodore Sedgwick, *A Treatise on the Rules Which Govern the Interpretation and Construction of Statutory and Constitutional Law*, 2nd ed. (1874; Littleton, CO: Fred B. Rothman & Co., 1980), 267–68.

6. Karen Orren, *Belated Feudalism: Labor, the Law and Liberal Development in the United States* (Cambridge: Cambridge University Press, 1991); Karen Orren and Steven Skowronek, "In Search of Political Development," in *The Liberal Tradition in American Politics: Reassessing the Legacy of American Liberalism*, ed. David Ericson and Louisa Bertch Green (New York: Routledge, 1999), 29–42; Steven Skowronek, "Order and Change," *Polity* 28 (Fall 1995): 95.

7. Karen Orren, "The Primacy of Labor in American Constitutional Development," *American Political Science Review* 89 (June 1995): 377–88.

8. Uday Mehta, *Liberalism and Empire: A Study in Nineteenth-Century British Liberal Thought* (Chicago: University of Chicago Press, 1999).

9. The selection of these three states represents some of the regional variation of reform of married women's property acts. No study has completed a close and comprehensive account of the nationwide waves of reform statutes, but if Zeigler is correct in noting uniformity in interpretation, then such a study is not necessary.

10. Reva Siegel, "Home as Work: The First Woman's Rights Claims Concerning Wives' Household Labor, 1850–1880," *Yale Law Journal* 103 (Mar. 1994): 1073–1217; Reva Siegel, "The Modernization of Marital Status Law: Adjudicating Wives' Rights to Earnings," *Georgetown Law Journal* 82 (1994): 2127–225; Amy Dru Stanley, *From Bondage to Contract: Wage Labor, Marriage, and the Market in the Age of Slave Emancipation* (Cambridge: Cambridge University Press, 1998).

11. *Journal of the Constitutional Convention of the Commonwealth of Massachusetts* (Boston: White & Potter, 1853), 35, 44, 61, 78, 175.

12. Harvey Fowler, Reporter, *Official Report of the Debates and Proceedings in the State Convention, Assembled May 4th, 1853, to Revise and Amend the Constitution of the Commonwealth of Massachusetts* (Boston: White & Potter, 1853), 2:384–85.

13. Massachusetts, *The General Statutes of the Commonwealth of Massachusetts* (Boston: White & Potter, 1860) ch. 108, sec. 1.

14. Massachusetts, St. 1864, ch. 197; St. 1869, ch. 409 (the condition that a married woman be joined by her husband in order to be an administratrix was repealed by St. 1874, ch. 184, secs. 4 and 5); General Statutes 1859, ch. 170, sec. 28; St. 1862 ch. 198 and St. 1863, ch. 165; St. 1869, ch. 304; St. 1874, ch. 184, sec. 1; St. 1874, ch. 184, sec. 3.

15. Indiana, *Revised Statutes of the State of Indiana passed at the . . . Session of the General Assembly* (Indianapolis, IN: J. F. Chapman, 1852–) St. 1852, ch.23, secs. 6 and 27.

16. Ibid., St. 1857, ch. 45, ch. 47; St. 1861, ch. 102; St. 1877, ch. 54.

17. Ibid., St. 1879, ch. 67.

18. Ibid., St. 1881, ch. 60, sec. 1.

19. *Bristor v. Bristor* 93 Ind. 281 (1883).

20. *Crawford v. Thompson* 91 Ind. 266 (1883).

21. *Haas v. Shaw* 91 Ind. 384, 389 (1883).

22. *Vogel v. Leichner* 102 Ind. 55, 59–60 (1885).

23. Linda Kerber, *No Constitutional Right to Be Ladies: Women and the Obligations of Citizenship* (New York: Hill & Wang, 1998).

24. A married woman could obtain *feme sole* status if her husband "abjured the realm." William Blackstone, *Commentaries on the Laws of England*, vol. 1, *A Facsimile of the First Edition of 1765–1769* (Chicago: University of Chicago Press, 1979), 431.

25. George Willis, *Kentucky Constitutions and Constitutional Conventions: A Hundred and Fifty Years of State Politics and Organic Law-Making* (Frankfort, KY: State Journal Co., 1930), 32.

26. Kentucky, *Acts of the General Assembly of the Commonwealth of Kentucky* (Lexington, KY: J. Bradford, 1792–); St. 1851, ch. 617, Art. II, secs. 1 and 3.

27. Ibid., St. 1852, Art. V, sec. 1.

28. Ibid., 1866, ch. 555, sec. 1.

29. *McAfee v. Kentucky University* 7 Bush 135 (1870); *Gatewood v. Bryan* 7 Bush 509 (1870); *Estep v. Commonwealth* 86 Ky 39 (1887).

30. *Campbell v. Galbreath* 12 Bush 459, 462 (1876).

31. *Pope v. Shanklin* 79 Ky 230, 231 (1881).

32. *Franklin, ex parte* 79 Ky 497 (1881) and *Moran v. Moran* 12 Bush 301 (1876).

33. Basch, *In the Eyes of the Law*, 206; Zeigler, "Uniformity and Conformity," 481.

34. The cases in the following pages rely once again on cases from three regions—the Northeast, the Midwest, and the South—adding one more state to each region, namely, Maine, Illinois, and Louisiana. Louisiana was a state with a civil-law system. In keeping with Zeigler's finding of uniformity, Louisiana courts interpreted the civil-law rules in keeping with trends in interpretation of common-law rules.

35. *Bradwell v. State* 83 U.S. 130, 141 (1872).

36. *Heck v. Fisher* 78 Ky. 643 (1880).

37. *Virgie v. Stetson* 77 Me. 520, 525 (1885), citing *Call v. Perkins* 65 Me. 439 (1876).

38. *Gibson v. Bennett* 79 Me. 302 (1887).

39. *Robinson & c. v. Robinson's Trustee & c.* 74 Ky. 174, 178 (1874).

40. *Franklin, ex parte* 79 Ky. 497 (1881).

41. *Gross & c. v. Eddinger & c.* 85 Ky. 168 (1887).

42. *Thomas et ux. V. Passage et al.* 54 Ind. 106 (1876).

43. *Bidwell v. Robinson & Wallace* 79 Ky. 29 (1880).

44. *Chaffe v. Oliver* 33 La. Ann. 1008, 1010 (1881).

45. Marylynn Salmon, *Women and the Law of Property in Early America* (Chapel Hill: University of North Carolina Press, 1986), 18.

46. *Sypert v. Harrison* 88 Ky. 461 (1889).

47. *Moore & Coleman v. Rush* 30 La. Ann. 1157 (1878).

48. *Jaffa v. Myers* 33 La. Ann. 406, 409 (1881).

49. *Darling v. Lehman* 35 La. Ann. 1186 (1883).

50. *Commonwealth v. Carroll* 1878 Mass. Lexis 218, 2 (1877).

51. *Commonwealth v. Roberts* 132 Mass. 267 (1882) and *Commonwealth v. Gormley* 133 Mass. 580 (1882).

52. *Jenkins v. Flinn* 37 Ind. 349, 353 (1871).

53. Kerber, *No Constitutional Right to Be Ladies.*

54. Reva Siegel has identified statutory reform as paradoxically serving to modernize the common law of marital status and masking it in modern guise, rather than liberating women from their common-law disabilities. "Home as Work" and "The Modernization of Marital Status Law."

55. *Vogel v. Leichner* 102 Ind. 55 (1885). In the liberal tradition, these are the classic categories of those who are unable to exercise their reason and thus remain under paternal — or, in the case of criminals, state — power. See John Locke, *The Second Treatise in Two Treatises of Government,* ed. Peter Laslett (Cambridge: Cambridge University Press, 1988), 308.

56. *Uhrig v. Horstmann & Sons* 71 Ky. 172 (1871).

57. *Succession of H. F. McKenna* 23 La. Ann. 369 (1871) and *McAfee v. Kentucky University* 70 Ky 135, 137 (1870).

58. *Chandler v. Cheney* 37 Ind. 391, 411 (1871).

59. *Sims and Others v. Rickets* 35 Ind. 181, 189 (1871).

60. *Hobbs v. Hobbs* 70 Me. 381 (1879).

61. Massachusetts, St. 1879, ch. 297.

62. *Moran v. Goodwin* 130 Mass. 158, 159 (1881).

63. *Estep v. Commonwealth* 86 Ky. 39 (1887).

64. *Succession of Boyer* 36 La. Ann. 506 (1884).

CHAPTER 5: THE DOMESTICITY OF THE DOMESTIC RELATIONS

1. Karen Orren, *Belated Feudalism: Labor, the Law, and Liberal Development in the United States* (Cambridge: Cambridge University Press, 1991), 100–101.

2. James Schouler, *A Treatise on the Law of Domestic Relations,* 3rd ed. (Boston: Little, Brown & Co., 1882), 664.

3. John Garraty, ed., *Labor and Capital in the Gilded Age: Testimony Taken by the Senate Committee upon the Relations between Labor and Capital,*1883 (Boston: Little, Brown & Co., 1968), 21.

4. Ibid., 149.

5. Amy Dru Stanley, *From Bondage to Contract: Wage Labor, Marriage, and the Market in the Age of Slave Emancipation* (Cambridge: Cambridge University Press, 1998), 77.

6. Michael Grossberg, *Governing the Hearth: Law and Family in Nineteenth-Century America* (Chapel Hill: University of North Carolina Press, 1985).

7. Garraty, *Labor and Capital*, 2, 31, 74–75, 39–40.

8. Orren, *Belated Feudalism*; Christopher Tomlins, "Subordination, Authority, Law: Subjects in Labor History," *International Labor and Working-Class History* 47 (Spring 1995): 56–90.

9. See Nancy Cott, *The Bonds of Womanhood: 'Woman's Sphere' in New England, 1780–1835* (New Haven, CT: Yale University Press, 1977); Paula Baker, "The Domestication of Politics," in *Unequal Sisters: A Multicultural Reader in U.S. History*, ed. Ellen Carol DuBois and Vicki Ruiz (New York: Routledge, 1990), 66–91; Carl Degler, *At Odds: Women and the Family in America from the Revolution to the Present* (Oxford: Oxford University Press, 1980).

10. William Blackstone, *Commentaries on the Laws of England*, vol. 1, *A Facsimile of the First Edition of 1765–1769* (Chicago: University of Chicago Press, 1979), 410.

11. Ibid., 411.

12. Ibid., 415.

13. James Kent, *Commentaries on American Law*, 11th ed., ed. George Comstock (Boston: Little, Brown & Co., 1867), 2:271.

14. Schouler, *Domestic Relations*, 646.

15. Ibid.

16. Ibid., 647.

17. Ibid.

18. See Stanley, *From Bondage to Contract*.

19. See Orren, *Belated Feudalism*.

20. Irving Browne, *Elements of the Law of Domestic Relations and of Employer and Employed* (1883; Littleton, CO: Fred B. Rothman & Co., 1981), 121.

21. Walter Tiffany, *Handbook on the Law of Persons and Domestic Relations* (St. Paul, MN: West Publishing Co., 1896), 451–52, quoting *Frank v. Herold* 63 U.S. N.J. Eq. 443 (1902).

22. W. C. Rodgers, *A Treatise on the Law of Domestic Relations* (Chicago: T. H. Flood & Co., 1899), 690.

23. Ibid., 690–91.

24. Edward Spencer, *A Treatise on the Law of Domestic Relations* (New York: Banks Law Publishing Co., 1911).

25. *Corpus Juris*, ed. William Mack et al. (New York: American Law Book Co., 1923), 30:1241, citing *Macfie v. Hutchinson* 12 Ont. Pr. 167, 179.

26. *Words and Phrases: Permanent Edition* (St. Paul, MN: West Publishing Co., 1971), 464, citing *Cinefot International Corp. v. Hudson Photographic Industries* 237 N.Y.S. 2d 742, 744 (1963).

27. *Trowbridge v. Carlin* 12 La. Ann. 882 (1857).

28. *Roby v. Murphy* 31 Ill. App. 599, 600 (1889); *Weaver v. Halsey* 1 Ill. App. 558 (1878).

29. *Common v. People* 28 Ill. App. 230 (1888).

30. Willie Lee Rose, "The Domestication of Domestic Slavery," in *Slavery and Freedom*, ed. William Freehling (New York: Oxford University Press, 1982), 18–48; Eugene Genovese,

The Slaveholders' Dilemma: Freedom and Progress in Southern Conservative Thought, 1820–1860 (Columbia: University of South Carolina Press, 1992); Jeffrey Robert Young, *Domesticating Slavery: The Master Class in Georgia and South Carolina, 1670–1837* (Chapel Hill: University of North Carolina Press, 1999). Peter Bardaglio distinguishes the southern patriarchal slaveholding family as an exception to the egalitarian mores of the rest of the country in *Reconstructing the Household: Families, Sex, and the Law in the Nineteenth-Century South* (Chapel Hill: University of North Carolina Press, 1995).

31. Elizabeth Fox-Genovese, *Within the Plantation Household: Black and White Women of the Old South* (Chapel Hill: University of North Carolina Press, 1988), 32. See also Bardaglio, *Reconstructing the Household.*

32. Young, *Domesticating Slavery.*

33. See Fox-Genovese, *Plantation Household.*

34. Carole Pateman, *The Sexual Contract* (Stanford, CA: Stanford University Press, 1988).

35. *Singelton's Will* 38 Ky. 315, 323 (1839).

36. Ibid., 358.

37. Ibid., 350.

38. Ibid., 323.

39. Ibid., 356.

40. Colonial jurists contested whether courts should conduct private examinations of married women when they wanted to dispose of their separate property to benefit their husbands; see Marylynn Salmon, *Women and the Law of Property in Early America* (Chapel Hill: University of North Carolina Press, 1986), 104.

41. *Swift v. Castle* 23 Ill. 132, 193 (1859).

42. Mrs. Castle had been a maid before she married, so the servants who testified on her behalf could be considered to be her friends.

43. *Godden v. Executors of Burke* 35 La. Ann. 160, 170 (1883).

44. Ibid., 168.

45. Ibid., 169.

46. Ibid., 179.

47. Ibid., 180.

48. Ibid., 182.

49. Ibid.

50. Ibid.

51. *Strawn v. Strawn* 53 Ill. 263, 273 (1870).

52. *Bigaouette v. Paulet* 134 Mass. 123, 124 (1881).

53. *Doyle v. Jessup* 29 Ill. 460 (1862) and *Yundt v. Hartrunft* 41 Ill. 9 (1866).

54. *Yundt v. Hartrunft* 12.

55. *Elijah v. Taylor* 37 Ill, 246, 249 (1865).

56. Although married women won the right to retain their own earnings for labor outside the home, they could not earn money for services rendered to family members. Courts reconceived these services as done out of love and affection. See Reva Siegel, "Home as Work: The First Woman's Rights Claims concerning Wives' Household Labor, 1850–1880," *Yale Law Journal* 103 (Mar. 1994): 1073–1217.

57. Because of the distinctive labor of the wife, Sara Zeigler has identified the labor con-

tract as the essence of the marital contract. "Wifely Duties: Marriage, Labor, and the Common Law in Nineteenth-Century America," *Social Science History* 20 (Spring 1996): 63–95.

58. *Miller v. Miller* 16 Ill. 295 (1855).

59. *Cooper v. Cooper* 12 Ill. App. 478 (1882).

60. *Johnson v. Johnson* 100 Ind. 389 (1885).

61. *Patterson v. Collar* 31 Ill. App. 340 (1888).

62. Daniel Sutherland, *Americans and Their Servants: Domestic Service in the United States from 1800 to 1920* (Baton Rouge: Louisiana State University Press, 1981), 30.

63. David Katzman, *Seven Days a Week: Women and Domestic Service in Industrializing America* (New York: Oxford University Press, 1978), 161.

64. Julie Novkov, *Constituting Workers, Protecting Women: Gender, Law, and Labor in the Progressive Era and New Deal Years* (Ann Arbor: University of Michigan Press, 2001); Suzanne Mettler, *Dividing Citizens: Gender and Federalism in New Deal Public Policy* (Ithaca, NY: Cornell University Press, 1998).

65. Gwendolyn Mink, *The Wages of Motherhood: Inequality in the Welfare State, 1917–1942* (Ithaca, NY: Cornell University Press, 1995).

CHAPTER 6: COMMON LAW LOST

1. Elizabeth Cady Stanton et al., eds., *History of Woman Suffrage*, vol. 1, *1848–1861* (1881; Salem, NH: Ayer Co., 1985), 292–306, 313, 746.

2. Richard William Leopold, *Robert Dale Owen: A Biography* (Cambridge, MA: Harvard University Press, 1940), 273.

3. Ibid., 273–77.

4. Ibid., 276.

5. Hendrik Hartog, *Man and Wife in America: A History* (Cambridge, MA: Harvard University Press, 2000).

6. *Report of the Debates and Proceedings of the Convention for the Revision of the Constitution of the State of Indiana H. Fowler, Official Reporter* (Indianapolis, IN: A. H. Brown, 1850), 479.

7. Ibid., 523.

8. Ibid., 484.

9. Ibid.

10. Ibid., 506.

11. Ibid., 527.

12. Ibid., 1172.

13. Ibid., 1176.

14. Ibid., 497.

15. Ibid., 476.

16. Ibid., 500.

17. Ibid., 1171.

18. Hartog, "Wives as Favorites," in *Law as Culture and Culture as Law: Essays in Honor of John Phillip Reid*, ed. Hendrik Hartog and William E. Nelson (Madison, WI: Madison House Publishers, 2000), 292–321.

19. *Report of the Debates*, 479.

20. Ibid., 481.

21. Ibid., 513.

22. Ibid., 1177.

23. Ibid., 520.

24. Ibid., 465.

25. Ibid., 465–66

26. Ibid., 1187.

27. Ibid., 521.

28. Ibid., 497

29. Ibid., 1187.

30. *Proceedings at the Presentation to the Hon. Robert Dale Owen of a Silver Pitcher, on Behalf of the Women of Indiana, on the 28th Day of May, 1851* (New Albany, IN: Kent Norman, 1851), 14.

31. Ibid., 15.

32. 83 U.S. 130 (1873).

33. 83 U.S. 36 (1873).

34. *Frontiero v. Richardson* 411 U.S. 677, 684 (1973).

35. 83 U.S. 130, 141 (1873).

36. Nancy Gilliam, "Professional Pioneer: Myra Bradwell's Fight to Practice Law," *Law and History Review* 5 (Spring 1987): 105–33.

37. Elizabeth Cady Stanton et al., eds., *History of Woman Suffrage*, vol. 2, 1861–1866 (1881; Salem, NH: Ayer Co., 1985), 602.

38. Ibid., 603.

39. Ibid., 610.

40. Ibid., 611.

41. Ibid., 616.

42. Rogers Smith, "The 'American Creed' and American Identity: The Limits of Liberal Citizenship in the United States," *Western Political Quarterly* 41 (June 1988): 243.

43. 83 U.S. 130, 137 (1873).

44. Ibid., 140.

45. Ibid., 141.

46. Charles Cook, *The American Codification Movement: A Study of Antebellum Legal Reform* (Westport, CT: Greenwood Press, 1981), 185–86.

47. Andrew P. Morriss, "Codification and Right Answers," *Chicago-Kent Law Review* 74 (1999): 361.

48. Gunther Weiss, "The Enchantment of Codification in the Common-Law World," *Yale Journal of International Law* 25 (Summer 2000): 506.

49. Lawrence M. Friedman, *A History of American Law*, 2nd ed. (New York: Simon & Schuster, 1985), 403; Daun van Ee, *David Dudley Field and the Reconstruction of the Law* (New York: Garland, 1986), 332.

50. Morriss, *"Right Answers,"* 362.

51. David Rabban, "The Historiography of Late Nineteenth-Century American Legal History," *Theoretical Inquiries in Law* 4 (July 2003): 541–78; Mathias Reimann, "The Historical School against Codification: Savigny, Carter, and the Defeat of the New York Civil Code," *American Journal of Comparative Law* 37 (Winter 1989): 98.

52. Rabban, "Historiography," 546.

53. Lewis Grossman, "James Coolidge Carter and Mugwump Jurisprudence," *Law and History Review* 20 (Fall 2002): 577–629.

54. See Morton Horwitz, *The Transformation of American Law, 1870–1960: The Crisis of Legal Orthodoxy* (New York: Oxford University Press, 1992), 117–23.

55. "Review of the Month," *American Law Review* 14 (1880): 726.

56. *The Arguments of the Honorable William D. Shipman and Frederic R. Coudert esq, before the Judiciary Committee of the Senate of the State of New York in Behalf of the Association of the Bar of the City of New York against the Adoption of the Civil Code*, ed. John R. Strong (Worcester, MA: C. Hamilton, 1881), 78.

57. Daniel Chamberlain, *Unanswerable Objections to Codification: Extract from an Address by Hon. Daniel H. Chamberlain* (n.p., [between 1896 and 1900]); George Tucker Bispham, *The Progressive Capacity of Unwritten Law* (Philadelphia: J. M. Power Wallace, 1886); Thomas Cooley, "The Uncertainty of the Law," *American Law Review* 55 (May/June 1888): 347–70; William Hornblower, "Is Codification of the Law Expedient? An Address Delivered before the American Social Science Association (Department of Jurisprudence) at Saratoga, N.Y., September 6, 1888" (n.p., [1888]); James C. Carter, *The Proposed Codification of Our Common Law* (New York: Evening Post Printing Office, 1884).

58. Norma Basch, "Invisible Women: The Legal Fiction of Marital Unity in Nineteenth-Century America," in *Domestic Relations and Law*, ed. Nancy Cott (Westport, CT: Meckler, 1992), 148n13.

59. *Association of the Bar of the City of New York, Report of the Special Committee to 'Urge the Rejection of the proposed Civil Code,' Reappointed November 1, 1881* (New York: Evening Post Printing Office, 1882), 16–17.

60. Frederic Coudert, *The Arguments of the Honorable William D. Shipman and Frederic R. Coudert esq, before the Judiciary Committee of the Senate of the State of New York in Behalf of the Association of the Bar of the City of New York against the Adoption of the Civil Code*, ed. John Strong (Worcester, MA: C. Hamilton, 1881), 92.

61. Ibid., 93.

62. Ibid., 96.

63. J. Bleecker Miller, *Destruction of Our Natural Law by Codification* (New York: H. Cherouny, 1882).

64. John Ruggles Strong, *An Analysis of the Reply of Mr. David Dudley Field to the Bar Association of the City of New-York* (New York: H. Bessey, 1881), 22.

65. Ibid., 24.

66. Jonathan Smith, *The Married Women's Statutes and Their Results upon Divorce and Society* (Clinton, MA: Clinton Printing Co., 1884).

67. Henry Hitchcock, "Modern Legislation Touching Marital Property Rights," *Journal of Social Science* 13–14 (Mar. 1881): 22.

68. Strong, *Reply of Mr. David Dudley Field*, 6.

69. Ibid.

70. Albert Mathews, *Thoughts on Codification of the Common Law*, 2nd ed. (New York: Baker, Voorhis & Co., 1881), 6.

71. Joel Prentiss Bishop, *Common Law and Codification* (Chicago: T. H. Flood, 1888), 8–9.

72. Robert Ludlow Fowler, *Codification in the State of New York*, 2nd ed. (New York: Martin B. Brown, 1884), 50.

73. George Hoadly, *Codification in the United States: An Address Delivered before the Graduating Classes at the Sixtieth Anniversary of the Yale Law School* (New Haven, CT: Law Department of Yale College, 1884).

74. David Dudley Field, *Legal Reform. An Address to the Graduating Class of the Law School of the University of Albany* (Albany, NY: W. C. Little & Co., 1855).

75. "Address to Law Students," *Albany Law Journal* 1 (Mar. 5, 1870): 166.

76. "Law Reform and Women's Rights," *Albany Law Journal* 10 (1874–75): 147.

77. Elizabeth Cady Stanton, *Solitude of Self: Address Delivered by Mrs. Stanton before the Committee of the Judiciary of the United States Congress, Monday, January 18, 1892* (Washington, DC: GPO, 1915), 1.

78. See Wendy Brown, *States of Injury: Power and Freedom in Late Modernity* (Princeton, NJ: Princeton University Press, 1995).

79. Stanton, *Solitude of Self*, 2.

80. Ibid., 1.

81. Ibid., 2. See Phyllis Cole, "Stanton, Fuller, and the Grammar of Romanticism," *New England Quarterly* 73 (Dec. 2000): 533–59.

82. Wendy Brown, *States of Injury*; Carole Pateman, *The Sexual Contract* (Stanford, CA: Stanford University Press, 1988).

CONCLUSION

1. Mary Becker, "The Sixties Shift to Formal Equality and the Courts: An Argument for Pragmatism and Politics," *William and Mary Law Review* 40 (Oct. 1998): 210.

2. *Frontiero v. Richardson* 411 U.S. 677 (1973).

3. Reva Siegel, "The Modernization of Marital Status Law: Adjudicating Wives' Rights to Earnings," *Georgetown Law Journal* 82 (1994): 2127–211; Becker, "Shift to Formal Equality."

4. James Stoner, *Common Law Liberty: Rethinking American Constitutionalism* (Lawrence: University Press of Kansas, 2003).

5. Mary Lyndon Shanley, "Just Marriage: On the Public Importance of Private Unions," in *Just Marriage*, ed. Joshua Cohen and Deborah Chasman (New York: Oxford University Press, 2004).

6. See Martha Minow, "'Forming Underneath Everything that Grows': Toward a History of Family Law," *Wisconsin Law Review* 1985 (July 1985): 819–97.

7. Martha Albertson Fineman, *The Autonomy Myth: A Theory of Dependency* (New York: New Press, 2004).

8. Wendy Brown, *States of Injury: Power and Freedom in Late Modernity* (Princeton, NJ: Princeton University Press, 1995), 106.

9. Hendrik Hartog, "The Constitution of Aspiration and 'The Rights That Belong to Us All,'" *Journal of American History* 74 (Dec. 1987): 1013.

10. David Strauss, "Common Law Constitutional Interpretation," *University of Chicago Law Review* 63 (Summer 1996): 877–935.

Index